With Open Eyes

Marguerite
With

*Conversations
with
Matthieu
Galey*

Yourcenar Open Eyes

*Translated by
Arthur
Goldhammer*

*Beacon Press
Boston*

French text: Copyright © 1980 by Editions du Centurion, Paris, originally published as *Les yeux ouverts: Entretiens avec Matthieu Galey.*

Translator's Preface and English translation: Copyright © 1984 by Beacon Press

Beacon Press books are published under the auspices of the Unitarian Universalist Association of Congregations in North America, 25 Beacon Street, Boston, Massachusetts 02108 Published simultaneously in Canada by Fitzhenry and Whiteside Limited, Toronto

Printed in the United States of America

(paperback) 9 8 7 6 5 4 3 2

Library of Congress Cataloging in Publication Data

Yourcenar, Marguerite.
  With open eyes.

  Translation of: Les yeux ouverts.
  Bibliography: p.
  L. Yourcenar, Marguerite—Interviews. 2. Novelists,
French—20th century—Interviews. I. Galey, Matthieu.
II. Title.
PQ2649.08Z47813   1984   848'91209 [B]   84—45074
ISBN 0—8070—6355—X

*Let us try, if we can,
to enter into death
with open eyes.*

MEMOIRS OF HADRIAN

Contents

Contents

Translator's Preface

Marguerite Yourcenar has described her first novel, *Alexis,* as the "portrait of a voice." It is to the French transcription of these wide-ranging conversations with Matthieu Galey that one might look for a portrait of Yourcenar's own voice, painted, as it were, from life. Of that portrait this translation can, in the nature of things, claim to be only a pale copy at best. But translations, as the subject of this book, herself an accomplished translator, is right to point out, are "indispensable" to most of their readers, a "necessary service" in an age when it is easier to cross borders than in the past but harder perhaps for most of us to make ourselves truly at home in a foreign tongue. To borrow an image from Mme Yourcenar: "A translator . . . is like a person packing a suitcase. The suitcase lies open in front of him. He puts in one item, then wonders if perhaps another wouldn't be more useful and so removes the first, only to put it back in after a moment's thought since it does seem clearly indispensable." I know no analogy that better captures what it feels like actually to be at work on a translation. Extending the conceit, may I therefore express the hope, reader, that you fill find in these bags everything you need, unencumbered by dead weight.

Before sending you on your way, however, I should surely point out that the citations given herein from Marguerite Yourcenar's two best-known works, *Memoirs of Hadrian* and *The Abyss,* are from the English translations by Grace Frick, done in collaboration with the author. Titles of works by Marguerite Yourcenar that have been translated into English appear in English in the text (full publication data appear in the Bibliography at the end of the book). With other French titles I've been deliberately inconsistent; some are given in French, some in

English. A few wordplays and etymological matters are treated
in brackets: some readers of translations are annoyed if the
translator assumes they know no French; others are perturbed if he
assumes they know any. I hope I have distributed the irritation
equitably.

Finally, to Walter Kaiser, whose translation of *Alexis,* done in
collaboration with the author, is soon to be published, I wish to
express my gratitude for being allowed to read not only the
manuscript of that translation but also his unpublished paper,
"The Achievement of Marguerite Yourcenar," from which I
greatly profited.

ARTHUR GOLDHAMMER

Introduction

"I knead the dough; I sweep the doorstep; after nights when the wind has blown hard, I gather fallen wood." These words, from Marguerite Yourcenar's *Archives du Nord,* are sure to awaken a memory in anyone interested in the author of *The Memoirs of Hadrian.*

A Frenchman familiar with some of the legends that surround the writer is all too likely to imagine her living on her American island in much the same way as women live on the isle of Ouessant off the coast of Brittany, with wooden shoes on her feet and a black kerchief over her head. Though Yourcenar's island retreat is known as Mount Desert, it is far less a wilderness than one might imagine. For some years now it has been linked to the coast of Maine by a bridge. Each summer the tourists invade, and scattered through the pines and maples are far more summer homes of the well-to-do than fishermen's huts.

Petite-Plaisance, as her house is called, cannot be compared to some of the other homes in the area, owned by the Rockefellers and other dignitaries, which seem to have been built to serve as backdrop to a novel by Fitzgerald or Henry James. It is closer to an idyllic shepherd's cottage of the past century: all wood, modest but livable, comfortable without affectation, full of books and other well-used objects—it is a house that is lived in, in which even the least significant item has its special history or symbolic importance. Outside, the countryside merges with the green silence of a broad lawn, bordered by a wood full of birds and friendly squirrels that will eat out of your hand.

For seven months out of the year, however, the island lives up to the name given it by Champlain: winter blankets everything, night comes early, and people settle down by the fire behind closed shutters. Just after the war, when Marguerite Yourcenar and Grace Frick, her translator, discovered this place, so old-fashioned that it seemed to stand apart from the rest of America with all its hustle and bustle, local people still traveled from village to village by horse-drawn sleigh. Something of this pioneering rural flavor remains. The house has no television and the radio is used but sparingly. A wood fire crackles in the fireplace. Only Zoé the spaniel dares disturb the calm with her yapping—she is as wild, active, and ardent as her name. To live in such a place one must choose to make do with the luxury of the essential. Here it seems almost as if contemplation is a given, according to the rhythm imposed by nature and the seasons.

This feeling of a peacefulness conquered and dominated can be read in Marguerite Yourcenar's blue eyes—her "Celtic" eyes—which study you with widsom that feels very deep indeed. Everything interests her, but people and events strike her as parts of an ordered (or disordered) whole that transcends them. If she frequently gives the impression of "talking like a book," this is no pose, nor is it an escape into abstraction; for this intelligence, constantly in touch with the universal, the humblest word or act can be fitted into a conception of the world that she holds constantly in view. When she speaks there are few hesitations: she is a woman of formidable intelligence, who could easily have been a philosopher.

Like Michel Tournier, one of the few current writers who can equal her for rigor and originality of mind, Yourcenar is a novelist only by chance. In another era *The Memoirs of Hadrian* might have been called a monologue, and *The Abyss,* a book written with the aid of techniques borrowed from the East and not unlike certain devices used by shamans, might have been called a meditation. Though few people have noticed their use, such hidden devices undoubtedly account for the unparalleled solidity of Yourcenar's works, as well as for the emotional power concealed beneath the smooth surface of her somewhat glacial style.

Marguerite Yourcenar never resorts to anecdote for the sake of mere embellishment. When she does use anecdote, it is always to reveal some detail of a character's nature—that, and nothing more. The stale accounts of anguished love and erotic exertion with which current literature abounds are, for Yourcenar, utterly devoid of interest, as nonsensical as talking about oneself at novelistic length. Lacking the proper perspective, "the reader," says Yourcenar, "is all too likely to rub his nose in the events of the story. Individual life is short, the self is porous; to conjure up an image of the whole from such things smacks of pure illusion."

The mystery and reality of sex are things too intimate to write about in a book, unless the writer happens to be rather ill-bred. That our books are full of such "gossip" indicates, to Yourcenar, a society in pretty bad shape: "Disintegrating societies appear to be free; but that is no guarantee of what the future holds."

When, at the age of twenty, Marguerite Yourcenar wrote her first novel, *Alexis ou le traité du vain combat,* she too believed that the sexual problem was the most important of all, the one that had to be solved first, after which the rest would follow naturally. Fifty years later, without going so far as to call for a return to old-fashioned repressiveness, she nevertheless sees dangers in this kind of liberation because it inevitably "fails to rise to the height of the sacred." When sexuality regains some of its former sacred quality, things will be better. But will that day ever come, and how?

When apprised that in some respects she seems to be swimming against the tide of history, she calmly rejects the observation as shortsighted: "All great battles are rearguard actions. And today's rear guard is tomorrow's vanguard. The world turns!" From her vantage point in the United States (and of course—just a little—from the standpoint of Sirius), France seems to her much too concerned with such unimportant subtleties. France is the country of fashion: "People there talk about ideas the way they used to talk about hats, when they wore hats."

In a world divided by conflicts that are, in her words, either "naïve or distressing"—such as that between the right and the left, for instance—chauvinism is harmful in all its guises, including that of feminism. The only worthwhile solutions are individual ones. And the only people who matter are those who say no: no to nuclear power plants and dams that destroy the environment, no to the blind worship of profit in a civilization where "having takes precedence over being," no to the pollution that is destroying plants and wildlife and works of art, and, if need be, no even to the Concorde. People must never give up trying to convince the masses: "When utopians begin to assume the role of government's bad conscience, the battle is half-won." Accordingly, the "good woman of Plaisance" is constantly sending telegrams and supporting one crusade or another with her pen and her pockebook.

When one assumes the standpoint of the universal, however, it is obviously not short-term results that matter most. As her personal moral principle Marguerite Yourcenar takes the dictum of Buddha that one must "work until the end, for everything is perishable." This is a double-edged moral precept, which can lead to hope or, just as easily, to despair, supposing it is true that we are mere droplets in life's eternally flowing river. At the very least it encourages a proper appreciation of the "little that one is" and of the vanity of all things.

I fear that Marguerite Yourcenar will indeed prove to have been one of the last writers to enjoy the dangerous privilege of not being poor. I say privilege because she was able, at her leisure, to travel extensively when and as she chose, mainly in the period between the two World Wars and in the Mediterranean countries that serve as backdrop and fertile soil for many of her works. But I say dangerous because the absence of routine worries in her life (she was forced to earn a living really only while living in the United States during the war, a period she apparently does not look back upon with fond memories) left her free to refrain from making the little concessions that might have won her an audience more quickly.

Indeed, the enormous success of *Memoirs of Hadrian* surprised her: she had not expected such enthusiasm for a work that was no easier than its predecessors in the demands it makes on readers. Why was it that the "happy few" suddenly became so numerous? Perhaps the only explanation is that many readers mistook the book for a love story because one of its minor, though essential, elements is just that, when in reality *Memoirs* is the story of an exceptional man at a unique moment in history.

Though famous now, Marguerite Yourcenar is still not well known to many of her readers; she remains a remote figure who takes no part in the literary games by which writers normally gain a place first in the reviews and then in the textbooks (academics being, regrettably, just as susceptible to fashion as anyone else). Not even winning the Prix Femina for *L'œuvre au noir* (*The Abyss*) in 1968 did much to change Yourcenar's rather peculiar situation as a writer celebrated but not in the limelight. Loved by a small but devoted following of readers who knew *Alexis* and *Le coup de grâce* (*Coup de Grâce*) even before the publication of *Hadrian,* and hailed as a master by a few good critics (by which I mean critics who don't confuse their tastes with their prejudices), she had yet a while to wait before receiving the attention of newspapers, radio, and television, where the eyes to discover true talent are rare.

Fame came suddenly to Marguerite Yourcenar with the publication of *Archives du Nord.* Why *then* remains a mystery. Even the most partisan newspapers and weeklies now decided the time had come to admit that while Yourcenar might be an aristocratic writer, she was an aristocrat worthy of praise. With luck she may receive as many lines as Robbe-Grillet in some future schoolchild's anthology. This is how reputations are made in France.

Nor was it wise, until recently, to reside too far from Paris's Sixth Arrondissement (where the major publishers are concentrated—TRANS.), with its schools, its vogues, its commitments. Yet on the shelves of the library at Petite-Plaisance one finds few works by Barthes and Lacan, and for that matter few contemporary French novels.

Like all truly inspired writers, Marguerite Yourcenar is mostly indifferent to what is being written nowadays, and the timeless tale of boy meets girl leaves her largely unmoved.

It would be wrong to conclude, however, that she is ignorant of the present. Whether she is kneading dough in her kitchen, petting Zoé, or writing a page of *Quoi? l'Eternité,* the next volume of *Labyrinthe du monde,* she is in constant contact with life. To a rare degree she gives the feeling of being in touch, aware of even the minutest details. No sooner does she pick up a wooden spoon than her thoughts turn to the craftsman who shaped it and from there to the tree from which it was made and on to nature in its entirety. For her, everything is part of a whole, and surely that is the source of the calm that emanates from her person as well as her work. With a rather dry but very beautiful gaze she contemplates creation with as little anxiety as reason will allow.

Don't for one moment think that this serene woman (if she is truly as serene as she appears) is insensitive or detached. She is capable of anger, just as she must once have been capable of passion—a rereading of *Fires* is enough to convince one of that—but on a level beyond the petty tribulations that make up most of our lives. Her intellect is a splendid edifice, unshakeable in its architecture, and it is this that endows her speech and her writing with their surprising power.

Nothing that she says or thinks is so unusual in itself. But most of us are unable to achieve such a strict harmony between conscience and contemplation. The currents that toss us this way and that seem not even to touch her. She is a rock ensconced in a conceptual fortress, and it is striking to see how similar are her answers to questions posed in different interviews, even years apart. All wisdom is patience: knowing how to suffer the world without forgetting the overarching perfection of which it is a part.

I t should come as no suprise that Marguerite Yourcenar, unlike most of her colleagues in the literary profession, has so persistently refused to talk about herself. Given her belief that the individual is to be valued only as part of an encompassing plan, it is not hard to understand her desire to avoid personal confidences and confessions. Not even the story of her own family was worthy of a book, in her mind, until she had found a way to link that story (as she does in *Souvenirs pieux* and *Archives due Nord*) to the history of the age, to cast it as not so much a pious souvenir as an exemplary case history. And as for writing about herself, two volumes of this family history have now been written and young Marguerite is still only six weeks old.

This determination not to be bound by the self's narrow limits has also led her to reject certain accepted or inherited ideas. This Flamande knows her ancient charters but doesn't care a fig for aristocratic origins or fancy genealogies. All her ancestors weren't enough to keep her at Mont-Noir, the family seat (destroyed during the First World War), nor did she stay very long in Brussels, where she was born, nor in Paris. Like her father, who led quite a vagabond life for a late nineteenth-century bourgeois, she regarded chance as a trustworthy deity and felt that, so long as she could pack her world in her valises, the place where she happened to be living had no particular importance. So much for the myth (promoted in France by the writer Maurice Barrès—TRANS.) of the writer with "roots," a myth that finds a present-day avatar in the flourishing of regionalism. "Wherever one may go, one must die on the planet Earth."

For similar reasons Yourcenar rejects anything that strikes her as simplistic, including feminism, which she comes close to regarding as a form of racism in reverse. Like many other women who have experienced no difficulty in being women because their intelligence forced men to consider them at least equals, she may have a tendency to deny the problem; by the same token, the author of *Alexis* and *The Memoirs of Hadrian* fails to see—arguing, as always, in the name of the universal—why anyone would want to make a distinction between homosexual love and love in general. In these attitudes of Yourcenar's there is enough to discourage any number of uninformed admirers who have set her up as spokesperson for their favorite causes, when in fact nothing could be more remote from her way of thinking. This also explains why Yourcenar remained for so long indifferent to invitations from the Académie francaise, whereas a feminist would probably have accepted membership at once for the sake of the cause.

The writer's solitude, which Yourcenar regards as essential, indeed indispensable, to the practice of her art, comes to her in consequence of her world view. She feels solidarity with humanity in general rather than with this or that social group or nationality. She takes an active part in campaigns to defend seals, whales, the ecological balance, the wilderness, the seacoast, and the ocean against all threats, current and future, but she shuns politics because she regards political activity as too ephemeral, a mere eddy in the current of history. As a result, the sympathies of this classical novelist, this writer whose style is carved in the marble of Latin, whose life is so orderly and regular, are directed mainly toward society's outcasts, those who disregard possessions and prejudices. Between reading Shakespeare and Saint-Simon, she sometimes listens to Bob Dylan.

Among her unforgotten dreams, tinged with a bit of nostalgic longing (for instance, she would have liked to have been a doctor, like Zeno, the hero of *The Abyss*), she harbors the thought of living on an American-style commune, which she had planned to do long before communes were in vogue. There she would have found time for quiet meditation while savoring a life close to other people and to things. And in truth, her life on Mount Desert Island (which is hardly a desert any more, having acquired a fairly considerable population since Champlain gave it its name) is not unlike the life of which she once dreamed. Each of her days is quietly witnessed by the likes of Joseph the squirrel (so-called because he wears a coat of many colors like Joseph in the Bible), the birds, the trees, and the sea.

Viewed from Mount Desert Island, our schemes for classifying writers seem rather silly. For Marguerite Yourcenar, such current catchphrases as "literary theory" and "literary research" don't mean a great deal. Conviction of this kind can sustain and justify a style just as much as it can sustain a thinker on a voyage of discovery. The writer of *The Abyss* never deliberately set a literary course for herself. She merely followed her vision wherever it led, as truly and accurately as she was able. This accounts for the density of her writing, which sometimes surprises readers accustomed to more padding or to pleasant devices of literary artifice. It is important to notice that the imposing style is inseparable from the whole enterprise. At the beginning of her career, still unsure of her path, Yourcenar experimented with other styles, drawing on the Gidian *récit* to develop the voice of her early works.

It would be wrong, however, to view her simply as a philosopher or historian who writes novels. Remember that she began as a writer by publishing poetry. In spite of appearances, dreams may play a larger part than intellection in Yourcenar's carefully crafted works. To borrow the title of one of her books, *Les songes et les sorts,* (a revised version of which is now in preparation, revision being a frequent practice of this perfectionist), dreams and the whims of fate (*songes* and *sorts*) have guided her creative life. Her great works of fiction were conceived, not in the tiny, book-lined office where she types her manuscripts, but at the whim of chance, in a night train or a waiting room, a hotel suite or a church, or while walking out of doors. This rigorous intellect has offered itself up to the irrational, without whose help it seems likely she would never have written a word.

But this openness to the mysteries of inspiration is also the product of a certain asceticism. Yourcenar strives to empty out the self in order to receive her creations, beings so alive in her thoughts that they are with her constantly. It is worth pointing out that two of her three great characters (Hadrian and Zeno, the third being Michel, her father, who figures in *Archives du Nord*) were born in her imagination by the time she was eighteen. The emperor and the physician have followed her throughout her life, first as mere sketches in a plan of future works, then as heroes of her novels, and finally as everyday companions, teachers, and accomplices, as much a part of her life as the most familiar of family and friends.

W hen a visitor, after passing under the corn tassels hanging from the porch roof (a local symbol of prosperity offered up to some forgotten god worshipped perhaps by the Indians), opens the front door of Petite-Plaisance and enters Marguerite Yourcenar's home, he feels that the atmosphere inside is completely different from that outside. The writer's eyes fix him, size him up, judge him. Her look is at once remote and courteous, tinged with irony. And she begins to speak, sure of what she believes.

Serene to the point of detachment—and yet tender. To understand, you have to see her pet a dog or pick up a pebble on the beach. She seems almost to belong to another realm, where words have meaning and humans reason, where the law is universally respected, and wisdom has its place and intelligence illuminates without shadows. She looks the world in the face, and the men in it, and contemplates what she sees with an abstract love which, like the love of saints, can be frightening. But it's not hard to guess at the fires that burn within her. Though on her lips you glimpse the smile of Minerva, so restrained, perhaps a little distant, you know that it is a visionary who is staring at you through blue eyes that reveal, beneath drooping lids, the child's glazed innocence in the face of a collapsing world.

N.B. These interviews, carried on over a period of years, have here been collected and organized for the sole purpose of providing the most accurate possible portrait of a writer for whom I have long felt a particular admiration. But I have read all too many supposed "dialogues" that turned out to be verbose, one-sided performances to fall into the role of the "interviewer" who attempts to upstage his subject. I trust that my readers will feel grateful for the brevity of my questions. I have deliberately reduced my role to one of picking up and tossing back, with the one aim of arranging the conversation so that one hears the voice of Marguerite Yourcenar and no other.

Childhood

MATTHIEU GALEY:
Do you feel that your childhood was a rather unusual one?
MARGUERITE YOURCENAR:
I have no basis for comparison other than accounts other writers have given of their childhoods. To me these don't ring true. There are only two possible conclusions: either my childhood was different from theirs, or else the writers in question have re-created novelistic or poetic childhoods for themselves by putting the past in some sort of order, not always with perfect accuracy.

G   Still, there are some points on which you might base a comparison. You knew other children, for instance.

Y   Yes, but my knowledge of them was superficial, confined to what I might call the conventions of childhood. Once they left me and returned to the privacy of their own rooms, what did they think, what did they dream about? I don't know. Take for example a person I regard as a very great writer, who also happens to be a woman—which is to say that one might expect to find some similarity between her life and mine. I'm speaking of Selma Lagerlöf. Now, it seems to me that her childhood memories are all right as chitchat, but everything important has been left out. The book she wanted to write has not been written. She might have written it, but she didn't. Her real depth is not captured on the page.

G   There is, though, one unusual thing about your childhood: you had no mother. Did her absence weigh heavily on you?

Y   Not in the least. I was never shown a portrait of my mother when I was a child. I never saw one until I was perhaps thirty-five. I visited her grave for the first time when I was fifty-five. I should tell you that my father was surrounded by bevies of women. So there were plenty of people to make me collars in *broderie anglaise* and to give me candy.

1

G   Still, your childhood was that of a solitary little girl.

Y   To a certain extent. Or perhaps I should say, at certain times, because sometimes I was alone, but other times I was surrounded by
other children and by the various people with whom my father
stayed. But you are right to say that sometimes I was all alone, and I
think that getting used to being alone early in life is of immense
value. It teaches you to some extent to get along without others. It
also teaches you to love people all the more. In any case, there is in
children a fundamental indifference that has rarely been described.
Perhaps awareness of this indifference embarrasses people; I don't
know. But it strikes me when I look at children: they live in a world
of their own. And my feeling is that I lived in a world of my own. I
think that most writers, even "serious" ones, deceive themselves
when they speak of childhood. Either they see the child from the
standpoint of the adult or they make a tremendous effort to put
themselves in the place of what they imagine a child to be. The
whole approach is too systematic, too much influenced by our own
conventions as adults. In my view the child has only a vague notion
of where he's going in life: like any young animal, the child who is
seeing—or rediscovering—something for the first time has some
surprises in store. Around him are grown-ups whose identity is not
always very clear. Someone says, this is your father, his name is
"papa" (but what is a father to the child?). And this is your
mother, and this is the maid or the cook or the postman. All of these
people are "grown-ups" who have some importance in the child's
life but who at the same time are not very closely connected to him.
He has a personal life that these people don't touch. But no one
wants to look at the relations that make up that personal life.
People want children to hate their parents or to adore them. The
truth of the matter is that I never "adored" my father, and it seems
to me that it was not until late in life that I even truly liked him.

G   Which "grown-ups" have lingered in your memories of childhood?

Y   I knew many grown-ups, but I felt very strongly that they counted
without counting, so to speak. I lived in a house in which there
were a great many people, as was common back then. There were
my grandmother, my half brother and, later, his wife, my uncle,
and various cousins. There was the household staff, which was
fairly large, since in those days there were no electrical or
mechanical appliances of any sort. There were the people of the

2

village, both adults and children. There were boys and girls I met on holiday at the beach. For me, each and every one of these people had as much existence as any other: which is to say, a great deal and yet at the same time very little.

G   You seem, though, to continue to harbor a certain resentment against your grandmother.

Y   A certain resentment! That's quite an understatement. But I've already explained my reasons in *Archives du Nord:* for me she exemplified the possessive bourgeoisie, as was perfectly plain in her way of saying, "Be careful of my armchair" or "Don't walk on my rug." I never really suffered at her hands, but I watched her and found her a curious person, not easy to like, like a bulky piece of furniture.

G   Was there ever a period in your life when you rebelled against your family?

Y   No, because my family didn't inhibit me enough to rebel against it. Except for my father, it didn't much interest me. I have spoken elsewhere of my half brother's antipathy toward me, but I seldom saw him. I've also described my relatives on my mother's side whom I knew or heard spoken about. Most of them were nothing more than interesting eccentrics, like my charming Uncle Octave. An exception has to be made for my great-uncle, also named Octave, who was obviously a great deal more: a mystic and a poet who was not granted the grace to express what he had in him. And there were other exceptions in the more recent generation, the one I knew, which contained a number of decent people worthy of respect for their courage, their endurance, or other qualities: for example, my paralyzed aunt, or the cousin who works as a nurse in a hospital for cancer patients. But the family didn't matter a great deal since I didn't see them often.

G   Where were you living at that time?

Y   I came to Mont-Noir when I was six weeks old. I have told the story of how my father, a few days after my mother died, sold the house he had bought in Brussels to accommodate his wife's desire to give birth near where her sisters were living and under the care of a physician, who, as it turned out, may have been careless and incompetent, given that my mother, like so many other women in those days of poor antiseptic technique, died in childbirth of puerperal fever. But Mont-Noir was never more than a summer home, even though people stayed there well into autumn. I'm told that I spent the first two winters of my life in the big house in Lille, but my memories of that house and its pretty garden are of course from a later period, when I made brief visits to my grandmother there. From the time I was three I spent every winter in the south of France until about 1912 (I can no longer be sure of the exact dates), and until 1914 spent the month of June in our large Paris apartment in a building, now demolished, on the avenue d'Antin, as it was then called.

From the time when I was very young we also went in the summertime to the beach—to Scheveningen in Holland and to various beaches in Belgium between the border and Ostende, where my father had friends, mainly lady friends. Sometimes we went to Brussels, for the same reason, and sometimes to Paris, even before my father moved there when I nine or so. My childhood was therefore scarcely what you could call "rooted." My most vivid memories, though, are of Mont-Noir, because there I learned to love all the things that I still love today: the grass and the wild flowers that mingled with it, the orchards, the trees, the pine groves, the horses, and the cows in their broad pastures. Then, too, there was my goat, whose horns my father had gilded. And there were the donkeys Martine and Printemps, which I rode, especially Martine, since I'd been taught quite early that the she-ass is the holiest of all animals (because she bears on her back the figure of a cross, commemorating the fact that it was a she-ass that Jesus rode on Palm Sunday). And I had a sheep that loved to roll on the lawn, and rabbits that ran free in the underbrush and for which I still feel an enormous affection—Zeno, you will remember, sets free a number of young rabbits just before he dies. I also had an old dog, whose death was heralded one morning by a loud gunshot. That was my first great sorrow (I was eight at the time). But I also loved the beaches with the endless plains that the sea left behind when it withdrew beneath the almost hypnotic rolling of the waves.

I have fewer memories of the south of France from this period, and those that I have have been overlaid by memories from adolescence, but I haven't forgotten the oranges we gathered in the yard (when there were no oranges my father hung some from the branches with string). As for people, I think that, apart from my father, who fortunately was with me, there were mainly those whom we then still designated in French by that lovely word, *les gens,* reminiscent of the Latin *gens,* the Roman tribe. Another thing I don't understand is how the fine word "domestic," which comes from the Latin *domus,* or house, could have lost its former sacred connotation (I suppose there simply must have been too many wicked heads-of-household). In any case, we lived with the domestics, *les gens,* under one roof. I can still picture Achille, the old coachman, and his replacement César the chauffeur, quite a lady's man; and Hector the gardener; as well as Hortense the cook; big Madeleine and little Madeleine, who sang in droning voices tunes that somehow had come to the village; little Marie, whose only chore was to churn butter in a chilled room, access to which was forbidden to all but the privileged; Joseph, the valet and butler; Melanie, Noémi's maid and as nasty as her mistress; and of course Barbara, my own maid. I learned very early in life that those people had as much of a life as I did and that it was good to be with them around the kitchen fire.

There was also the village procession, where I was dressed like the other children as an angel or a saint. And there was a sacred well into which coins were thrown to win the favor of I can't remember what saint, who must have taken over that spot from various Gallic nymphs. Since then I've tossed coins into quite a few places myself, in such diverse locales as Iceland and even here on Mount Desert Island, where there is a certain spring; and of course the Trevi fountain, into which Clement Roux tosses his coin (in *A Coin in Nine Hands*—TRANS.). And all over the world the small coins that people toss into the water are somehow symbols of human hope. I should add, though, that when I was a child the sacred well was less interesting to me than a certain shop nearby, which sold horrible chocolates with a sweet, creamy filling.

As for Mont-Noir, its great virtue as far as I was concerned was the rural life, the possibility it offered of knowing nature. It was quite important for a child to have grown up in the midst of nature, to have lived with animals, to have had daily contact with people of all kinds, to have lived a great deal among common, ordinary people. I say "common, ordinary people" because nothing better comes to mind to describe people who belong to no particular set or circle and whose lives are governed by necessity. A child living a fairly solitary life in a large house is obviously thrown into constant contact with the gardener, the coachman, the milkmaid. These people were my earliest acquaintances, and frequently I find that it is their present-day equivalents with whom I prefer to spend my time here on Mount Desert Island. It may be that the only people I like are those wrongly thought to be very simple folk.

G   You've led a nineteenth-century life, the life of a "model child" of privileged background.

Y   No, because I have no class feeling whatsoever. Nor was I a "model child"; the idea of being a "model" or of having one never occurred to me. I should add that I've always detested the books of the countess of Ségur; to this day the Bibliothèque Rose (a series of French children's books—TRANS.) makes me ill whenever I see a copy: the children in those books used to irritate me, and they never seemed real, sullied as they were by all the conventions, which I perceived quite clearly.

G   Yet those children lived lives remarkably similar to your own.

Y   No they didn't, precisely because Mme de Ségur did have class feeling and was conceited about family connections. Her books are full of cousins, people "of good family," distinguished guests. What did she see in such people? I, too, had cousins, but they were no more important than the gardener's son. No, class feeling is something utterly foreign to me. When I spoke this morning to the driver who delivered the clothes I had sent to the cleaner, my conversation was just the same, absolutely the same, as it would have been had I spoken to Churchill in his heyday. It was a matter of human contact, pure and simple. Some people are more pleasant than others, but that has nothing to do with class or even with culture. Let me take a moment to name a few of the residents of Northeast Harbor, whom I may not have occasion to mention elsewhere: Eliot McGarr and his wife, the gardeners who live next door—though not a hunter, this man knows or intuits everything there is to know about animals and plants. People say that he has Indian blood in him. Bernice Pierce, who used to clean house for us, is and always will be a friend. Then there are the three nurses, Ella, Ruth, and Didy, all so different from another. Ella is a sturdy and sensible New England bourgeoise. The other two are our neighbors. Ruth, born of Norwegian peasant stock, is fierce in the face of adversity. And Didy, a proud woman, extremely refined, has a sensibility similar to my own. (Without these three women, I doubt that I would have survived the repeated bouts of exhaustion I suffered while caring for Grace through a long and frightful illness). Jeannie, who is now my highly efficient secretary, I look upon almost as a daughter bestowed upon me by a stroke of good fortune. Then there is the old watchmaker, who loves to talk, over a spot of drink, about his youth in Transylvania. Dick, the fisherman-carpenter, is full of sarcastic wisdom. George K., now quite old, fled Armenia at the age of eighteen to escape the massacres in which his entire family died. He is almost illiterate, in English at any rate, yet quite an artist—he restores carpets, and many of the carpets in the Metropolitan Museum have had the benefit of his attention—his sense of color rivals that of many painters. Old Harry is fond of bending the elbow but never fails to appear for every occasion, happy or sad, with flowers or fruit from his garden or honey from his bees. And so many others, ranging in age from eighteen to eighty. Obviously I'm not talking about the literary people, "intellectuals," and artists in my own immediate circle or from earlier periods in my life. Some of them are very dear to me. But as far as human sympathy and respect are concerned, I see no difference between them and Bernice or Dick or Harry. That would be unthinkable. We are all alike, and the same fate lies in store for all of us.

Father

MATTHIEU GALEY:
In reading *Archives du Nord* one forms some idea of your father's character, and it begins to seem as if his character shows through, in a sense, in you.
MARGUERITE YOURCENAR:
I'm beginning to think you may be right, but only now that I'm practically at the end of my course. My father is a difficult sort of person to pin down for people of the present generation. As a type, he belongs to the past, and even in the past his type was, I think, rather rare. In *The Abyss* there is a character named Henry Maximilian, a soldier of fortune who loves literature and educates himself through experience, and, even though the two men were physically quite different, in describing the fictional character I sometimes thought of my father. He was one of those Frenchmen of a bygone era who were literate, straightforward, adventurous, incredibly impulsive and independent, quick to make up their minds, and impatient of the slightest interference or limitation on their freedom, and, to a degree scarcely imaginable today, totally unconcerned about the future. At times I've felt that Rimbaud—the real Rimbaud, not the Rimbaud of legend and literary anthology—must have been a lot like this.

My father was a man who lived by impulse and whim, a man of letters of the old school who read because he loved books, not for the sake of "research" or even learning, in any systematic sense. He was an extraordinarily free man, perhaps the freest man I have ever known. He did exactly what he wanted to do and liked to do. About the rest he concerned himself very little.

When I was fifteen, whenever anything went wrong, no matter what, he used to sum up the situation in a phrase that he probably learned in the army, where he had been a cavalry sergeant prior to his desertion—but that is another story. He used to say, "Oh, that, that's nothing to worry about! We're not from these parts, and in any case, tomorrow we're clearing out." This saying evidently captured his philosophy of life. Actually, what he said was closer to, "That's nothing to worry about! Who gives a damn? We're not from these parts, and in any case, tomorrow we're clearing out." He combined boldness with generosity and, for all his ardor, with deep indifference, with an ability to shrug his shoulders: time after time he did whatever his women wanted, whether wives or mistresses.

G   But how was he with you?

Y   He was very good but hardly a father. Just a gentleman somewhat older than I was—I wouldn't call him an old man because I've never paid any attention to differences of age—with whom I used to walk for hours, talking about Greek philosophy or Shakespeare or sometimes about things he remembered or stories he'd heard from people still older than himself, which gave me the advantage of a memory extending back over nearly two generations prior to my own. He was a friend with whom I used to visit churches and digs or discuss horses and dogs, a man who late in life reminded me of an old vagabond sitting by the roadside with knife in hand, eating a sandwich.

G   Did you ever have the feeling that he was a rather unusual sort of father?

Y   I never asked myself the question: he was the way he was. That was the long and the short of it.

G   At what point did you begin to think of yourself as your father's contemporary?

Y   Very early, from the time I was thirteen, perhaps, we thought of each other as equals, because age didn't matter to me. I'm not aware that I speak any differently to a child of six than to a man of sixty. And I don't feel any age. From time to time I notice that I'm no longer as strong as when I was twenty, but such weaknesses might have afflicted me when I was forty. I might have suffered from sciatica or circulatory problems at that age just as easily as now. Apart from that, age means nothing. If anything I feel that I'm still a child: eternity and childhood are my ages.

10

G   Such equality between father and daughter was a kind of privilege, wasn't it?

Y   A privilege, yes, but was I aware of it at that age? By the time I was fifteen or sixteen, yes, I probably was, and then, too, the best things, the most obviously valuable things such as intellectual companionship, had been taken for granted for so long that the question never arose. Later, after I shed tears over his death (which came when I was twenty-five), I confess that I almost forgot him for nearly thirty years. Which wouldn't have shocked or surprised my father, because a young person should forget and should live. It wasn't until much later that my father again occupied my thoughts for fairly long periods. But during my adolescence and early youth, our relationship was excellent and we had some fine exchanges. For one thing, it was my father who first developed my taste for truth and precision. He liked people to know exactly what they knew, and he liked them, when they formed judgments of a book, to proceed slowly. If we read something together, say a play by Ibsen, he insisted that we carefully put ourselves in the place of each character without letting our own feelings enter into the picture. And then, he never contradicted me, which I think is a great art when it comes to dealing with the young.

He never said, "Why did you do that? You shouldn't have done it, you were wrong." His sole desire was to forge ahead, and I still think there's no other way to carry on a conversation: drop the disputed issues and proceed in the areas where there is agreement.

G   And things remained this way to the end of his life? You stayed with him until he died?

Y   Yes, to the end. I took care of him, not very well, mind you, because at the age of twenty-four a young woman has her own concerns, her own preoccupations, and is a mere novice when it comes to sickness and death. I left him far more often than I left Grace Frick when she was ill, but never without asking myself, anxiously, What might happen? Should I be there? At the age of twenty-four one still has far too much confidence in life. But in the end I was with him: I saw him die. That taught me one lesson right off the bat, that he had lived a fine, successful life, when someone judging from outside might say that it had been a mad life of missed opportunities.

I felt this immediately. I was old enough to judge. And he, too, felt it. He felt that his life had been very full.

G   Do you remember any special moments in your relationship?

Y   It's very difficult to say, because we saw each other so frequently. No, I can't say that there were any special moments. There are moments from which I retain a particularly vivid image of him. I can picture him in Rome and certain other places in Italy of which I harbor fond memories. I recall some of his thoughts. He had never seen Florence before we went there together when I was twenty-two, and I remember him standing in front of Michelangelo's sculpture and saying, "For a man of my age, what is most impressive about this moment is that I shall probably never have the opportunity to return to this place, but these statues existed before me and will remain after I am gone."

G   A philosophy not unlike your own. But did you feel that you brought something to him?

Y   Yes, a great deal. By nature he was not an intellectual—not that I pretend to be one—but what I mean is that he could very easily have done without reading or seeing anything. He would have been perfectly content to walk in the forest looking at the trees, and I think that the sort of intellectual ardor that goes along with adolescence, such as I displayed, reawakened him, gave him a new lease on life. We helped each other.

Education

MATTHIEU GALEY:
Was it your father who made the decision not to send you to school?

MARGUERITE YOURCENAR:
No one made the decision, which in some ways was a non-decision. At that time it wasn't unusual for a child to be educated at home. Of course I had a series of governesses, but they didn't count for much, you might even say they didn't count at all. They taught me arithmetic and French history, but I always felt that I learned better on my own, which was in fact true. I wasn't good at arithmetic. The problems seemed stupid to me: How much fruit will you have if you fill a basket with three-quarters of a pound of apples, an eighth of a pound of apricots, and two ounces of something else? I didn't see the problem. I just asked myself why anyone would choose to arrange a basket in such a manner. So there was no answer.

G   Did you read a great deal?

Y   Oh, yes, a very great deal! At that time you could already buy pocket books for ten centimes (not the same as today's centime, of course). I probably still have one of those, which I've kept since I was eight: Aristophanes' *The Birds,* which I bought in the métro station at the Place de la Concorde. I read those books with passion.

G   How old were you then?

Y   Eight or nine. Obviously I didn't understand the plot, the moral, but it didn't matter since the stories seemed beautiful and the characters were grown-ups, interesting to think about. I liked *Phèdre,* for example.

G   Racine's *Phèdre,* at age eight?

Y Yes, I thought it was beautiful. Now, mind you, I didn't care much
about who exactly Thésée and Hippolyte were. The play was
beautiful, it appealed to me. I remember that some time between
1954 and 1958 I was in Paris and ran into Mme Pierre Abraham,
Jean-Richard Bloch's sister,[1] a woman who by now seems a character out of another era, a descendant of a literate, liberal, and
profoundly French family of Jews, some of whom died heroically
at the hands of the Gestapo (one niece was executed). Now, this
woman had published, more or less privately, a book about another
woman, her speech teacher if I'm not mistaken, one Jenny de
Vasson, daughter of an old family of the Beauce, also literate,
without the slightest desire of fame or success, and, on account of
her utter independence, a true aristocrat (in the etymological sense
in which I use that word, meaning "the best"). This Jenny de
Vasson had been educated at home, as I was, in a country house near
that of George Sand, and she had known Sand when the writer was
an old woman and she was a little girl. Now, in the curious and at
times remarkable material collected by Hélène Abraham you will
find that Jenny too at the age of eight or nine was reading
Chateaubriand or a translation of Dante, which no doubt left her
better off for the rest of her life. People nowadays ignore the genius
of childhood and deny that it exists.

G But did your father allow you to read whatever you wanted?
Didn't he advise you in your choice of reading?

Y He sometimes read to me, from Chateaubriand particularly. And he
read me Maeterlinck, including *Le trésor des humbles* (The treasure of
the humble), from which I acquired a taste for mysticism that has
been growing ever since. I felt that Maeterlinck's writing was
somehow a source of light, and defects such as a certain monotony
in the style which now seem perfectly apparent evidently didn't
strike me at all when I was nine or ten.

He also read to me from Marcus Aurelius, but the circumstances
were rather unusual: it was 1914, August 1914. We had just arrived
in England, having escaped from northern France via the Belgian
beaches because we were cut off from Paris, to which we would
have preferred to return. Somehow my father took it into his head
to teach me English, and he conceived the curious notion, significant

1. Jean-Richard Bloch, 1884–1947, novelist and playwright.—Trans.

perhaps of things to come, of using an English translation of Marcus Aurelius's *Manual* for my lessons. My father was no teacher, though. Imagine the effect of Marcus Aurelius in English on a child of eleven who didn't understand a word of the language. I stammered incoherently and after two lessons he threw that Marcus Aurelius out the window, which proves that the wise Roman emperor had not taught my father patience.

G When did you begin studying Latin and Greek?

Y I began Latin when I was about ten and Greek at twelve. My father taught me the rudiments and then we had two teachers who came to the house. But it was really my father who started things off. This was also during the war and it was quite cold. I have never been as cold as I was during that winter of 1915 in Paris, to which we finally did return after spending a year in England. We had been living in Paris since the sale of Mont-Noir in 1912 or 1913. My father had gone away in 1912, shortly after his mother's death. Selling the house caused him no distress, as it had been for him the scene of so many family difficulties and disputes. He found a place on the avenue d'Antin, which later became the avenue Victor-Emmanuel III, and, still later, the avenue du Président Roosevelt—who knows, some day it may be renamed yet again, avenue Mao. The wing of the building in which we lived has since been demolished. Six or seven years ago I revisited the site and didn't recognize it at all.

   We lived at number 15 in a beautiful old nineteenth-century house with an inner courtyard. We had a second-floor apartment overlooking the courtyard. I read a good deal during the time we lived there, but most of all I went to museums. That prewar move from the country to Paris was a wonder to me, because in Paris I discovered the museums.

G Didn't you miss Mont-Noir?

Y I was too young. For a child any novelty is wonderful. In Paris I had the Louvre, I had the Cluny, with its excavations, its Roman baths. For me it was the beginning of a great dream, the dream of history, which is just another way of saying the world made up of everyone who has ever lived in the past. At Mont-Noir I had only the church, which was not very pretty, and, in the park, a cave that had been transformed into a chapel. In the house were a few paintings and some bronze statuettes that my grandfather had brought back from Italy. Not much compared to the churches of Paris and the Louvre.

I should perhaps make it clear that in speaking of love of the past, what I really mean is love of life, for there is so much more of life in the past than in the present. The present is of necessity but a fleeting moment, even when the fullness of that moment makes it seem eternal. When one loves life, one loves the past, because the past is present insofar as it survives in human memory. Which is not to say that the past was a golden age: like the present it was at once frightful and grand, brutal and merely ordinary.

I should add, though, that even when we were living in Mont-Noir in my early childhood, we went fairly often to see the beautiful sights in the surrounding towns such as Arras and Furnes. Furnes especially impressed me with its giltwork and its beautiful churches. We also went to Bruges and occasionally to Brussels, where I stayed with one of my aunts—but I never liked Brussels. Then, when war broke out and we found our route blocked after the German armies had outflanked the French, we went to London.

We went by refugee-packed steamer via Ostende and stayed for one year in a place near Richmond. This is a time of vivid memories for me, for it was the first time I'd really lived in a big city from morning till night, and my childhood was three-quarters over. It wasn't only or entirely the big city, either: it was above all Richmond Park, the deer, that sort of thing. But we also saw a good deal of London, the National Gallery, the British Museum. There I saw Hadrian for the first time, a virile, almost brutal, bronze depicting the emperor at age forty or so, which had been fished out of the Thames in the nineteenth century, and I also saw the Elgin marbles.

G You talk about museums the way someone else might talk about the movie he saw last Thursday.

Y It's not altogether different, really. What I experienced in the museums was the birth of imagination. I toss that off rather lightly, because heaviness is always to be avoided, but it leaves a lot of questions unanswered: the imagination accepts the objects to which it attaches itself, but there are also things that it—I won't say rejects, but ignores, passes over. There are affinities, choices, which are not easy to account for. I should add that I, too, had a period of enthusiasm for the cinema, between the ages of twenty-five and thirty-five. Then I lost it, though obviously there are a few great films that I still admire. But I remain somewhat suspicious of shadows on celluloid, as I've explained in *A Coin in Nine Hands*.

G Do you recall any special moments in your visits to museums?

Y I remember quite well my first visit to Westminster. In the Gothic tombs I discovered the mystery of the Middle Ages. I have equally vivid memories of other things from around the same time, like a show of Meštrović, which was my first encounter with Slavic art and, I think, the awakening of an interest that was to take me later to the Balkans, to the Slavic east that furnishes the backdrop for my *Nouvelles orientales*.

G You've alluded several times now to the Middle Ages, but this doesn't seem to be a period that has especially inspired you.

Y It's true that I haven't written anything about the Middle Ages, but chance plays a large part in what one actually writes. For a long time I dreamed of writing an *Elizabeth of Hungary,* which would have been set at the height of the Middle Ages, around 1220, and would have revolved around the major figures who in a sense dominated the life of the young saint: Francis of Assisi, her inspiration though they never met; Frederick II of Hohenstaufen, a relative of hers and an atheist with an almost sublime intelligence yet a hard, cruel man whom Elizabeth nearly married; and Conrad of Marburg, the Grand Inquisitor who had been assigned as her confessor, which must have been frightening at times. (From the few words of hers that have survived, one feels that she came to judge him, with her feeble invalid's smile.) And there is also her husband, a typical simple-hearted German lad, on whose bed the chroniclers tell us Elizabeth "threw herself with joyful laughter" and whose death was one of the misfortunes of her brief life.

Had I written this book, obviously I'd have been immersed in the Middle Ages. I didn't write it, largely because I never returned to Germany, at any rate not to that part of Germany, East Germany, and also because I don't read German well enough. I would have needed too many intermediaries between the old chronicles and myself.

G At what point did you plan this project?

Y Oh, it was shortly after I finished *Memoirs of Hadrian*.

G   The book would have spanned the gap between Hadrian and Zeno—the Middle Ages between antiquity and the Renaissance.

Y   I never thought of it that way. What interested me was that it would have been fascinating—which brings us back to the mystery of childhood—to see the little girl Elizabeth suddenly discover herself as a little Christian, not in name only but in the true sense of the word, a little girl who shed tears at the sight of Christ on the cross when she went to church, while other little girls I suppose sucked their thumbs or thought about what they would have for lunch or about the dolls they had been promised. Once again you see the mystery of choice at work. You have the little girl who chooses to love the poor, who chooses to live the Christian drama by loving Christ in the poor and the incarcerated.

But it must be granted that she was an exceptional little girl. She had a crude father, a nobody, a thick-headed Crusader of some sort, and a German mother, a very arrogant, authoritarian woman, killed while her husband was away by Hungarian lords unwilling to be ruled by a German woman. Elizabeth had to judge her mother in the obscure way that children do judge, for when she was nineteen her mother's ghost returned from purgatory and asked her to pray for it. This was a kind of judgment, you see, since the little girl imagines that her mother is in purgatory rather than heaven!

G   Did you, as a child, have any mystical anxieties of your own?

Y   I would say rather that I had mystical intuitions. Let's say that I had an interest, a capacity to participate, in mystery, an interest that was fundamentally religious (in the true sense of the word, from *religare,* to bind together). It may be that I was born not for anxiety but for pain, for the infinite pain of loss, of separation from loved ones, for the pain and outrage that I feel for the suffering of others, animals as well as people, and for the pain of knowing that so many human beings live in such abject poverty and alienation from the light.

As a child I was very moved by religious festivals, by images of angels and saints. In an unsophisticated, naïve way I had a very strong sense that these stood for another world—how shall I put it?—a radioactive world in some sense, a world at once invisible and very powerful. My religious education came to an end very early, but I feel lucky to have had it, because it showed me the way to the invisible, or if you prefer, the "interior" world. People who have had no religious instruction, or whose education has been too baldly secular or even Protestant, remain cut off from mythical truth, from the everyday manifestations of the sacred. It's a big point in favor of the Catholic religion and a few other religions, that they have stayed in touch with such things. My father greatly enjoyed Slavic music and went often to the Russian church in the rue Daru in Paris because he had many Russian friends. I myself was quite moved at a very early age by the beauty of the Orthodox service and Orthodox rites, which I encountered again later on in Greece, and much later, but in an unforgettable way, at services in an Orthodox church in the Soviet Union.

All rites are beautiful, though. I love ritual. My culture is built on a foundation of religion, something of which my readers are completely unaware—they don't see it.

G To what extent is your culture religious?
Y That's difficult to say. During the period of my life that you called turbulent a while back, my Greek and Italian period, the appeal to myth was the sign of my fervor, my sense of being bound up with the whole. Somewhat earlier, in *Alexis,* religiosity expressed itself in the form of scruples, in the desire to do one's best, a desire tinged with religion and coupled with a certain tenderness, as in the character's feeling of pity toward his flatmate Marie, part servant, part prostitute, or in his emotions upon hearing peasants singing hymns in the night. I can't remember any more whether Alexis was Protestant or Catholic. At one point he says to his wife, Monique, "I used to be a Protestant, you used to be a Catholic." I rewrote that sentence three times. In the second edition it read, "I used to be a Catholic, you used to be a Protestant." And then I went back to the first version. In the end it scarcely mattered. The important point is that both characters come from backgrounds that were not what I shall have to call "materialistic" for want of a less idiotic word. In the next period of my life, myth became the chief vehicle for expressing all of this—that is, humanity's constant closeness to the eternal—through the Greek gods. These feelings have never left me and continue even today, more than ever, though now I've turned to oriental and, again, to Christian myths and away from the Greek.

G I can't explain this very well, but it seems to me that there is in you, in your requirements and concerns, a Protestant element. Am I wrong?

Y If I appear to be neglecting Protestantism in this discussion, the reason is that I was not exposed to it in childhood. Beginning when I was twelve, however, I came, happily, under the influence of a Protestant woman friend of my father's. This woman, whose influence came to me sometimes directly, sometimes indirectly by way of my father, has in my eyes always stood for an ideal of womanhood. Rather than "religious" in the narrow sense (though she was, as I learned later on, some sort of Lutheran), this woman was profoundly mystical, putting others above herself and finding in them manifestations of God, by whatever name you want to call Him.

Such an influence never wears off. Much later I came to know how much America's unfortunate black slaves benefited, in the nineteenth century, from the naked fervor of a certain kind of Protestantism, despite the fact that most of the white slaveholders were also Christians. And I also gained respect for the Quakers, for their social and humanitarian role and their admirable silent prayers, which strike me as a Western form of the Asian practice of meditation.

Finally, in the American friend who was my companion during the second half of my life, a period of nearly forty years, a woman who was a stranger to every sort of religion, what I appreciated more than anything else was her flawless integrity, the absence of all subterfuge, and her respect for the dignity of others, all virtues more Protestant than Catholic (which is not to say that all Protestants have them, far from it: there is always a mass of people, a mob sometimes, whose only service to the religion whose name they bear is to discredit it).

In some respects, I think, it's true to say that Protestants tend to be more open-minded than Catholics. On the subject of birth control, for example, the Catholic church refuses to acknowledge that the world has changed and must change. In another respect, I am supremely grateful to the Protestant minister of Northeast Harbor, who agreed to celebrate a memorial service for Grace Frick even though she belonged to no church, a service based on texts I selected, ranging from the Sermon on the Mount and the Canticle of the Creatures to the meditations on life and death of the

Taoist philosopher Chuang-tzu and the four Buddhist vows of
dedication to study and charity. I'm not sure that a Catholic parish
priest would have done the same.

What I want to say by way of explanation for the thoughts
expressed in the past couple of pages is that my own sensibility—I
was going to say, my emotional makeup—is not fundamentally
Protestant.

G So you're still moved by Catholic mysticism?

Y I like the mysticism that emanates, as it were, from ritual, provided
the ritual is beautiful and has not for one reason or another been
spoiled. I'm also fond of sacred images, and today whenever I visit a
certain church in Bruges and look at the statue of the suffering
Christ, the man of many sorrows, I experience exactly the same
feelings as when I was a little girl of eight in a village church in the
north of France. What moves me in the church ritual, though, is a
certain effort of participation, at a level accessible to all—which is
important, because there's nothing at all comparable in the realm of
the intellect. In church each person interprets the concepts in his or
her own way. Rituals in which people feel a sense of togetherness
are beautiful, because they represent a more fervent form of life
(and virtually the same thing can be said of festivals). This is true as
long as the rite doesn't degenerate into a sort of mass chauvinism,
whether it be Catholic, communist, fascist, racist, or whatever, in
which fervor quickly gives way to arrogance and hatred.

I have attempted to explain the mystical significance of ritual in
discussing a poet about whom I wrote a poor essay when I was still
much too young, just eighteen years old: Pindar. Upon finishing the
book that I recently published on Greek poetry, I said to myself that
the time had come to make it up to poor Pindar and that I would try
to elucidate this aspect of the Greek conception of religion, which
is not so very different from Catholicism, itself not unlike Shin-
toism in this respect: namely, that it is the splendor of the service,
the ritual, the feeling for the sacred that is important, because this is
what unifies the participants for a period of perhaps half an hour,
by exhibiting the various aspects of life in all their beauty. Such
beauty scarcely exists any more in religion, especially in Catholicism, which seems to shun it in favor of electric guitars and the like.
I think this is wrong. I think it is based on a misunderstanding of the

nature of religion, which as I mentioned earlier is "that which binds." The point is to bind each man to everything that is, has been, and will be, not just to the fashions of the hour.

G   Still, it seems to me that the aim of the Catholic church was to clarify its practices, at least insofar as the decision to say the mass in the vernacular is concerned.

Y   The question I ask myself then is, What is left of the religion? I think that the old words, which had been fixed for a very long time and which had served thousands upon thousands of human beings, carried a very high emotional charge, which has now been lost. They were in a sense mantras, and as soon as you replace them with ordinary everyday words it becomes difficult to root them in the human soul, in the human mind and sensibility.

G   But for you, as one who has always claimed to understand, to try to understand, this whole line of thought strikes me as rather odd.

Y   Yes, of course, one must try to understand, but not everyone is obliged to understand, and no one is obliged to understand all the time. There are certain areas, such as religion and poetry, that must remain obscure. Or dazzling, which comes to the same thing.

G   As a child did you have faith or was it merely emotion?

Y   I don't believe in faith, at least not in the sense in which believers use the word nowadays, almost aggressively. They seem to be saying that they believe, or that they force themselves to believe, in something that has not been proven, so that their great virtue becomes their willingness to continue to believe despite this absence of proof. One feels or suspects that their faith depends on an effort of the will, and indeed on a will to set themselves apart: we have the faith, it belongs to us, and anyone who doesn't have it is either pitiable or execrable. Nonbelievers are to be converted without regard for their traditions or personal feelings. Such sentiments are a long way from my own.

In the past faith was more instinctive and therefore more acceptable. Miracles, ghosts, apparitions—why not? This bird might be an angel, after all. And why can't it be so even now, since the word "angel" means messenger and every creature comes to us with a message of its own? Since the world is vast, why not accept realities such as these? Simple folk used to make no distinction between the marvelous and the real, the visible and the invisible. Both belonged to their imaginative life, and at bottom there was no mistake about what was what.

G   Do you think that different religions used to share comparable kinds of faith?

Y   Yes, I believe that fundamentally all religions share a common basis. When we study them in books or analyze them in depth, we are intimately aware of the differences, and these differences are real. But in a simpler sense it is the contact with the invisible, the unexplained, that is obviously omnipresent and always has been, even in antiquity.

In *La couronne et la lyre* (The crown and the lyre) there is a short poem, erotic but in a very discreet way, that depicts an amorous Greek who naturally hopes to seduce his beloved and prays for help to his minor household gods. This reminds me of François I, the king of France, who prayed in church that the woman who preoccupied his thoughts would turn up for an assignation. For both the Greek and the king, the miraculous was a natural part of life. In another sense these stories show that the very structure of reality was permeated by the sacred.

"Sacred" is a word to be taken very seriously. I always feel sorry for people who did not experience the religious myth as a natural and straightforward part of their childhoods. My own education was quite liberal, and no one ever said that I had to accept this or that dogma, but somehow it has left me with a lively feeling for the vast realm of the invisible and the incomprehensible that is all around us.

G   You stopped following the religious path while still quite young. Was this a reaction, a rejection?

Y   When I was still very little, I felt—wrongly perhaps, because there were ways to combine the two, but nobody told me about them—I felt that I had to choose between religion, such as I perceived it in my immediate vicinity, that is, the Catholic religion, and the universe. I preferred the universe. I felt this way even as a child, when upon leaving church I went to walk in the woods around Mont-Noir. At that time these two aspects of the sacred—religion and the universe—seemed incompatible. One seemed far more comprehensive than the other: the Church hid the forest from view.

23

I'm not saying that everyone must necessarily face such a dilemma. I have no difficulty imagining a Catholic capable of combining the two, particularly the more broad-minded Catholics you find today or, even more, those you used to find ages ago. But in the rather attenuated Catholicism of the turn of the century, such a thing was scarcely possible. Later I discovered that Ireland's "antique saints" (to borrow Renan's phrase) did combine the two. A few of them, at any rate, harbored both a feeling for nature and a feeling for transcendence.

G Which Irish saints do you have in mind?

Y Saint Columban, for example, whose death was announced by a white horse that came and lay its head on the saint's breast. Or the eremite who reads his breviary alongside the entrance to a cloister attached to his little church: when he spots a deer fleeing its pursuers, he opens the gate to the cloister and the deer hastens inside and disappears. The man then closes the gate and resumes reading his breviary. The lord arrives with his huntsmen, all in a lather, and says, "Which way did the deer go?" The eremite replies, "God only knows," and turns back to his breviary, enjoying his play on words to the full.

Christianity of this sort could easily combine the concepts of nature and transcendence. In the third century Saint Blaise, who is mentioned in a note in *La couronne et la lyre,* took himself off to the forest after suffering various political reverses. One fine day, the emperor's huntsmen appear in the forest and find Blaise in the midst of a crowd of animals, to which he is preaching. The huntsmen want to draw their bows and fell their plentiful prey right then and there, but Blaise simply immobilizes them, much as a Hindu fakir might have done. Discomfited, the huntsmen go off to tell the emperor what has happened. The emperor then sends men to arrest Blaise, and this time, unfortunately, the miracle fails to work and the eremite is sentenced to death. "I see that God has not forgotten me," he says, and I think he must have said it with a smile. But what became of the animals in the forest?

These beautiful stories are part of a Christianity that I instinctively accept, much as I accept the overwhelming and utterly human story of the Passion of Jesus. The trouble is, these weren't the things my village curate taught. As a result, I came to the conclusion that I had to choose between a set of dogmas on the one hand and the universe on the other. I chose the universe. Later on, the study of oriental religions influenced my judgment; I became fascinated and utterly absorbed, and this helped to bring me full circle to the Christianity of my childhood, which I was now better able to appreciate.

No one, or almost no one, has yet noticed that the Prior of the Cordeliers (in *The Abyss*) is Zeno's *paradrome,* and his equal; that the Christian and the would-be atheist "meet beyond all contradictions"; and that, when Zeno, near the end of his death agony, thinks he hears steps coming toward him ("This person who was coming to him could be only a friend"), it is the prior, for whom Zeno had cared in his final days. The dying physician cannot tell whether it is he who has once again been called to aid the prior or the prior who has been summoned to aid him. They meet again in an eternity which may be no more than a supreme moment.

Some Influences

MARGUERITE YOURCENAR:
In the course of preparing to write *Quoi? l'Eternité,* the third volume of *Labyrinthe du monde,* I had occasion recently to list some of the books I read as a child and adolescent. Two periods are sharply differentiated: the childhood influences have nothing in common with those that follow. In the end there were so many influences, they must have cancelled one another out.

To begin with, there were the fairy tales, of which I was very fond. Like any other child I attempted to act them out, for instance by walking around with a magic wand, touching it to some object, and commanding it to turn to gold. The objects may not have changed much, but it was a wonderful game.

Then there was the reading I did out loud with my father of books that he liked, such as *Le trésor des humbles,* which I mentioned earlier. I was eleven when he read me the historical novels of Merezhkovski, which were then in vogue; that mysterious man, though somewhat effete and something of a high-society figure, just may have exerted some influence on the direction I was to take. These readings took place in our Paris apartment. I didn't understand them very well, but the books left me with the sense of a crowd that all Russian novels give, whether by Merezhkovski or Tolstoy.

I also read Shakespeare. I read all my classics in cheap editions that I purchased myself, as I told you earlier: Racine, La Bruyère, and the rest. I remember an impression I had just after I began reading, or, rather, when I had just learned how to read and reading was still an entirely new experience for me. I must have been six-and-a-half, seven at most. It was a day when we were moving, and my father had left me alone in his bedroom while he busied himself with sealing our trunks. He had handed me a book that happened to be lying on the table: it was a novel by a woman who is completely forgotten today, whose name I happened to run across on a plaque affixed to the house she had occupied in Montpellier when I was

staying in that beautiful city some years ago. Born of a good
Languedocian family, Protestant I think, her name was Renée
Montlaur and she wrote novels based on the Gospels and the Bible.
Books of that sort were never among my favorites, but I remember
that this one was set in Egypt at around the time of Christ. I barely
knew where Egypt was, and I've forgotten the plot, but my eyes
happened to fall on a passage in which several of the characters
board a boat on the Nile at sunset. That is the impression I remember: the glint of sunlight on the Nile, when I was six or seven. And
that impression stayed with me, though it took quite a while before
it became an episode in Hadrian's travels through Egypt. It stuck in
my memory. I'm sure it would have astonished the author of the
pious novel from which I borrowed it.

MATTHIEU GALEY:
What other French novels did you read?

Y   In early adolescence virtually none. It was not until later, when I
was almost fifteen, that I began to read everything. I read Barrès,
of course. He was the man of the hour. The patriotic side of his
work didn't interest me. *Les déracinés (The Uprooted)* struck me then
as forced and artificial, and that opinion still holds. But the Barrès
of *La colline inspirée (The Inspired Hillside)* was overwhelming, again
because it combined the invisible world with another world, that of
the peasant's everyday reality. I still think that it is a great book.
Obviously there are slack passages, places where Barrès merely
tosses off a bit of Barrès, but there are other places where he
achieves the level of truly great art: the Lorraine landscapes, so
wonderfully described, and especially the solitude and old age of
Leopold, the magician and practitioner of occult arts, and his devotion unto death to Vintras, half fanatic and half charlatan, despite
the fact that Vintras is the cause of all his woes.

G   Did Barrès's style have any influence on your own?

Y   It's hard to say. Certainly not at the time of my first "major
experiments," when I was twenty, and not when I was writing
Alexis either. But after that, maybe a little. Overall I have had two
or three periods in which I wrote in different styles, which I can
pinpoint fairly accurately. The first includes my early sketches, my
Pindare, written by an adolescent who knew practically nothing, the
first "Hadrian," the first "Zeno," the two other short stories in *La*

mort conduit l'attelage, first drafted when I was twenty and subsequently rewritten in a style that was, though still immature, something approaching the "free" style I finally settled on. I hope that these stories, which I wrote or, rather, rewrote in this free style from beginning to end, will soon be published. It pleases me to think that one's style improves throughout life, as one sheds the scale of imitation, simplifies, finds one's path, while the underpinnings remain, shored up or, rather, strengthened by experience.

Then came my first published attempts to write in the genre known in French as the *récit,* very reserved, moderate, limited in scope: this was the period of *Alexis.* The development of my own personal style came to a halt until I was almost twenty-five, as I attempted to get in step with contemporary literature, especially the *récit* form as it was being used by Gide and Schlumberger;[1] I wanted to confine myself to a more literary, more restrained form of art, which was in fact an excellent sort of discipline.

This was followed by a reaction against *Alexis.* In the next period I wrote *Fires* and the original *Coin in Nine Hands,* in an ornate style that may have been influenced by Barrès but that was certainly also influenced by many others, Suarès[2] for example and all the baroque painters and poets of Italy. And after that I think I more or less found my own voice, beginning with *Hadrian.*

G   Did your father have literary enthusiasms that he passed on to you?
Y   He was very fond of reading and had his favorite authors, but enthusiasms, no, I think not. He loved Shakespeare and Ibsen, for instance. We read Ibsen together when I was sixteen or seventeen: he wanted to teach me to read out loud, and he conceived a sort of musical notation to mark the places where one should pause and where the voice should rise and fall. Ibsen taught me a great deal about man's total independence, as in *An Enemy of the People,* where the hero is the only person who sees that the town is polluted. The great nineteenth-century writers were often rebels, subversives, opponents of their age and their society, of all mediocrity. Ibsen, Nietzsche, and Tolstoy were like that, and I might add that it was with my father that I read all three.

1. Jean Schlumberger, 1871–1968, novelist.
2. André Suarès, 1868–1948, poet, playwright, and essayist.—Trans.

On the other hand, my father didn't read much Balzac. Though it may appear arrogant to say so, I would even go so far as to suggest that it was I who forced him to read a part of nineteenth-century French literature. For example, I was the one who said, "Let's read *La Chartreuse de Parme.*"

We read together a great deal, out loud. We passed the book back and forth. I would read, and when I became tired my father would spell me. He read very well, far better than I: he put much more of himself into the characters.

G   When did you discover Proust?

Y   Shortly after his (i.e., Proust's) death. I must have been twenty-four or twenty-five. But my father didn't go along with me there. It was his age that refused: he hated the thought of reading the latest books. For him Proust was the incomprehensible. He preferred the Russians, of whom we were enormously fond. And Selma Lagerlöf, about whom I was later to write an essay and whom I still regard as a writer of genius.

G   And Dostoevsky?

Y   I read him later on and admired him so much that I was virtually dumbstruck. How shall I put it? At times he took my breath away, so great did he seem. But he didn't exert much of an influence on me. His Christianity was—or at any rate seemed to me—poles apart from what mattered to me, though I was moved by the starets, Zosima. Yet I've never gone back to reread much Dostoevsky, and that's the real index of influence.

We read some French writers too, such as Saint-Simon. My father particularly liked the seventeenth-century writers. I read almost all of Saint-Simon with him. He introduced me to whole crowds of humanity, and I thought of him as the great observer of what happens and what passes by. As for style, his is so great that, unless one is a writer, one doesn't notice that he has one. His diction is admirable, but I sometimes wonder if it's because of the moment of history in which we now find ourselves that I find it particularly impressive.

G   And what about poets?

Y   Poets? The seventeenth-century poets, of course, and the Renaissance poets, and Hugo. I've always liked Hugo a great deal, despite the vagaries of fashion. I recognize that at times he can be heavily rhetorical, but there are also tremendous, dazzling moments. All the other poets, Rimbaud and Apollinaire, I discovered later in life. As I wrote in the preface to *Alexis,* I think that young writers are quite often not particularly involved with their own age, unless they happen to belong body and soul to a "school" with its finger in the wind, which tries to anticipate or at least latch on to every change in outlook. Generally speaking, the young writer takes his nourishment from the work of preceding generations. You see this very strikingly when you study the work of the Romantics. They hark back not to their immediate predecessors but invariably to artists somewhat further back in time.

G   Who were your predecessors?

Y   Oh, perhaps Yeats, Swinburne, and D'Annunzio. D'Annunzio was widely read at the time. Mainly the poems, many of them quite beautiful, which I read in Italian. I was capable of distinguishing between his novels, which are very dated, and those of his poems that have stood up well, provided, of course, that one is willing to overlook the rhetorical passages and baroque ornamentation which are as embarrassing in D'Annunzio as they are in Barrès.

Who else? Péguy? I never got very far with Péguy. I didn't like his aggressive brand of Christianity any more than I did Claudel's. Neither one really mattered to me. Baudelaire? Yes, but I didn't sample him until rather late, as a connoisseur—I read him with the eye of the professional, appraising the extraordinary perfection of the Baudelairean line. It was too late for naïve enthusiasm, so to speak.

My enthusiasm was reserved mainly for the seventeenth-century and Renaissance poets: Racine, to a lesser extent La Fontaine (it was not until much later that I came to appreciate the rhythmic beauty of La Fontaine's verse), and the English poets, especially the Metaphysicals, whom I read, of course, in the original.

If you're looking for influences, you'd probably do better to look to the philosophers. It would be impossible to overestimate Nietzsche's influence, for example: the Nietzsche not of *Zarathustra* but of *Joyful Wisdom* and *Human, All Too Human,* the Nietzsche who had a certain way of looking at things, from close up and at the same time from afar, a man lucid and acute as a writer yet light of touch.

31

G   What about someone like Schopenhauer? Was he important to you?

Y   Yes, but his influence soon became confused with that of Buddhism, because basically Schopenhauer represents the earliest attempt to develop the philosophy of Buddhism in a European climate. Still, I am moved whenever I think of Mann's Thomas Buddenbrook, discouraged after a long life lived according to the conventions of his time, discovering in Schopenhauer not only the meaning of despair but also, perhaps, the utmost peace.

Poems and Projects

MATTHIEU GALEY:
Despite your rather philosophical background, you, like many other novelists, first came to literature by way of poetry. In 1922 you published a small book of poems entitled *Le jardin des chimères,* which few people can boast of having read. What sort of book was it?

MARGUERITE YOURCENAR:
No sort of book. I wrote it in 1919, when I was sixteen, and it consisted of a "very ambitious, very long, and very boring" little poem—I'm quoting verbatim, I believe, from a review written by a polite and distinguished gentleman, a little precious as a writer, perhaps, but discerning and at the time quite fashionable, by the name of Jean-Louis Vaudoyer. His judgment was not mistaken. It was a poem about Icarus, regarded not as a precursor of air travel but as the symbol of an ascent toward the absolute. You can see that it was an ambitious effort. The cut of the poem was greatly influenced by Victor Hugo, almost to the point of plagiarism, and there was an epigraph consisting of two beautiful lines from Desportes, the best lines in that very slim volume:

> Le ciel fut son désir, la mer sa sépulture,
> Est-il plus beau dessein ou plus riche tombeau?

> *(Heaven was his desire, the sea his sepulchre. Is there a design more beautiful or a tomb more sumptuous?)*

Not bad choosing for a girl of sixteen. Except for this there was nothing; the poem consisted of Icarus's reveries. There was, though, one rather good, and rather touching, scene—my first portrait of an old man—depicting Daedalus conversing with Death.

G   What led you to your choice of subject?

Y Possibly Brueghel's *Icarus,* though I couldn't have known the painting very well at that time. I don't know, unless I imagined an Icarus
   of my own age, enamored not of flying but of the sun and eager to
   approach it. My father generously paid 3000 (old) francs to have the
   book published by Perrin—a subsidy publication. I followed this
   with another slim volume of verse, still worse than the first, since
   the poems in it were done earlier and in fact lifted straight out of my
   schoolgirl's copybook: this was entitled *Les dieux ne sont pas morts.*

   These poems contained overtones of just about all the poets of
   the late nineteenth century. Of course artists must learn their trade
   just like anyone else, but at least musicians practice their scales in
   their own rooms and don't bother anyone outside the family, while
   young writers sometimes publish too soon. It would have been
   better, I think, to have thrown those early works in the waste-
   basket. Still, I have often gone back to the same subjects I treated
   then: some of the poems that appeared in *Les charités d'Alcippe* in
   1956 were based on those early themes. So the themes did interest
   me. I had by this time already written a "Villa Adriana," but it was
   quite poor and naïvely "literary," like most precocious work of
   adolescents in too much of a hurry to write.

G How did you envision the future at that time?
Y I didn't envision anything, but I felt that I was someone who
   mattered because I *existed.* I remember that when I was eight,
   perhaps—I'm trying to picture how old I was by the clothes I was
   wearing and the furniture in the room—I looked in the mirror and
   said to myself, Look, I *exist,* I'm important, and these people don't
   even suspect. By "these people" I meant all the people around me. I
   had a strange certainty—strange considering the fact that as a child
   I was, as I have described Alexis, "naturally humble," and some of
   that natural humility lingers on, I think, even today—I had a
   strange certainty that I *was* somebody. I also had some vague notion
   of glory, as in the seventeenth century. But I had no way of imagining what that might be or how I would obtain it, even after I published those two slim volumes of verse. They didn't mean a great
   deal to me.

   Most writers begin, or used to begin, by writing poetry. Which is
   quite natural, since rhythm sustains as well as constrains. There's an
   element of song in poetry, and an element of play and of repetition,

which makes things easier. Prose is an ocean in which one could easily drown.

G Was this when you hit upon your pen name?

Y My father and I made a game of it. We had a good time trying to figure out what could be be done with those few letters (Yourcenar is an anagram of Crayencour, the writer's family name—TRANS.). My father offered to pay for the publication of my Icarus poem as a sort of Christmas present, and he asked me if I would prefer to publish under a pseudonym. I answered, "Yes, of course." In the first place, a pseudonym puts some distance between you and the family tradition, assuming there is one, and in any case frees you from possible family fetters. My father naturally respected my wishes. So we set about looking for a name and passed a pleasant evening making anagrams of the name Crayencour, moving words and letters around on a sheet of paper until we came up with the name Yourcenar. I'm very fond of the letter Y, which is such a beautiful letter. Someone like Louis Pauwels or Julius Evola will tell you that Y stands for all sorts of things among the Scandinavians or the Celts: a fork in the road or a tree—yes, especially a tree, with arms spread. So, we said, "Fine, good for the Y." And, as it turns out, I've stuck with that pseudonym through thick and thin. At one point I even adopted it as may legal name. But you see the role that chance plays in such things!

G Did you think of changing your first name?

Y No, because my first name is very much *me*. I don't know why. It's hard to imagine yourself with a different first name. Perhaps because you heard it so often when you were a child. After all, you hardly write your last name at all until you reach the age where you have to sign checks and official documents.

   I liked the name Marguerite well enough. It's the name of a flower and comes to us via the Greek from an old Persian word meaning "pearl." It's a mystical first name. But it was given to me, as I explain in *Souvenirs pieux,* mainly because my mother's old German governess was named Gretchen, or Marguerite. Thus I owe it to that most virtuous and almost unbearable old woman that I have the name that I do. I like it because it belongs to no particular period or class. It's a name that has belonged to queens and peasants

alike. It would have bothered me to have a name like Chantal, for
instance; it, too, is a saint's name, but it smacks too much of the
Sixteenth Arrondissement.

G Regardless of the pseudonym, I see that you were interested in
   ancient mythology right from the start.

Y I first came into contact with ancient myth when I began studying
   Latin and Greek. In addition, I was lucky enough when still quite
   young to be able to travel, to discover the ancient world in its
   natural habitat, as it were. When I was eighteen—no, sixteen—I
   saw the Roman ruins of Provence, as we were then staying in the
   Midi: the arena of Fréjus especially, and the Alyscamps at Arles.
   And then, when I was eighteen, I made my first visit to Italy.

G Did it come as a shock to you?

Y A shock? No. But I found it quite beautiful, particularly the ruins,
   and the feeling that time's passage had made it possible to judge the
   events of the past, to separate out the dregs, as it were, through
   some mysterious process of decantation. I soon came to feel quite
   strongly that each period, each era, is like a cloud: it gathers,
   acquires certain features, and then its imposing bulk begins to thin
   out and disperse until it has disappeared forever. The next cloud
   will make a different impression, its shape won't be the same. I've
   often wondered what we would think of the Parthenon if we could
   see it as the Greeks did, brilliant with gold and color. And wouldn't
   Saint Peter's in Rome be wonderful in ruins, while it is merely
   overwhelming in its present gilt splendor? So, yes, I found Italy
   beautiful. Not shocking.

G But one might have thought that it would be shocking to a person
   from the north of Europe, from a very different sort of country.

Y Yes, but I must have had some of Italy in my genes, or perhaps I
   benefitted from some subtle sort of interference, some ancestor's
   acquaintance with antiquity or the humanist tradition. At any rate,
   in the past, many people from the north went to Italy. Musicians
   like Roland de Lassus and painters, including many Flemish and
   Dutch masters from Rubens and Van Dyck on down, have always
   flocked to Italy. At that time, though, I knew nothing whatever
   about them. Chance alone dictated my course. I might have gone to
   Spain. I almost went to India, because my unfortunate *Jardin des*

chimères and my *Icarus* had pleased a great writer whom I admired. I had sent a copy—or someone had sent a copy—to Rabindranath Tagore, who wrote me a beautiful and cordial letter inviting me to come to his university, Santiniketan, in India. But in those days a seventeen-year-old girl did not leave her family and run off to India. The time when busloads of hippies would wend their way eastward to Nepal was still far off. Since I'm acutely aware of the fact that every action, even the most trivial, both opens and closes doors, I've sometimes regretted my decision. My life would have been different. I would have lived among different people. Would I have reached the place where I am now, or not? Who knows?

G   By this time you must have already had in mind what you earlier called "projects of my twentieth year."

Y   Among the projects I had outlined were *Hadrian* and a plan for *The Abyss,* which at that time was entitled *Remous.* My ambition was to write long books. For *Hadrian* I wrote out several complete versions, some close to a historical novel, others more of a dialogue in the manner of Gobineau.[1] Fortunately I discarded all of those attempts. With *Remous* I went further, practically to the point of publication, which is to say that I wrote long drafts of a novel that would have spanned several eras. It would have been an *Archives du Nord* and an *Abyss* rolled into one. The book contained several imaginary characters who were to represent humanity at its finest. But when I reread my draft at the age of twenty-eight, it no longer seemed to hold together. There were major gaps and I didn't think I had it in me to fill them. I didn't know enough history. So I slashed it into pieces and made three stories out of it, which were published in 1934 as *La mort conduit l'attelage.*

The first story, entitled "D'après Dürer," was really the point of departure for *The Abyss.* In the first few pages of the novel traces of the original story are still fairly recognizable: the workers' uprising was already there. What is more, the last two pages of the story served as the germ for the last three hundred pages of the novel. Three other pieces remained from the original draft, and these I've recently rewritten.

G   Under what title will they be published?

1. Count Gobineau, 1816–1882, essayist and racial theorist.—Trans.

Y   The first story was called "D'après Greco" and was about incest. In its new form it will be called "Anna Soror." I didn't make many changes because the theme was too simple to allow it. I merely added a few details and loosened up certain conversations, nothing more. When I looked at the 1934 text of the second story it struck me as overly vague, flat, confused, and pallid. So I told myself that I would have to write a new story on the same subject. Which I did, and I'm just now in the process of finishing it. I still have a few pages to go. For a moment the title is "Comme l'eau qui coule" (Like water that flows), because it is about life's passing and because a man who is poor, sensitive, virtually without education and yet never taken in by appearances or clichés, is willing to let it pass. As in my adolescent draft, the hero is a Dutch workman, but I know much more now than I did then about the life of the worker and about Holland, to say nothing of life in general. The collection itself will be entitled *Comme l'eau qui coule.* The final piece, "Une belle matinée," will be a dream story just a few pages long, in which a child dreams of what its future life will be.

G   When and why did you decide to abandon these major projects of your youth?

Y   It's difficult to remember. One strange thing—on this point, no one can contradict me, since I'm the only person who has read these manuscripts—is that the dialogues in the first version of the Hadrian story were not bad at all, in their Gobineau-like manner, both immersed in and detached from their period. A book could have been made out of them. I really don't know why I decided to scrap the idea. I must have felt that I was very far from the reality of the situation, that Hadrian was not altogether the way I had depicted him, and that one could depart only so far from verisimilitude.

Why? How does it come about—it's something of an intellectual scandal, actually—that by altering the distance between oneself and a particular aspect of reality, say the fact that there is a glass on this table in front of us, one can utterly change all one's thinking, and even the quality of one's perception. Certain painters have been aware of this. Close contact with reality is, I think, absolutely essential, essential even in an almost mystical sense. In an almost physiological sense, truth, insofar as we are capable of approaching it, depends on our keeping faith with reality, in the same sense as

Nietzsche spoke of keeping faith with the earth. What I had to do was to learn enough about Hadrian to know the circumstances surrounding his visit to the Spanish mines, what legal judgments he handed down, what illnesses he suffered from, what poets he liked. From these facts a phantom arose.

So you see, it makes no difference whether we're talking about people in our immediate vicinity, people who actually lived in the past, or fictional characters: it's as if we were guided not just by our thoughts and feelings, as they are or were, but also by a system of sympathies, by I don't know what affinities that force us down into the realm of the senses or, rather, the realm of contact.

I realize that there is no way to explain what I mean when I say that reality (whatever we mean by that vague term), the most detailed possible knowledge of everything that exists, is our point of contact with, our gateway to, things that transcend reality. As soon as we lose touch with certain very basic realities, we begin to concoct fables and degenerate into rhetoric or sterile intellectualism.

I must not have been very clearly aware of these things in my early youth, but in the end I did begin to sense them. Probably also there were various events in my personal life, changes of locale and circumstance, that led me to abandon my early book projects, begun at a time when I was not yet capable of incorporating enough of the real.

G The reality you're speaking of—is it really that important for a novelist?

Y Oh, yes, terribly important, just as important as for the author of a tragedy or for the epic poet, of whom the novelist is the present-day heir. The novelist needs to believe in what he does. In my case, at any rate, the important revelations about the nature of my characters came to me through certain true details, certain contacts, certain incidents, certain objects.

With Hadrian, for example, the important moment came when I stumbled upon certain little-known documents from which I learned that on such and such a date at six o'clock in the morning Hadrian happened to be at such and such a place in Egypt. From those few details a whole day in the life of the emperor was conjured up.

G But why did you burn all the early versions?

Y   The safest way to get rid of something that isn't good is still to destroy it. The early versions of *Hadrian* emphasized the mystical aspects of Greece, the initiatory rites. In *Les charités d'Alcippe* as well as in my translations of the Greek poets there remain certain broken lines which I inserted to serve as intervals of rhythmic silence. In particular, in *La couronne et la lyre* there is a poem that Antinous was asked to recite by Chabrias, his initiator in the Orphic rites, entitled "Poème trouvé dans une tombe d'initié orphique: Sur le seuil de la porte noire" (Poem found in the tomb of an Orphic initiate: On the threshold of the black gate). What I discovered was that even though there is a certain truth to all of this, since Hadrian did spend a good deal of time with various mystical philosophers and seers, in my writing it was more poetic than historical, and there was a lot I missed. For one thing, I had nothing about Hadrian as prince. So I dropped the project.

As for *Zeno,* my other project at that time, again I felt that I wasn't yet mature enough, that there was too much that I didn't know. I had charted a course but there were still large gaps in my knowledge of history and my knowledge of life. When it comes to making a book, you've got to know how to wait.

G   You have written somewhere that it is impossible in this day and age to avoid falling into "the rut of the novel." Why? Why write a novel and not a monograph or a historical essay?

Y   Because I wanted to show things from a certain angle, I wanted to offer a certain image of the world, to depict a man's fate in a certain way which I could do only by telling the story of a man or a group of men. I believe in the immense freedom that history grants us when it demonstrates to our contemporaries that what they believe to be unique is in fact part of the ebb and flow that is the human condition, and that the solutions to problems that people today put forward, or fail to put forward, are not the only possible answers, that others have been tried in other times and other places that might work better.

At the same time, however, I am wary of the fact that historians systematize, that history is often no more than the historian's unavowed personal interpretation or an ephemeral theory aggressively presented in the guise of truth. Historians conceal the origins of their work, whether personal or ideological or sometimes both, the one camouflaging the other. Yet no historian studies anything without having a reason for doing so: one may be a nineteenth-century bourgeois, another a German militarist who admires Roman imperialism, still another a Marxist who invariably discovers communism, or the absence of communism, wherever he looks in the past. Historians are ruled by theories, sometimes without their even being aware of it. But if, in fiction, you have a character speak in his own name, as Hadrian does, or if, as I did in the case of Zeno, you use diction that stays fairly close to the language of the period and an indirect style of narration, which is really a monologue in the third person singular, then you end up putting yourself in the place of the person evoked. You find yourself in a particular situation, that of this particular individual, at this particular time, in this particular place. This roundabout course is the best way to capture both the human and the universal.

G   Your stories often use a well-defined frame such as a letter or a monologue, devices rather seldom used in contemporary fiction. Why do you feel this need?

Y   Because a frame imposes limits, and because the subject wouldn't survive outside the frame. I said this about *Coup de Grâce,* but it's true in general. *The Memoirs of Hadrian* could only have been set in a moment of history when things looked relatively bleak, a period of exhaustion—the exhaustion of the ancient world figures prominently in the book—and yet a period when it was still possible to believe that things would continue the same way for some time to come. Fifty years later and it would have been too late, fifty years earlier and it would have been too soon: people wouldn't have been aware of how fragile things were. What the frame gives you is a precise location of a moment in the past; it's because of this ability to locate the moment precisely that lessons drawn from the study of the past still have validity for us, even if the conclusions seem to be based on a letter or monologue in which a historical figure appears to speak merely for himself.

Alexis

MATTHIEU GALEY:
You began your career as a writer, of prose at any rate, with a historical work devoted to Pindar, which you now disown.
MARGUERITE YOURCENAR:
It was more of a literary biography than a historical study. It was, in its own naïve way, purely and simply a potboiler. Fictionalized biographies were a popular form at that time, and I said to myself, I know some Greek, why not write about a Greek poet? It was André Maurois who inaugurated this fashion, and he was quite successful at it, increasingly so as he grew older, and gradually reduced the dose of fiction that he mixed in with the biographical facts. His late works are very good, in my opinion, especially his *Balzac,* but I was a long way from achieving such heights. I chose Pindar as my subject without the slightest notion that it would have taken me twenty years to understand the meaning of Pindar's world view.

G   How did you come to write *Alexis* after this detour through history?

Y   How can you ask me such a question? I was twenty-four years old and was beginning to learn enough about what people call "life" to take an interest in one of my contemporaries. Alexis was someone I knew and loved, but in describing him I wanted to achieve a certain distance, to set him in another period, twenty years earlier, separated from where I stood by the abyss of World War I. This was necessary to sharpen my view, to detach my character sufficiently from the all-too-vivid impressions of the moment. Another reason for my choice was that the present is so limited—it's now, you and I, here in this room, talking to one another, nothing more—and it's already different from the moment when you arrived this morning. This present moment, brief as it is, is also vast and full of relationships that elude us, which we can begin to unravel only by achieving a certain distance from it.

This, I think, is something I've always been aware of. I've always been suspicious of immediacy in literature, in art, and in life. At any rate I've always been suspicious of what people take to be immediate, which is often only reality's most superficial aspect.

G It's also a rather common practice in classical literature, isn't it, to set a story in an earlier time?

Y In an earlier time, or as Racine put it when he was writing *Bajazet,* "at a distance." The point is to sharpen your view, to place the subject where you can see it best.

G Paradoxically, though, *Alexis* is perhaps the most dated of all your works. It's a "period piece." It strikes me as rather Gidian in character.

Y Much less Gidian than people think. Rilkean, rather—I'll come back to that. The story concerns a young man who, after two years of marriage, writes to his wife to explain why he is leaving her. I wrote this "intimist" work in reaction against the vastness of my earlier projects. It also represents a sharp turn away from *Pindare,* which was crudely designed to fit the taste of the moment for "fictionalized biography." For the first time I attempted to concentrate on a story which, though narrowly delineated, would allow me to delve as deeply as I was able into my character's psychology. The book has been likened to Gide's work for the obvious reason that it concerns a homosexual (if you care to use the word) who loves his wife yet feels compelled to leave her. Homosexuality—a word I find annoying, by the way—has been much written about since. I'm still happy with the way I presented the subject, because in my opinion it corresponds perfectly to the sensibility of the character. And this sensibility is not confined to the period in which I wrote the book: abundant correspondence, much of it anonymous, proves the point as far as I am concerned. Of course there is much else that could be said, and said more directly, but then it wouldn't be Alexis who is speaking.

G Another reason for comparing you to Gide is the book's title, *Alexis ou le traité du vain combat,* which is reminiscent of Gide's *Traité du vain désir.*

Y The title, yes, that was Gidian; it came from a youthful work of his, whose title struck my imagination, though the book itself was rather disappointing. The truth of the matter is that there was a much stronger influence than Gide's, namely, Rilke's. Rilke was my great discovery in those years: not yet the Rilke of *Duino Elegies,* not quite, but the Rilke of *Malte Laurids Brigge.* He has the same tone as Alexis, the same scruples as Alexis—not just with regard to one particular subject but in general. Alexis's religiosity, the tenderness he bestows upon living and inanimate objects—these are much closer to Rilke than to Gide. Obviously, the basis of the comparison with Gide is that the work was cast in the form known as the *récit,* which in our day is virtually synonymous with the name of Gide. Anybody who wrote a *récit* was automatically compared to Gide. Gide's great contribution was to show the young writers of his day that that apparently outmoded form, which people had associated with *Adolphe* or even *La princesse de Clèves,* was still usable, still had something to offer.

G Didn't it also, perhaps, offer you a kind of self-assurance as a writer, particularly since its style was so polished, so glacial?

Y I don't think that the style of *Alexis* is glacial in the slightest. It's tremulous. A few months ago I read a bulky dissertation by a scholar who has noticed that the style of Alexis is one of withdrawal. His analysis shows that there is constant vacillation in the writing, backing off, almost to the point of stammering, something you also find in another short work of mine which is far less well known, the *Dialogue dans le marécage* (Dialogue in the swamp). The deceived husband speaks in the same way: "I am jealous, that is, I was jealous, or I almost was, or at any rate I think I remember being jealous." It's a way of grasping something without quite grasping it, while still groping about.

G But why choose what you once called "a subject fraught with taboos" to make your entrance into literature?

Y That didn't bother me.

G Nevertheless, you once wrote that "the world of sensual realities is hedged about with prohibitions, the most dangerous of which are perhaps linguistic." What did you mean?

Y Yes, I did write those words, but twenty years after *Alexis,* at a time when I had thought a great deal more about what other people think, or profess to think. I would point out that now when we discuss the sexual problem we use a Freudian or post-Freudian jargon. In other words, we still focus our vision of reality quite narrowly, we still enforce the use of certain words that seem indispensable because everybody uses them. But how closely do they actually correspond to reality? Do they perhaps distort or conceal it? Somehow we never ask ourselves these questions.

I think that, without intending to, I succeeded in solving the linguistic problem in the case of this twenty-four-year-old Alexis. Through an extraordinary series of lucky breaks, I found solutions that were, I wouldn't say facile, but plausible. The tremulous, hesitant style was able to convey a vacillating psychology. Moreover, since the story ends when Alexis is only twenty-five, the problems he raises are really only the beginnings of problems. Where would he be at age forty? My book wasn't obliged to say. Alexis's future didn't concern me, and I felt myself under no compulsion to consider what changes he might undergo. I didn't think about such things myself, and I was the same age as Alexis. I had little or no notion of what my character might become in the future.

G   Weren't you tempted to take the point of view of Monique, Alexis's wife?

Y   I often thought of it but was prevented by the frame I had chosen for my story. In order for Monique's story to introduce a new element, rather than simply merge with Alexis's story after she comes inwardly to accept his love, I would have had to focus on a period in their lives ten or twenty years later, at a point when, though still in love with him, Monique would have begun to judge Alexis and possibly also to judge herself. But I had set Alexis's story in the past, even though the personal experiences on which it was based occurred in 1928. The Monique of the novel would have been forty in 1930, too old compared with me. We fell between two eras, as it were. I've often thought of writing a *Monique* and still toy with the idea from time to time, but the problem now would be so different that the book would no longer be a "companion volume" to *Alexis*.

To begin with, the central problem would no longer be sexual. What has happened with *Alexis* is what always happens with books that endure. To give you an example of what I mean, I was recently reading the *Journal* of the Greek poet Seferis, who observes that in the work of Cavafy, who was one of the masters of his generation, it was the sexual aspect that aroused or shocked readers when the poems first appeared. To some extent this is still true, as I see now that the first translations of Cavafy's work are beginning to appear in France, my own and several others. People invariably get caught up with that issue. Whereas in Greece, as Seferis points out, nobody talks about the sexual content any more. It's comparable in some ways to Baudelaire. When *Les fleurs du mal* was first published, people talked about the trial and the censored sections. Nowadays anyone who dwelt exclusively on such details would be judged an imbecile. What counts is Baudelaire's genius, nothing else. In the same way, you'd be taken for a fool if you analyzed *Madame Bovary* as a portrait of adultery, as lawyers and judges did in the nineteenth century.

The case of *Alexis* is in some respects comparable: what remains an issue is the question of how a musician or poet is born, how a person, in order to raise himself to the condition of artist, draws on everything that he has in him, including his sensual underpinnings, and who repudiates, at least for a time, everything that he is not. The book might also be seen as a poetic cycle of departures and homecomings, Alexis hastening to Monique's side only to abandon her again a moment later.

G   Yet this is one of the rare works that you've never attempted to rewrite.

Y   Because *Alexis* seemed to me to be sufficient unto itself. The only books I've rewritten are those I judged to be botched or incomplete for one reason or another. I rewrote *Hadrian* because I wasn't happy with the early versions. I rewrote the beginning of *La mort conduit l'attelage* for use as yeast in brewing up *The Abyss* because I saw clearly that what I had done originally did not hold up. I rewrote *A Coin in Nine Hands* because I found that the protest against fascism that I had wanted to make had come out more stylized than heartfelt. The horror of that period of Italian history had not penetrated me profoundly enough at first. And that about does it for rewriting, except for the two short stories I mentioned earlier, which I reworked for similar reasons.

There are a number of books that I've never rewritten—*Alexis, Coup de Grâce,* and *Fires*—because I felt that I'd said what I had to say. I couldn't have gone any further with them. I've dreamed of writing a sequel to *Coup de Grâce,* depicting Eric as an old man, in much the same way as *Monique* would have been a sequel to *Alexis.* But in both cases, and in various other "sequels" that I've imagined writing for the characters in *A Coin in Nine Hands,* so many contemporary issues become involved that the books would turn out to be something quite different from sequels, unrelated to the works that inspired them. I would have to shoulder the burdens of a whole new world. If I live, maybe I'll do it some day.

G   How could you be sure, though, that you'd "said all you had to say" in the books that you didn't rewrite?

Y   Increasingly I've noticed that the way to penetrate most deeply into another person is to listen to his voice, to understand the melody of his being. Hadrian has one voice, Zeno another, and it is impossible to confuse the two. A voice consists of a specific tone, a specific way of expressing things, a specific way of establishing a relationship between the person speaking and the person being spoken to. Zeno speaks to Henry Maximilian or to the prior, and Hadrian speaks to us across the centuries.

You've got to work to hear, you've got to create a silence within yourself in order to hear what Hadrian or Zeno would say in a particular situation. And you must take care never to put in your own voice, or at least see to it that what you do put in of yourself is at the level of the unconscious: you nourish your characters with your being as you might feed them your flesh, which is not at all the same thing as feeding them your own petty personality with all the idiosyncrasies that make us who we are.

I had no trouble hearing the voice of Alexis. I remember writing the novel under difficult conditions, in a hotel room somewhere in one of the rare moments I had to myself, but I wrote it straight off, on the typewriter, without revising. Even today I work only when I have the time. You've seen my house, which is always open. I can be writing the death of Zeno, and the gardener or the carpenter will come knock at the door and say, "I have something I want to talk over with you," and I'll reply, "Fine, come in and have something to drink," or "Sure is cold today, isn't it?" Eventually the visitor will leave and I can get back to the death of Zeno—which has been continuing all the while.

G When you wrote *Alexis,* did you feel that your true work as a
writer had begun, that you had found your way and your voice?

Y I don't think so. Surely not "my voice," at any rate not in its full
range. All I had found was Alexis's voice. When I'd finished the
manuscript, I told myself, Now it's time to find a publisher. But it
was around this time that my father died, and naturally my memory
is blank as to other details. My father did read the manuscript
before he died. He never discussed it with me, but I found a slip of
paper stuck in the pages of the last book he opened, the letters of
Alain-Fournier to Jacques Rivière. On it he had written, "I've
never read anything as limpid as *Alexis.*" You can imagine how
happy I was! That final message contained all the friendship and
understanding that my father and I shared.

 After that I can't remember much, but I do remember that I sent
Alexis to a publisher almost immediately. One publisher rejected
it—I won't name names—and I then sent it to René Hilsum and
Martin Chauffier, whom I admired because they had recently
started a new house (Sans Pareil) open to young talent and had
published a number of books that interested me. They accepted it at
once. It was my second try.

G Did it give you great pleasure?

Y Of course, I felt a flush of personal satisfaction. This all took place
in the fall of 1929, an agitated period for myself and for the world in
general. The day the book was accepted was fair and cold. I left the
publishers with the munificent sum of 100 francs (or was it 150?)
which I had been given as an advance—in those days an advance
still meant something—and then, well, it was a first novel, they
were really quite generous to give it to me. I walked, I think, along
the rue Froideveaux to the place Vendôme, enjoying Paris and
telling myself, It's just a little book, you never know what will
happen, but still, now I'm a writer, I have my place alongside
everyone else who has ever written in French. I was a happy
woman. I went into the Lalique store, which still existed at that
time, and bought, for precisely 150 francs, a blue vase. It was a
milky blue, like the color of that wintry day. I still have it.

Love

MATTHIEU GALEY:
There is, in *Alexis,* a theme that is quite important, I think, because it occurs in a number of your other works as well: I'm speaking of the distinction that you make, or rather that Alexis makes, between pleasure and love.

MARGUERITE YOURCENAR:
Yes, you're right. The same theme figures in Hadrian, although, in the end, it is Hadrian's destiny as a lover that wins out. Hadrian is a man of abundant carnal experience who late in life basks in the sunshine of love. Such a thing is not uncommon; one sees it in many lives. But we must also reckon with what I like to call "the obscure portions" of a character's life, which no long novel can avoid. As an adolescent and while serving in the army, Hadrian surely knew love (I'm thinking of the army friend who, as Hadrian tells us, "went dragging himself about on bloody legs"). He loved or at any rate enjoyed with some considerable zest, as he himself admits, the young women who were his mistresses when he was in his twenties. Afterward, however, he discovers that those affairs have faded into oblivion or succumbed to skepticism. But when at the age of forty-seven he meets Antinous, the older Hadrian almost immediately feels that this is a unique encounter, even though he soon notices that his passion occasionally lapses or wanes. Finally, death places its seal on Hadrian's sense that, of all his loves, this one was unique. Something should also be said about the moments of fatigue in his grief, moments during which Hadrian feels "spellbound" by this memory and suffers for it. In such a case it is only poverty of language that forces us to make a distinction between pleasure and love. Doubtless the two are indissolubly fused.

In *Alexis,* though, I think I introduced the distinction mainly in reaction to the clichéd French notion of love, which I felt, and still feel, did not ring true. The French have in a sense stylized love, created a certain style of love, a certain form. And having done

51

that, they proceeded to believe in what they had invented, they forced themselves to love in a particular way when they would have experienced it in an entirely different way had there not been all that literature behind them. In my view, it's only in France that La Rochefoucauld could have said "there are many people who, had they never heard of love, would never have felt it." I don't think that such a statement makes any sense here and perhaps in many other parts of the world. It's different in France because there everyone is exposed to the notion of love à la française, which runs through our literature from *Andromaque* to *L'éducation sentimentale*. Convention plays a large part.

Alexis's purpose is to keep the two sentiments distinct. The first thing is to know what one means by love. If love means to adore another person, if it means the conviction that two people are made for one another, that they complement one another by virtue of their unique qualities, then a thoughtful person is likely to see it all as a mirage and to say to himself, Look, there's nothing that exceptional about my beloved either. Let's take a good look at what we are, and love each other for that. This sort of love might be called "sympathetic" and it comes close to what the Gospels call agape; the senses have their part in it, to be sure, but a great deal of self-denial is essential. But is this what goes by the name of love in France? I doubt it.

G   What is sympathetic love?

Y   Let me put it this way: a deep feeling of tenderness toward another creature who (or which) shares our condition, with all its risks and vicissitudes. Such feeling is quite strong in me, but it isn't precisely what people call love in books or on the stage. Nor does it have anything to do with what is so inaptly referred to as "Platonic love." It is a bond—which may or may not be carnal but, like it or not, is always sensual—in which sympathy takes precedence over passion. I should add that one thing that has always troubled me in the French notion of love, and perhaps in all European conceptions of love, is the absence of the sacred; somehow, owing to our Christian, or perhaps I should say post-Christian, education and to all the psychology of the past fiteen hundred years, we have lost the sense that love, or, more simply, sensual bonds between two people, or for that matter ordinary everyday relationships, are sacred. Sensual relations are sacred because they are universal. Few Western women share the sentiments of the Hindu bride who, in marrying, feels momentarily that she is a goddess, a representative of Siva marrying Rama. In the West, if one member of a couple does have a feeling for the sacred of the kind I've been describing, it is highly unlikely that the other member will share it. Even more, there is an inward sense that sensuality is something coarse. The sacred element seems to be lacking, and in its place there is only prudery or ribaldry.

G   Has the sacred aspect of love as you describe it ever existed in a Christian culture?

Y   No, I don't think it has, perhaps not even in the marriage ceremony, at least not in a fully developed form. Christianity has always been divided on the subject of love, it has always been hostile, doubtful, disapproving of the flesh. But the Greeks may have had such a feeling for the sacred. They had great respect for marriage. What did that mean in practice? The first thing to bear in mind is that Greek marriage—what I am about to say may seem scandalous— always bordered on pederasty. A girl of fourteen would marry a man of thirty, so there was always a generation gap which made the man the dominant partner in sexual matters as in all others. It wasn't a matter of female inferiority but one of age, as in all forms of love among the Greeks.

Obviously, though, the Hindu *maithuma* was the most highly developed expression of the sacred in love (but how widespread was it in practice?). This was a rite in which the lover gradually accustomed himself to the presence of his beloved (who, incidentally, was generally a professional) by spending the night in the same room with her, dressing and undressing her, slowly achieving greater and greater intimacy and a higher degree of sacredness, up to the moment of full union. Maithuma was a very complex thing, a work of art. It was union with the divine through the agency of a human individual.

Alongside this I would place what one might call "charitable love," in which one person bestows love upon another without particular regard for the nature of that other, simply because the other is "a poor creature like myself, subject to the same obligations, the same dangers, the same ends." This is what I understand best, but I see no example in literature other than Price Genji in Murasaki Shikibu's novel, a sort of Don Juan worshipped by all women, who bestows his favors upon the ugly, red-nosed princess. And I might add that, for perfectly natural, physiological reasons, this form of love seems to be little practiced by men.

G   In an era such as ours, in which the religious spirit has waned, don't you find a sort of divinization of pleasure, which is now in the process of recreating itself?

Y   Yes, but generally as an end in itself, not as an instrument of knowledge or sympathy. And anything that is an end in itself usually turns out badly. What needs to be restored is the feeling that pleasure is a gateway to knowledge or to God, if you want to put it that way, or to another being in all its divine poverty. I am convinced that pleasure can serve as such a gateway, though no European poet or novelist has ever used it that way, or even felt the possibility. The Russians may have come a little closer. But I am certain that it can be so and that very simple people do in fact sometimes experience pleasure in just this way. You see something of the sort in that much despised but in her own way very moving character of Flaubert's, Madame Bovary.

This takes us quite a long way from love as it is generally depicted in French novels, love of the sort that Félix de Vandenesse thinks he feels for Mme de Mortsauf, to be precise, love that is really just an artificial form of adoration. At best it's a love of God that mistakes its object or that is filtered through a series of romantic spectacles.

G   But love in the French novel is always unhappy love.

Y   Yes, and it cannot be otherwise, in the first place because it is almost always love born of vanity. This is still true even in our feminist age. A short while ago a feminist journal, *F. Magazine* (to me the initial F calls to mind words other than *femme*, woman, but leave that aside), republished one of my *Nouvelles orientales*, "Le dernier amour du prince Genghi." I wrote to the editor, Mme Servan-Schreiber: "I'm somewhat surprised that you have introduced your readers to so devoted, so tender, and so humble a woman. They must have been shocked." The response I received, logical in its own way, asserted that, on the contrary, the story offered an excellent object lesson: "Don't be so devoted: look what happens when a woman is so devoted to a man!" For my part, I find the woman of the Village of Falling Flowers who figures in the story to be an exemplary figure. True, she suffers when she learns that the prince, on his deathbed, has forgotten the first moments of their love. Obviously this discovery is painful. But she comes back to the prince, who has gone blind, and takes care of him, nurses him, helps him to die. Thus she fulfills to perfection the lover's role for which she was destined, and everything is as it should be. Whether he remembers their early love or not is of no importance.

G   If you had to write *Alexis* today, it would probably take a totally different form. Do you think that the problem it treats still exists?

Y   It may still exist, but it wouldn't be posed in the same terms. It would be distorted by the very fact that nowadays sexual freedom appears to exist, but this freedom is more imaginary than real, more a fashion or social convention than a reality. I'm not sure that so-called liberations do much to alter the practical problems, if you look at them closely. Maybe things have changed in certain segments of society, but probably not in Alexis's milieu, nor for someone with his scruples. Had I written *Monique* I would surely have shown Alexis regaining his wife and then losing her once more as he lived out the consequences of his chosen course, happy and unhappy by turns because nothing is ever perfect or complete. But ultimately I just lost interest in this couple's fate.

Eurydice and Marcella

MARGUERITE YOURCENAR:
After *Alexis,* events in my life were such that I was unable immediately to begin writing again. Then I retraced my own steps, which was a mistake. Telling myself that the time had come to begin my career as a writer (how conventional youth is!), I wrote a bad novel—*La nouvelle Eurydice.* This novel, written I think in 1930 and published in 1931, has its loyal admirers, but I'm not one of them. I wanted to "do" a novel, and of course nothing came of it because I was then convinced that to be a genuine novelist one had to find a subject in reality and transform it into fiction. I had formed my own idea of what a novel ought to be: it needed episodes of this or that kind, a love interest, landscapes, this, that, and the other. You can imagine what a mess I got myself into! Incidentally, I plan to discuss this disaster in *Quoi? l'Eternité.*

MATTHIEU GALEY:
But you did publish the book nevertheless.

Y   I did. At the time I didn't realize how bad it was. You have to consider the circumstances. It was a time when publishers would publish anything, and Grasset was producing sumptous editions for all its writers. It wasn't long, though, before I saw what I had done. I had taken from my own life an episode that might have made an interesting and rather unusual novel precisely because it would have been so unlike the usual novels of love, ambition, or vanity. Instead, it should have been a novel of influences, showing how different influences combine to affect a young person. But I told myself, No, you must somehow make a "real novel" out of this material. At the time I was incapable of sticking with the naked reality. I believed that what I was doing was setting out to write a real novel, learning my trade. It was as if a painter with some talent, who had already done some fairly good work, set out to learn technique in the studio, started painting according to the rules, and wound up producing work of the most tedious academic sort.

It was an extremely "literary" work, and I intend that as a reproach. *La nouvelle Eurydice* is the story of a young man who sets out to find a young woman with whom he had once been vaguely in love and discovers that she has married and subsequently died. At first he has great difficulty finding out what he wants to know. He goes from one place to another, attempts to locate her grave, in the end does locate it (or perhaps he doesn't—I can't remember any more), and in the course of looking picks up contradictory bits of information about the dead woman: some people say that she was as faithful a wife as could be, while others say the exact opposite. So that, in the end, the man has a hard time making up his mind what he thinks of her, a hard time deciding who the woman whose loss he is mourning really was. The characters were stereotypes; even the woman was a composite of two stereotypes, one virtuous, the other not. Her rather mysterious husband was not badly drawn, but the young man in love was quite vague and might have been taken from any nineteenth-century novel. It was a complete blunder.

G   What suggested the subject to you?

Y   A quite different story which I plan to tell in *Quoi? l'Eternité.* It has to do with my respect and affection for a woman whom my father nearly married but in the end had to give up because she refused to divorce her husband. When my father fell ill, I happened to be near where this woman had lived. I was then twenty-two, and, like the character in the book, I sought out her friends (she had died in the interim). Naturally the information I turned up was not always consistent. I went to see her physician and finally discovered her husband, with whom I had several conversations about her. It would have been quite beautiful had I told it as it was, the story of a young person's attachment to someone older, to whom she looked as a model.

G   Did you know her only through your father's stories?

Y   No, I knew her a little. I judged her chiefly through the stories my father told. And when I was fifteen, I saw her again briefly. Then, sometime in the next few years, she died.

Something beautiful might have come of it, but it would have taken some judgment and tact in matters of adolescent psychology

which I lacked at age twenty-nine. The subject was too unlike that
of the novels I knew.

G   Was it this comparative failure that led you to try your hand at a
    quite different genre in *A Coin in Nine Hands?*

Y   No, once again, it wasn't I who went off on a tangent, it was life. I
    was living in Italy, in different circumstances from any I had known
    previously. Before me was a different set of models. For the first
    time in my life I felt aware of current events, of what was going on
    in that particular year of history, and I had to improvise my tech-
    nique as the scene around me changed. I wasn't very sure of what I
    wanted to do.

    The book originated (as I've described in great detail in the pre-
    face to my play *Rendre à César,* which was drawn from the second
    version of the novel) with observations I made of various characters
    during a visit to Rome when I was twenty-two or twenty-three.
    This was either at the time of or shortly after the assassination of
    Matteotti, and feelings were running very high. Hence several of
    the novel's characters, especially the heroine, Marcella, who is
    based largely on an Italian woman I knew at the time, were mem-
    bers of militant antifascist groups, and it was through them that I
    shared in the excitement and emotion of the moment.

G   Didn't you feel that French writers were slow to notice what had
    happened to Italy?

Y   They didn't notice a thing. They—how shall I put it?—they suffered
    from a sort of lyrical attitude toward Roman Italy and Romanness in
    general, which they saw from a distance and described in the most oro-
    tund way. They spoke of what they liked to call a "tradition of
    grandeur" and saw nothing of its bombastic, fraudulent side. What I
    tried to show in my book was above all the life of the common
    people and the way they reacted to events.

G   Was the book written out of an inner necessity? It isn't like any of
    your others.

Y   Actually it's rather like *Fires* in some of its themes. But each book is
    born with its own quite special form, rather like a tree. An experi-
    ence transplanted into a book carries with it moss and wild flowers
    mixed in with the clump of earth adhering to its roots. Each
    thought that gives birth to a book conveys a whole set of circum-

stances, a complex of emotions and ideas that will never appear in quite the same way in any other book. And each time the method is different. To begin with, *A Coin* is based on a specifically Italian theme and therefore involves what I am tempted to describe as opera, the baroque, that sort of melody in plaint which is so peculiarly Italian and which I don't find in any of my other books, or elsewhere in reality for that matter.

G But the technique itself wasn't all that unusual.
Y I can't think of another book that uses the device of a coin passed from person to person. I have no idea why I chose this device. Obviously, as the idea took shape and I really got into the composition of the book, the ten-lire coin quickly came to stand for the external world, the state, in the sense of "render unto Caesar" (which is what I called the play based on the book, written thirty years later)—in other words, everything that stands in contrast to the secret, intimate life of individuals. And, as I came to put it much later, I was very much struck by the fact that so many of our encounters, so many of our human relations, are based on nothing more than the exchange of a coin or bill for a postage stamp or evening newspaper, an exchange that takes place with a person of whom we know absolutely nothing. In an act of this kind there is something purely automatic that can occasionally become fit material for a novel, though this happens rather rarely because in general we don't think about what we are doing.

But in *A Coin in Nine Hands* there is something else: a strong desire to draw a parallel between the characters of the novel and the figures of Greek mythology—the characters are seen as avatars of legend. The novel is constructed on two levels: one level is that of Roman popular life and concerns very, very simple people as well as openly subversive groups; the other level is, as always, mythological—the characters are assimilated to the figures of mythology. This was to make the reader feel the grandeur of their actions, not unlike the grandeur that one finds in ancient legend and myth, and in the year 1933 legend and myth were quite prevalent in Rome's "modern" center.

Marcella has something of Phaedra in her and something of Nemesis. Massimo is of course Thanatos, the angel of death, as well as Harlequin of the commedia dell'arte and medieval legend.

Marinuzzi is Dionysus. All of these parallels are maintained in the second edition, though in a much less pronounced way, because the realistic level of the novel is given greater prominence. As far as I was able, I tried to fill the book with the realities of that period as I remember them.

G   You were in a sense contradicting your own theory that we can get a clearer view of things by projecting them into the past.

Y   In this case I was projecting so far into the past that the story swerved toward myth. But I have no objection to the present, as long as the subject requires or lends itself to such treatment. Writing in the present is infinitely more difficult, however. The eye you need to filter events as they are happening is extremely difficult to acquire. The danger is that you wind up doing journalism.

I had a rather clear image of Italy, but the problem was that I didn't know what details to use to convey that image. That's undoubtedly why I redid the book years later with the same details decanted or further developed. I saw fascism as something grotesque. I had seen the march on Rome: gentlemen of "good family" sweating under their black shirts and beating people who didn't agree with them. It wasn't pleasant to look at. And I was never taken in by the claims of unanimous support. No country is ever fully in agreement with its government. It never happens. Rural people and workers weren't won over. They simply kept quiet.

G   Were you never tempted to become politically active?

Y   I am not Italian. It is difficut to become involved in the politics of another country unless you're deeply tied to it. But I knew quite a few people who were active, people who fought with the Italian resistance. Marcella was based on a real person. So was Carlo Stevo. Many of these people were anarchists. The anarchist tradition was, and still is, quite strong in Italy. It may be that it's too strong, given the terrorism that Italy has been experiencing recently. Italians have long believed in the possibility of individual action, including terrorist acts by individuals. But a writer can contribute to the political struggle simply by saying what he or she has seen. Dostoevsky's *House of the Dead* was a powerful instrument of combat against the czarist regime in Russia, and so was Tolstoy's *Resurrection*.

G Do you think that *A Coin in Nine Hands* had any influence?

Y No, in the first place because the original version of the book was
   not very widely read—and, to tell the truth, judged as a work of
   literature, it didn't deserve to be read. In the second place, the
   battle was already over, if such a battle can ever really be said to
   end. It might have exerted an influence had it been read as a
   warning of things to come, but people never, or only rarely, heed
   such warnings. Even *The Abyss* is a warning, but few people have
   noticed.

Money

MATTHIEU GALEY:
At the time you wrote *A Coin in Nine Hands,* were you living primarily in Italy?
MARGUERITE YOURCENAR:
No, I went there often, but I went other places as well. I traveled a great deal in Switzerland and Austria and, later, in Greece. I subscribe to the words of Zeno: "Who would be so besotted as to die without having made at least the round of this, his prison?"

G Maybe that's something you inherited from your father, who also seems to have been quite a traveler.
Y Quite a traveler indeed, but my father was the last man to bequeath anything to anyone. One of his favorite dicta was, "Where is one better off than in the bosom of one's family? Anywhere." And, "A man is at home only when he is away." No, he wasn't a man to think of passing on a tradition, assuming he had one to pass on.
G How did you live? Didn't you have any material worries?
Y None whatever. I've told how it was in *Archives du Nord.* It was a rather embarrassing chapter to write. It's always embarrassing to talk about money. My father didn't leave me anything. The fortune left me by my mother had been badly administered, by someone other than my father. As for what remained, I simply said to myself, Spend it—afterwards, we'll see. The question of money never came up. I spent freely, sometimes beyond my means, sometimes not. And I'm glad of it. It was a stroke of luck, I think, to have enjoyed such absolute freedom for a period of time. It might have turned out badly if it had gone on too long: things would have been too easy. But the war interrupted my period of freedom, and it was just as well: the experiment was finished once and for all.

It was a privilege, but a privilege that can be enjoyed even by those without great wealth. I see it frequently enough in that segment of society which in French is called *le peuple,* the common people. The desire for security is bourgeois. In the first place, there is no such thing as security, for you never know what the future will bring. Not long ago I heard about a family of fairly modest means that was unable to pay the interest on various mortgages and loans and was faced with the loss of all its property. I was struck by the willingness of the couple involved to do whatever had to be done. "I will work as a waitress in a restaurant," the woman said. "And I will work as a gardener or a house painter," said her husband, "and if we can't stay here, we'll go somewhere else." Such spirit offers a kind of liberty. I admired them: they were free.

G   Is work also a form of liberty?

Y   Yes, provided one can accept it with this kind of simplicity. The person I pity as a kind of slave is the one who, whether a company president earning $150,000 a year or a clerk earning $10,000, is scared to death of quitting his job even though the plant in which he works is poisoned by pollution and produces products that are dangerous, stupid, or even useless, simply because he is afraid of losing his health insurance or his retirement benefits. That is slavery, for such a person does not dare to raise his voice in protest, come what may. The slave of his "position," he can't even engage in collective social or political action.

For myself, whenever I had to choose between liberty and security, I always chose liberty. When it comes right down to it, I have always loathed possessiveness, acquisitiveness, and greed, and I despise the notion that success is equivalent to amassing a fortune. During my first few years in the United States, I told myself, I really should set something aside in case of emergency—we all have our moments of naïveté. So I bought some shares in something or other with the little money that I wasn't using at the time. Then I happened to see a picture in a newspaper of a factory spewing out huge clouds of black smoke: I glued that photograph to my little portfolio of stocks and gave up all thought of buying any more.

You can't win, either, because if you simply deposit your money in a savings account, the bank will invest it in businesses that you would prefer to have nothing to do with. But at least there are three or four intermediaries between you and the use to which your money is put, which reduces the feeling of greed and the horrible sense of being implicated in industrial misdeeds.

G So your position with regard to money is in the end quite an aristocratic one.

Y If that's what you call aristocratic, well, then bravo for the aristocracy! I'm not sure that you're right, though, because the aristocrat who needed money and went into debt to get it was no less dependent on "lucre" than if he had amassed the sum as a capitalist. A person is aristocratic in this respect only if he is capable of putting on an old coat, packing a small valise, and walking out the door, thinking to himself, All right, that's the way it is, I'll do something else, I'll sell newspapers. But if you're talking about the aristocrat who owes money to his tailor and bows and scrapes in order to extract a pension from the king at Versailles, then that aristocrat is just as greedy and servile as anyone else.

From Literature
to Passion

MATTHIEU GALEY:
This period of financial freedom was also quite a productive period
for you.
MARGUERITE YOURCENAR:
It was a period of chaotic production. My work in those years was, I
think, based on a highly poetic notion of what life was about, and my
characters were, as I said earlier, very close to mythical figures. So
much is evident in the first version of *A Coin in Nine Hands* and also, to
the extent that I remained faithful to the original idea, in the second
version. It is visible too in *Fires* and in *Les songes et les sorts* (*Dreams &
destinies*), which is a study of mythical dream-composition (and
which I intend to revise one day). In other words, my metaphysical
thinking in those days expressed itself through myth. *Coup de Grâce*
is somewhat different. Reality, because it was so powerful, takes
precedence. But some of the characters—the Portglaives and heroic
Sophie—are to a certain extent still represented as figures of
mythical magnitude. Myth for me represented a way of approaching the absolute, a way of delving beneath the human surface to
discover what was durable, or, to use a rather big word, eternal.

G   Wasn't there also a certain period flavor in those works?
Y   If it's Cocteau and Giraudoux you have in mind, it's better to
consider the two separately. Cocteau, whom I rank quite high as a
poet, was to my mind much closer to myth than Giraudoux. In
Giraudoux there is disparagement of myth: his characters are more
caricatures than they are mythological figures. You will object that
there are plenty of broad-brushed caricatures in my own *Qui n'a pas
son Minotaure?*, but my grotesque Minos and cringing Theseus are
there, in mythical guise, in order to bring out a certain irreducible
vileness that is part of the human condition. I don't think Giraudoux was much concerned with the vileness of the human condition.

In Cocteau there are moments of greatness: a peculiar greatness, akin to a kind of occult power. He was a medium. Too often, though, he allowed himself to be sidetracked by trifles, by the desire to cut a brilliant figure in Paris, by embarrassment at the sight of his own gifts.

But his talent could erupt quite suddenly. Take *La machine infernale*, for example: there are some unforgettable scenes, such as the half-sleep of the son and the mother, along with unfortunate theatrical platitudes. Perhaps this was inevitable, given what theater was then and is now, but some of the more trivial touches are embarrassing, because you feel that Cocteau made concessions. I knew him slightly, or rather I had fairly lengthy conversations with him on two or three occasions. I liked him a great deal, and his judgments of my work (when he wanted to, he could be a very judicious critic) were important to me, but my feeling was that he was torn in several directions at once by his many gifts, and I daresay by his genius ("Plain-chant" is surely one of the most beautiful poems in the French language), not to mention his efforts to stay in fashion as a poet. I don't think he ever fully let himself go; he never fully cast off his shackles.

G   You seem to take a greater interest in literature than in writers.

Y   I have always been happy to know the writers I have met, such as Cocteau, Martin du Gard, Schlumberger, and others who are still living, because knowing a writer personally allows you to make certain judgments that you couldn't make otherwise, judgments of the person rather than the work. But at bottom it's all rather illusory: such judgments add nothing as far as the work is concerned. The problem, the mystery of the work remains. Besides, I've never felt any particular desire to know writers as distinct from other people I've had the opportunity to meet.

For one thing, I always felt that I would bore other writers to death. Even today, I'm not absolutely delighted to open my door every time a young writer appears on the doorstep: many have nothing to say. And then, so little goes on between two people in a half hour's conversation. Why not spend the time rereading the books of a writer you admire? The writer's solitude is profound indeed. Each writer is unique, with his own problems and his own technique, painstakingly acquired. And every writer has a life of his own. There isn't much to be gained from talking about literary subjects with writers you happen to know (or don't know, for that matter).

G   Broadly speaking, you're quite hostile to literary schools and coteries. I'm thinking, for example, of Gide and his friends, who read their works to one another.

Y   I must confess that I don't understand that sort of thing. Which is not to say I'm shocked—everyone has to find a style that suits. But really, Gide's little circle gathering to read their works out loud— imagine! Think of the embarrassment, the shame, the artificiality that such meetings could engender! Gide had no reason to be astonished that Madame Gide chose that day for her dental appointment: how right she was! That manner of working I don't understand at all.

G   But aren't literary movements rather like the lyceum, like the Greek philosophers with their disciples? Haven't you ever been tempted to seek out someone's intellectual heritage?

Y   I've never sought out a person whom I looked upon as a master, the way some people looked upon Gide as a master. I'll grant you that I may have gained a considerable amount from knowing certain writers, even writers whose work I don't appreciate. For example, Jaloux's[1] work as a novelist meant nothing to me, but as a critic and simply as a person to talk to he was important, but no more, in a way, than the carpenter who lived next door. My purpose in saying this is not to disparage Jaloux. On the contrary. What is important is a lasting relationship with any person. The accent here is on *lasting:* I'm talking about people one sees every day, or with whom intensity of exchange makes up for periods when contact is lost. Literary groups and movements never contribute anything but wind, and plenty of it! Wind full of dross and dust.

G   *Fires* stands out in this period as an unusual book.

Y   Yes, it was unusual from the standpoint of technique, because it's a personal monologue that is—how shall I put it?—somehow externalized, disembodied. It's not me so much as myth again, the grand vistas of human existence. Of course I'm also present, but what you have in addition is access to various possibilities, to a number of imposing images of human life.

1. Edmond Jaloux, 1878–1949, novelist.—Trans.

Nearly all of the stories in the book depict characters from Greek and occasionally Christian history (there is one story about Mary Magdalene, but with the same Near Eastern setting as the others). I was traveling frequently in the Near East at this time, and the setting of all the stories is based on what I saw.

To take one example, "Léna ou le secret" is about a woman who is part of a conspiracy and who allows herself to be tortured rather than betray her coconspirators. The real tragedy, though, is that, in my presentation of the situation, she doesn't really know the group's secrets: for reasons of security she has not been told everything. Yet she won't admit, even under torture, that she doesn't know everything and isn't a full-fledged member of the group. Plutarch, it seems, took a different view of the matter: he saw the woman as the lover of one of the conspirators, fully cognizant of the plans of Harmodius and Aristogiton. But in my story, Léna, like nearly all my female characters, is both humbler and more humiliated, yet at the same time a woman in love.

Even though the story actually took place almost a century before Pericles, I present it as though it might have taken place at around the time of writing, in the Greece of 1936. When you think about Greece and the Near East, whether in the past or in the present, you see that partisan struggles of the sort described in the story have been going on continually, or nearly so. Needless to say, at the time of writing Spain was also much on my mind.

G   This is possibly the only book of yours in which the word "I" occasionally occurs.

Y   No, there are brief passages in which I use "I," speaking in my own name, in my prefaces and notebooks, as for example in the notes accompanying *Hadrian.* I did use "I" on occasion in *Fires,* but in much the same way as a musician tunes his instrument before a concert. I wanted to go beyond the narrow framework of the tale and to attempt to show what lay behind it, a joyful, durable passion. Passion in many guises: love *tout court* as in *Phèdre;* love of the absolute, as in the *Phaedo;* love of God, as in the story of Mary Magdalene; or love of justice, as in *Antigone.*

G   The book contains almost no adjectives.

Y   That may be fortunate, because adjectives generally play such tricks on you! When we reread the writers we admire, it's usually their adjectives that bother us. Still, adjectives are surely necessary.

G   The tone of the book is dry.

Y   No, it's altogether ardent, it's truly *Fires*. I suppose you regard fire as a dry element. Champagne is also "dry." And as far as I know, precious gems don't exude moisture either.

G   Why, in discussing this book, did you say, "I hope it will never be read"?

Y   Because people will probably mistake its nature or fail to enter into the emotions that still overwhelm me whenever I reread it. To some extent every writer has to balance the desire to be read against the desire not to be read. The same thing is also true of many poets. Otherwise they wouldn't fill their poems with so many obstacles to discourage potential readers. I put a few such obstacles into *Fires*—the situation lent itself to doing so. Writers have always liked to toy with enigmas. But the lines of force in *Fires* are quite visible. They're all related to passion, but passion tugs in many directions. Including, of course, the direction of transcendence.

G   What do you mean by passion? How do you distinguish it from love?

Y   Most people see no difference, viewing passion simply as love pitched one degree higher. But it would be more accurate to say that the two emotions are close to being opposites. In passion there is a desire to satisfy oneself, to slake one's thirst, in some cases coupled with a desire to control, to dominate another person. By contrast, in love there is abnegation. When I wrote *Fires* I combined the two, sometimes describing love-as-abnegation, sometimes love-as-passion. Ultimately, though, passion has more to do with aggression than with abnegation. Etymologically speaking, it should be the other way around. Passion comes from a word meaning "to suffer," a passive condition, as when we speak of the "Passion" of Jesus Christ, the flagellation and crucifixion. Love, on the other hand, is an active condition.

G   Time also plays a part. Passions are briefer.

Y   I suppose so, though one does find instances in history and in life of great loves that have endured, and from my point of view it is difficult to distinguish between a great love and a great passion. There are women who've managed to sustain love for difficult men for more than forty years, like Mrs. Carlyle.

G   Was her love reciprocated?

Y   Reciprocity may not be very important: Laura wasn't especially preoccupied with Petrarch. His was a case of love-as-fervor, in which Laura somehow figured as an image of God. The same remark applies to Beatrice. When it comes to reciprocity in love, there is always a question of how much reciprocity, and reciprocity in what respects. Did Hugo, for example, love Juliette as much as Juliette loved Hugo? Certainly not. For two or three years, perhaps, they enjoyed what they thought of as mutual love, following which she became the great man's humble servant.

   The impression one gets is that she was never uppermost in his mind except for a very brief period. Many other women must have found themselves in similar circumstances. With men, love-as-abnegation is less common, because men have always felt that there were other things in life and in the world than love.

G   In that case, how do you account for the fact that all literature, including your own work, revolves around this problem?

Y   Not *all* my work, surely—far from it—and not all literature. Love plays only a minor role in *The Abyss*. In *Hadrian* many readers focus on the story of Antinous, which is of course a love affair, but in fact it only takes up one-fifth of the book, admittedly the most moving part. It's very important, I grant you, since it must have been very important, too, in Hadrian's life. But in no way is it typical of the book as a whole. It is possible to imagine writing Hadrian's memoirs without dealing at all with the subject of love, in which case they would describe a life incomplete to be sure but still great.

G   But the book would then lack its crucial radiance. And if Hadrian's story could be told without mentioning love, why does the happenstance of the emperor's meeting this Bithynian shepherd change everything?

Y   To begin with, Antinous was probably not a shepherd (nor was he, in all probability, a slave, as we have been told). Antinous as I have tried to describe him was closer to a "middle-class" Bithynian adolescent of his day. As for the change that comes over Hadrian and what you call the episode's "radiance," I would say that both have to do with the fact that the encounter with Antinous is the only point at which Hadrian renounces his lucid self-mastery, the only point, apart from certain occult experiences, at which he feels that life transcends him. Love is a disorder in the same sense in which Thomas Mann maintained that genius is a disorder. Or, to put it another way, love is dangerous. Of course it's also a kind of happiness—fundamentally, happiness is also dangerous. Hadrian collapses when Antinous dies but later regains control of himself, after a hard struggle, by dint of what he calls "Augustan discipline." But some traits of his character very likely die forever, along with Antinous.

Even before Antinous dies, however, Hadrian had begun, I fear, to blunder quite frightfully on the subject of love. He mistakes the amount of happiness and security that he is able to bring to his young friend. He behaves quite badly toward the end of the relationship, mired as he is in a routine of business mixed with facile pleasures that makes him a rather odious and rather ordinary character. Then comes the death of his friend, when he comes close to losing his grip entirely, after which he gradually proceeds toward the *patientia* of his final years. I have always viewed Hadrian's story as having a sort of pyramidal shape (though few of my readers have noticed this): the slow ascent to self-possession and power; the years of equipoise followed by the brief period of intoxication, which is also the peak of his ascent; and then the collapse, the rapid descent, followed by a new beginning in the final years, when his feet are once again firmly planted on the ground; after the earlier years of exotic experience, lavish building, and suffering, Hadrian finally comes to accept Roman customs and religion.

But the death of Antinous is not the only cause of collapse in Hadrian. Hadrian gives the impression of being a man who tended to push his strength to the limit and beyond. He came quite close to collapse during the period of uncertainty surrounding the imperial succession prior to the death of Trajan and was saved only thanks to Plotina. As an old man, even after his misfortune, he needs to muster all his self-control to surmount the despair that seizes him during the war in Palestine. Then, however, it is his body that collapses as heart disease takes hold. Frightfully ill, he suffers bouts of despair that bring him within an inch of suicide. His collapse on the ship's deck after the death of Antinous was not Hadrian's only experience with an affliction affecting both body and soul.

G   You often assimilate love to disease.

Y   The ancients did it before me, for the very reason that I mentioned earlier, namely, that love involves danger. I do not subscribe to the notion, common to so much of French literature, that "love" is the center of life, the center of human existence—not continuously at any rate. It may be life's nadir, rather, or its summit. Love brings good and ill alike, but it is not necessarily what matters most, or, if it is, it is something more than love, something that words lack the power to express.

G   Do you really think that French literature is unusual in this respect?

Y   More, I think, than anywhere else, French thinkers have developed a closed frame of mind, all too often unreceptive to outside influences. Frédéric Moreau is so taken up with Mme Arnoux that he scarcely has time to concern himself with anything else. Madame Bovary is a little different, because she is beset by ambition. I may as well confess that I've always been shocked that Racine, in *Andromaque,* chose to show us an Orestes in love with Hermione without once, even for an instant, having him recall his father Agamemnon or his mother Clytemnestra, Aegisthus the murderer, or Electra. For Orestes, victim of both love-as-passion *and* love-as-vanity, nothing seems to matter except Hermione's rejection.

G   Was Racine wrong to attach so much importance to love?

Y   It is very embarrassing, in France, to reproach Racine for anything. Owing to the matchless perfection of his language, he is our greatest poet. But if you set *Phèdre* alongside the *Hippolytus* of Euripides, you see at once all that has been lost. True, there is a marvelous gain in the description of Phèdre's passion; Euripides' Phaedra is merely a proud young Greek woman who feels desire but is interested mainly in avoiding dishonor. That's all, and as such she is profoundly feminine and Greek. She is genuinely typical of young Greek women even today—I've known many like her. But she in no way resembles the Phèdre of Racine. In Euripides, however, we have much more, which Racine completely ignores: the love of the father and the son, the deep relationship between the two men. We also have the sanctity of Hippolytus, a very high holiness indeed, the very archetype of the pagan saint, about which Racine has nothing to say. Instead, he gives us a conventional young man, courtly to be sure but lacking in genius. One has the impression that, if Racine's Hippolyte were a contemporary young man, and if he married the well-brought-up and rather dry young woman Racine gives us in Aricie, you'd have an average young couple of the sort who like to ski in winter and live in Parisian high-rises with well-equipped kitchenetts. Whereas Euripides' Hippolytus is an example of the grandeur of the human race.

Virtually nothing matters in Racine other than amorous passion and jealousy. When these elements are missing, ambition in one form or another becomes the only important motive, as with the characters of Acomat, Agrippine, Mithridate. The beauty of *Hippolytus,* by contrast, lies in the hero's utter freedom with respect to the passions; his is a soul aware of the gods and constantly in their presence. The forgiveness he feels in the end toward his father and even toward Phaedra is also quite moving. In *Antigone* (at which none of our great seventeenth-century poets tried their hand), you also have the heroic beauty of a perfectly pure soul.

G How is it that you don't prefer Corneille to Racine?
Y It isn't a question of preference. Corneille's grandeur is rugged, Racine's is polished smooth.

G But Corneille is the most Roman of our French classical writers, and you are the author of the *Memoirs of Hadrian.*
Y Corneille's Romans are beautiful in their way but also conventional. Besides, Hadrian was a long way from being a Roman of the type people usually imagine. The young Hadrian's contemporaries referred to him as "the Greek." Spain, where his ancestors had lived for centuries, may also have left its mark. Remember that Hadrian was Andalusian. We have no information about Spain at this time, so it is absurd to try to imagine what it was like. Still, people in Rome made fun of young Hadrian for speaking with what they identified as a "Spanish" accent. And some of Hadrian's light, almost weightless, verse on the subject of death reminds me of the

temperament of Seville, where one finds the trivial coexisting side by side with the tragic. On the tragic side, there was Hadrian's worship of the dead, his passionate involvement with death. Remember that Hadrian, contrary to imperial custom, went into mourning for Plotina, the wife of his predecessor. He also built or rebuilt tombs for many of antiquity's most distinguished men. And finally, he caused to be built an enormous mausoleum for himself and his successors, the nucleus of the future Castel Sant'Angelo, which was in a sense his Escorial.

No, Hadrian was quite different from the typical Roman. He was basically a rather austere and sober character, with a passion for hunting and a taste for the wilderness and harsh climates. Hadrian combined the height of Hellenistic sophistication with elements of the post-Roman world to follow. If you compare him with Augustus or Julius Caesar, the difference is striking. They don't resemble him at all, those two clever Italians.

Dreaming
and Drugs

MATTHIEU GALEY:
What was your purpose in writing an essay like *Les songes et les sorts*
(Dreams and destinies)?
MARGUERITE YOURCENAR:
It was a study in the aesthetics of deams. Why are dreams struc-
tured as they are? To answer this question I recounted a series of
dreams at some length, trying to give full details and not merely to
say, "Last night I dreamed that I was walking in a town," which
proves nothing. Instead, I tried to describe what the town looked
like, where I walked, and so on. I plan to continue this with a new
series of dreams, if time enough is left to me. The virtue of *Les
songes et les sorts* is that, when I wrote it in 1938, I didn't subscribe to
any of the then dominant theories. They all struck me as woefully
inadequate, and still do.

G   Do you have your own theories about dreaming?
Y   No, it's almost always too early to start spinning theories. I'd rather
do without. I touched on this subject again in *The Abyss*. If I should
republish *Les songes et les sorts* I plan to include as an epigraph the
page from *Hadrian* in which he speaks of his last dreams (as recorded
by a chronicler) and observes that life itself has something of the
inconsistency of a dream. I will also include the page in which
Zeno, in prison, makes the observation that before we can hope for
a theory of dreaming, we must analyze the elements of which
dreams are made. He lists them: "At the bedsides of his patients, he
had often heard dreams recounted. He, too, had dreamed dreams.
Folk are usually content to draw from such visions portents which
sometimes prove true, since they reveal the sleeper's secrets; but he
surmised that these games the mind plays when left to itself can
indicate to us chiefly the way in which the soul perceives things.
Accordingly, he sought to enumerate the qualities of substance as
seen in dreams: lightness, impalpability, incoherence, total liberty

with regard to time; then, the mobility of forms which allows each person in this state to be several people, and several to reduce themselves to one; last, the sense of something akin to Platonic reminiscence, but also the almost insupportable feeling of necessity. Such phantom categories strongly resemble what Hermetists claim to know of existence beyond the grave, as if the world of death were only continuing for the soul the awesome world of night."

That was my plan, more or less, but I never carried it out, and when I wrote the essay on dreams in 1938 I limited myself to recounting a few dreams and to making a few observations along the way.

G Did that book arouse an interest on your part in practical means of communicating with "the world of the dead"?

Y The only such means known to me are terribly crude, such as necromancy. There is no proof that they really accomplish what they claim to accomplish. I've observed such methods quite closely, and there's always some flaw. At some point you always find yourself wondering if it isn't the person asking to receive a message who has actually reconstructed the personality of the deceased, or if there isn't some influence of memory, imagination, or, if you like, unknown entities at work.

This is a realm of phenomena that cannot be verified. All we can do is watch, with a cautious eye. I've often thought that it would be interesting to conjure up Hadrian using spiritualistic techniques, but then it occurs to me that a mind, a spirit, is similar in nature to a ghost (even the words are to some extent interchangeable: we say, I saw a spirit). So if we put our minds to work conjuring up another mind by means of all the verifiable techniques at our disposal, why bother trying to conjure up a ghost to boot? Let me hasten to add that however far experimentation of this sort may take us (and the real question is *where* such experiments can take us), it seems to me rather futile to attempt to communicate with the dead when, as things now stand, we communicate so poorly with the living.

It is true that in my work I make every effort to subdue my own personality, to efface myself, so that I may better hear, better give myself over to, the character I'm trying to comprehend; and admittedly this sort of method is reminiscent of spiritualism. It is also true that my method won't work unless there is some sort of relationship between the character and myself. Otherwise I wouldn't have chosen to conjure up that particular alien personality. Or, if you prefer to make matters more mysterious than they really are, the personality wouldn't have chosen me.

Nevertheless, a certain distance remains. I showed you earlier a piece of paper on which I attempted to forge the signature of Zeno a dozen or more times. What I was trying to do, really, was to imagine what his handwriting might have looked like, with its tense, obscure, angular Gothic script, the rapid stroke of an extraordinarily impetuous man who made his way through life in a very vehement manner. The writing on that paper isn't mine. You also saw the sheets on which I tried, in a Greek that would probably cause a purist to shudder, to write down the main points that Hadrian would have liked to confide to us: I said to myself, Why, Hadrian wrote in Greek, after all. Let's try first to get in touch with him in that respect. Actually, though, the writing on those pages is neither Greek nor Latin nor any other language but the stammerings of a person in the grip of a vision, the results of an early attempt to make contact with a human personality.

One day I conducted a strange but simple experiment. A professor, from the University of Toulouse, I think, sent me a copy of an assignment he had given his students (those poor souls must have hated me that day!): the exercise was to choose a page from *Hadrian* and translate it back into Greek. A fascinating assignment. So I said to myself, Fine, I'll follow the students' example and try my hand at the same exercise. What I soon discovered was that certain French sentences went into Greek quite readily, but one or two did not, because they were my sentences, not Hadrian's.

G   Why do you want to rewrite *Les songes et les sorts?*
Y   No, you misunderstood me, I don't want to rewrite anything; I want to add something new. I intend to leave the book as it is, with the 1938 preface, and to add a new preface with further explanatory comments. The original preface was written at a time when I still believed that all prose, even expository prose, had to achieve a certain lyrical beauty, verging on song. This time I would like to explain in greater detail when, and in what circumstances, I dreamed the dreams in the book. And I plan to add, say, ten more-recent dreams not contained in the original version. It will be interesting to see the differences, even though the essential phenomenon is necessarily the same.

The book contains those of my dreams that I thought most striking, dreams of the sort that stay with you, unlike less vivid dreams
which are generally forgotten within the hour. These were dreams
that recurred with some frequency, occasionally with variants.
That kind of dream one always remembers. Two or three nights
ago, for example, I was awakened by what seemed to me a startling
dream, which I plan to include in the new book. The vivid dreams
are seldom anxious ones. By and large they're filled with scenery of
extraordinary beauty. Sometimes there are human characters as
well, but these are less important than the scenery. Specialists have
argued that dreams are always in black and white. But based on my
own inquiries I would say that many people dream, as I do, in vivid
colors.

G   Did your dreams influence what you wrote?

Y   I would say rather that writing and dreaming paralleled one
another. One dreams in more or less the same style as one writes.
One thing that's very odd but confirmed by my own experience and
by artists I've questioned is that almost no one dreams about what
they are writing or painting. Dreams parallel art, they don't imitate
it. Very few people seem to dream of loved ones, their parents, say,
immediately after they've died, but they do dream about them
twenty, thirty, or forty years later. Observations of this sort might
well lead to something. Before any new theory of dreams is pro-
posed, however, much more research is necessary.

Here's another interesting observation: I don't dream about
Hadrian any more than I dream about my closest friends (including
both those who are dead and those still living), which is to say, quite
seldom. This vanishing in sleep of the thoughts that constantly
occupy one's waking mind is quite interesting. No doubt our dream
images consist of what Jung called archetypes, but archetypes of
what?

G   In what sense do you intend the word *sorts* in the title *Les songes et les
sorts?* (The question may require further explanation for English
readers. The word *sort* is ambiguous in French: it can mean "lot," in
the sense of "one's lot in life" or "drawing lots," and by extension
it connotes "fate" or "destiny." But it can also mean "spell," as in
"to cast a spell upon." I earlier translated the title *Les songes et les
sorts* as *Dreams and Destinies,* which preserves both the alliteration of

the French title and the meaning that Marguerite Yourcenar singles out here as the correct one.—TRANS.)

Y   Destinies (*les destinées*). A person's lot in life. That's the etymological meaning of the French *sort* (from the Latin *sors, sortis,* "a lot," "part"—TRANS.). The lot that falls to you. There is certainly a connection between a person's destiny and what he or she dreams. There is something magical in dreams, where by magic I mean inexplicable associations. The word *sort* in French has something of an evil connotation (like the English "fate"—TRANS.), particularly in colloquial usage, since people always try to ascribe a definite meaning to a word that is essentially ambivalent, like "luck," for instance, which in itself is neither good nor bad. When I used the word "luck" (in French: *chance*) in *Archives du Nord,* in the phrase "the luck not to exist," everyone assumed that what I meant was that not to exist would be a stroke of good fortune. Leave that question aside—it's not very well formulated in any case. The point is that, linguistically, luck is neither good nor bad. But everyday speech congeals the meaning of words.

G   Why did you publish *Les songes et les sorts* in 1938?

Y   Because I had written it, quite simply. The book has its virtues, but there isn't enough explanation. For example, the conditions under which I dreamt these dreams aren't mentioned, nor does the book say anything about the method of transcription. The reader might well suppose that I had transformed the dreams into something like prose poems, which is not the case. But as soon as one tries to describe the colors of a dream, one is forced to go beyond a simple linear account. "I was walking in a garden" is not enough. The garden has to be described with all the colors it had in the dream. The reason why most accounts of dreams don't amount to much is that the dreamers lack the ability to recount all the actual details. Some dreams, of course, are quite mediocre, but some are very beautiful, similar in nature to visions. Some dreams are stupid, foolishly literary, mere plot summaries no more interesting than a pulp mystery. For instance: you dream you've lost your passport, and you run into an obliging chap who lends you his, but then you have to get a new picture taken or a new stamp, and so you need to find a photo shop, etc., etc. The photographer, it turns out, is also a veterinarian or a shoemaker. What's more, it isn't a passport that you lost but an exhibition catalogue. And so on, ad nauseam.

Dreams of this kind are highly verbal. You hear yourself talking, even chattering away. By contrast, in the magical type of dream, you don't hear yourself talking, you see something. An example is Dürer's dream, of which we have both Dürer's account and a sketch made shortly after he awoke on the night of 7–8 June 1525. This was obviously a painter's dream. But it was also a moving-picture dream. I won't call what he saw the end of the world—that would beg the question; he saw the destruction, by torrents of falling water, of the place in which he happened to be staying. Whirlwinds devastated the countryside, which he took the trouble to draw in his sketch. It bears some likeness to the Lombard plain, which he must have known since he traveled frequently in Italy. The details he gives are remarkable: he even attempts to gauge the distance between himself and the scene of devastation. It's quite fascinating to watch this very observant man's mind at work in a dream. Particularly in a dream so striking that he immediately sat down to describe it in words and pictures.

We also know something about the dreams of Leonardo da Vinci, but in his case we can't be sure that they weren't daydreams. They may be not so much dreams in the true sense of the word as recurring myths or reveries.

G What you're describing has a great deal in common with the experiences of people who take certain drugs to stimulate their dreams.

Y Perhaps. Only with drugs the experience is fraudulent from the beginning. Whatever is stimulated or willed is partly false. Drug-induced dreams may strike their roots into the dreamer's own soil, yet they generally look either wilted or wildly exotic, like plants grown under artificial conditions. People who use drugs aren't usually made for the kinds of dreams they produce. What is peculiar, I grant you, is that mescaline-induced dreams exhibit most of the characteristics of magical dreams obtained without stimulants, such as unusually complex, labyrinthine architecture and landscape. Why does a sleeping person's mind construct such incredible edifices?

G What do you think of people who "trip" with drugs?

Y I am against anything that is artificial. In my opinion the mind must act on its own, in accordance with its own laws, without crutches, and most definitely without stilts.

In Mexico, stimulant-induced dreams are no doubt a part of normal ascetic practice, used in connection with religious ritual and ceremony. In such conditions the drug user is protected to some extent. But when people start doing the same thing in their own homes, alone or with others who don't know what they're doing, I'm very skeptical. What is more, the results of such experiments are not always very clear. Aldous Huxley, for example, wrote *The Doors of Perception*—which, like all of his work, is a supremely intelligent book—after one experience with mescaline, the only experience of his life with the drug. Now, Huxley, a man blessed with a very sharp, very shrewd mind, was not very gifted when it came to the faculty of imagination, as his novels partly reveal. But after taking mescaline, he had, for once in his life, imagination; he felt things emotionally. All at once, the colors of flowers became vivid for him, and he saw and heard the music that was played for him in an utterly new way. The experience made him a poet for three-quarters of an hour. After which he again became Aldous Huxley, the admirable essayist, all the more admirable because he took an intelligent interest in an unusual realm of experience to which his native gifts had not granted him access. Still, he couldn't remain high on mescaline for the rest of his life.

G But one does remember what one has seen.

Y Of course we do all remember something of our vivid or overwhelming dreams, and these memories stay with us like a buried treasure. But, even apart from the fact that these memories surface only intermittently and are eroded by time, if we knew that they were originally obtained with the aid of stimulants, then that very knowledge would introduce an element of doubt. True dreams must well up from the depths of our souls, without any trickery on our part. Adepts of the inner life, of mental life (the lack of a precise vocabulary makes it even more difficult to speak about these matters), warn their disciples against miraculous gifts, against what the Hindus call *siddhis*. They must learn to look upon such things as utterly commonplace and completely uninteresting, of no importance whatsoever. To go to great lengths in order to have powerful dreams by artificial means is to go against the wise counsel of those who know.

From the Orient
to Politics

MATTHIEU GALEY:
Dreams, visions, and the Orient—a common thread runs through all three, it seems, and indeed it was in this period that you published your *Nouvelles orientales*. Was there a common link, a relationship?
MARGUERITE YOURCENAR:
The collection *Nouvelles orientales* includes not only stories from the Far East ("Comment Wang-cho fut sauvé," "Le dernier amour du prince Genghi") and Hindu tales ("Kali décapitée," which is the worst story of the lot) but also several stories set in Greece and the Balkans. Thus Asia and the Near East meet in these pages.

The title is rather ambiguous: I obviously had Gobineau's *Nouvelles occidentales* in mind, but Greece and the Balkans, after all, were considered by many in the eighteenth and nineteenth century to be part of the Orient. To Delacroix and Byron, for instance, what was most striking about the Balkans was that they had for so long been Islamic territory.

The book was written in a period when I traveled frequently to Greece, often by way of the Balkans. The Balkan stories originated in the various stops I made along the way. "Wang-cho" and "Prince Genghi" attest to my passionate interest in Chinese and Japanese literature. "Wang-cho" is based on a Taoist tale; I didn't make it up. Obviously a writer always adds a touch here and a touch there. "Le dernier amour du prince Genghi" is an attempt to conjure up what might have been written on that blank page in Lady Murasaki's novel, the page that bears only the simple title, "Disappearance into the Clouds." The subject is the death of Genji). We have been told that he has retired to a monastery; of what comes after we kow nothing, except this title. I simply tried to imagine what took place.

G   At what point did you discover Japanese literature?

Y   Very early, at the age of twenty or so. Very little had been trans-
    lated into French, but much more was available in English and I
    used to read a great deal in English. *The Tale of Genji,* for example,
    had been translated, very well indeed, by Arthur Waley.

    The stylistic principles on which the recent French translation is
    based are interesting, but I'm not fully in accord with them. Broadly
    speaking, the point is to translate the Japanese by approximating
    the flavor of medieval French. A case can be made for this, no
    doubt. Nevertheless, I prefer a translation that avoids putting our
    own sense of the medieval between us and the original. The current
    translation is a kind of tour de force, but it leaves me only partly
    satisfied, as does Victor Berard's translation of the *Odyssey,* which
    has Penelope living in a "castle" and refers to various characters as
    "squires" and so on. For the same reason, I don't like J.-M.
    Edmunds's translation of Theocritus, which takes its inspiration
    from English pastoral poetry of the Renaissance, even though I'm a
    great admirer of Edmunds's translations of Greek poetry.

G   What did you find particularly attractive in the Japanese novel
    Genji Monogatari?
Y   It's one of the richest novels I know, for the complexity of its
    female characters and for the extraordinary subtlety of Prince
    Genji's portrayal in his relationships with several women and in his
    awareness of how varied those women and his feelings for them
    are. Again, we come back to the distinctions I made earlier be-
    tween love-as-compassion, love-as-sympathy, and love-as-play:
    play of a very high order indeed, the play of a civilization that
    blends love with all the arts—poetry, painting, calligraphy—other
    than those of the bedroom. The novel offers us a wonderful mix of
    fragrances as well as contact with the invisible.

G   What in Western literature might be compared with it?
Y   Nothing whatsoever. The book is written with incredible subtlety,
    not only as to the psychology of relations between men and women
    but, more profoundly, in the manner of depicting the ambiguity of
    life, the passage of time, the way love has of combining tragedy,
    delight, and a certain fugitive quality in all its episodes. The
    opening is admirable. The emperor, having lost his mistress (who,
    because she was not a member of one of the court's powerful clans,
    was subjected to mental torture by palace intriguers and rivals),

sends a lady-in-waiting to find out what has become both of the
child he had by the former mistress and of the woman's elderly
mother. The lady-in-waiting returns and describes a more or less
abandoned house, open to the rain, a deserted garden, a tearful old
woman, mother of the former mistress, who is unable to explain
anything, and a child who is, on the contrary, gay, lively, and very
handsome. The feeling this gives of the transition from generation
to generation, of the solitude of each generation along with the ties
that bind one generation to another through life and death, is
magnificent.

Whenever I'm asked what woman novelist I admire most, the
name Murasaki Shikibu comes immediately to mind. I have extraordinary respect, indeed reverence, for her work. She was truly the
great writer, the great novelist, of eleventh-century Japan, which is
to say, of the period when Japanese civilization was at its height. In
a word, she was the Marcel Proust of medieval Japan: a woman of
genius with a feeling for social gradations, love, the human drama,
and the way in which people will hurl themselves against the wall
of impossibility. Nothing better has ever been written in any
language.

G   Did her work influence you in any way?

Y   Well, one thing is certain: I've never written anything of the kind!
To have achieved such variety I would have needed a subject that
allowed it. And of course Lady Murasaki's genius is inimitable. But
there can be no doubt that her exemplary work helped to refine my
sensibilities. Very early I developed a feeling for the unique tempo
of her work, which is informed by a sense of time quite different
from our usual Western sense. But my subjects were totally different from hers, and perhaps my thoughts were different too.

G   The time, or rather the atmosphere of the period, must have been of
some importance when you wrote *Coup de Grâce* in 1938. You must
have sensed the imminence of war.

Y   One would have had to have been deaf and blind not to have seen
the war coming in 1938. And remember that I knew Germany fairly
well and Austria even better, and that I had personally witnessed
the growing anxiety in the Near East. But whenever I returned to
France from either Greece or central Europe, I saw people sitting in
the cafés who gave no sign of suspecting that anything was amiss.

In those days I had a very strong feeling of imminent danger, heightened by the war in Spain and by what I knew of the underside of Italian fascism. The scenes of torture in "Léna ou le secret" and *Fires,* along with Antigone's suicide, also in *Fires,* seemed almost to anticipate what history was to enact.

France seemed relatively safe. In part this had to do with life's being so agreeable there, certainly much more noticeably so than elsewhere. No one seemed to anticipate what lay ahead. But a trip on the Orient Express in those days was enough to reveal the hatred that festered in every country along the line, a clear sign that terrible things lay in store. My purpose in writing wasn't to describe the current situation, however.

With *Coup de Grace* I made the discovery that it was better to work toward a certain perspective in time and space, as I tried to do by evoking the Baltic Wars of 1919–21 (which of course I had not lived through). This was already history, and I was therefore forced to deal with a specific social setting at a specific point in time, far enough in the past so that the resolution of at least some of the issues of that period could already be discerned—which for me may be the essence of what history is about.

Incidentally, the story was a true one, told to me by a friend and subsequently by the brother of the person involved, who is called Eric in the novel. The story appealed to me because it concerned a love affair involving three young people left isolated in a country devastated by war. I sensed in this situation a tragic beauty, together with a unity of place, time, and danger, as the French classic canon so wonderfully puts it. The place was Livonia, or rather Kurland, and the time that of the German putsches of 1919–21, directed against the Communist government. As for danger, there was the drama, the human drama, of three isolated young people set against the larger drama of war, poverty, and conflicting ideologies.

Eric, the main character, the voice in the monologue, looks on as the world into which he was born crumbles around him: Germany collapses in the wake of its defeat in World War I, the Baltic world collapses into chaos, and even the French world of his ancestors falls apart—because his German father was killed on the French front. Finally, the world of ideology, the foundation on which he might have built his life, collapses under him. His only bulwark against the general ruin is the castle in which he is living with his friend,

Conrad, and Conrad's sister, Sophie. With the stage thus set, all that remained was to involve these three characters in the action.

I'm still quite interested in the character Sophie, who is a very generous woman, generous even to the man she loves—not as common a thing as one might think. The story ends in the book as it ended in life, in the kind of tragic incident that is inevitable in the ferocity of guerrilla warfare. But love, loyalty to a way of life, and the close bonds that unite three human beings of similar type— these are the things that count, far more than the political background.

G   What sort of welcome did *Coup de Grâce* receive, given that its main character, a German, is portrayed with a certain amount of sympathy?

Y   Many readers liked it a great deal. A critic once told me that Eric was, for some people, the young Werther of his generation. What he had in mind was probably the character's emotional makeup, which resembles Werther's to the extent that "romanticism" is possible in this day and age. Politics is not important to Eric. He is an adventurer, as well as a champion of lost causes. At the very beginning of the book he dismisses all ideologies.

G   I'm sure I won't be telling you anything you don't already know if I remind you that a person who describes him or herself as apolitical generally stands politically on the right.

Y   Let me think a moment about that statement, which strikes me as too cut and dried to accept on its face. . . . What your proposition proves is simply that, for the time being, left-wing ideology is dominant over right-wing ideology, or at any rate is attempting to assert its dominance. Any minority appears apolitical to the surrounding majority. Mussolini, for example, surely looked upon any writer who did not subscribe to his imperial policy as an "apolitical" person with anarchist tendencies.

In this respect, people described as "left wing" are all too often as naïve as the early Christians, who believed that their answers had to be right and who dreamed, as true believers invariably do, that Eden was at hand—even though Eden always turns out in the end to be inaccessible, because man is imperfect and because any halfway attempt to establish perfection invariably brings violence and error in its wake.

I am not arguing that such eschatological fantasies are wrong because they are left wing; I am saying that they are wrong because, inevitably, they are distorted and turned into hollow formulas. I am utterly convinced that there is no form of government that cannot be perfect, provided that both ruler and ruled are also perfect. An ideal communist would be divine. But an enlightened monarch of the sort Voltaire desired would be equally divine. Where are they, though? A monarchy with a sublime king would be able to find sublime, perfect advisers! Show me such men. That's the error of the monarchists, if there are any monarchists left. They don't see that their king would soon call upon someone like Mr. Giscard d'Estaing or Mr. Mitterrand to serve as prime minister and that the post office would still be staffed by the same people as today, or by others just like them. And as far as I'm concerned, the capitalist technocrat who claims that by using the methods of a sorcerer's apprentice he can bring happiness to human kind is in the same boat. The old political labels have outlived their usefulness, or ought to have.

G But in the period just after the Popular Front, when many writers, like Gide, Malraux, Bernanos, and even Mauriac, suddenly became "committed," what was your attitude?

Y One of indifference. I was spending so little time in France then that it seemed more remote to me than Spain or Greece. Of course, you're right, at that time people like Malraux were pouring forth torrents of eloquence, but I detected a certain rhetoric in that eloquence. To my mind, Malraux was never very sure of what he was doing until he discovered de Gaulle. Underneath it all, I always felt, was *Les conquérants*, Malraux's same old poetic anarchism.

I greatly admire Malraux in certain respects, but he never impressed me as being a convinced man. He was a great actor. In the end it all had a rather hollow ring, as one senses in *Antimémoires*. It's impossible to tell truth and falsehood apart in that book, and Malraux doesn't even seem to care since he can no longer tell the difference himself. In *Les chênes qu'on abat* (based on Malraux's conversations with de Gaulle—TRANS.), it's impossible to say who's asking the questions and who's giving the answers. It's all

Malraux, always and everywhere, and in many places he is indeed superb. Both his commitment to the left and his later commitment to General de Gaulle seemed a magma of words, that formed and reformed like clouds in the setting sun.

Interlude

MATTHIEU GALEY:
Did the publication of *Coup de Grâce* mark the end of a period in
your writing career?
MARGUERITE YOURCENAR:
That period came to an end largely owing to the force of events.
Coup de Grâce was published a month or two before the outbreak of
World War II. But the important change in my life during the
period 1939—48 was that I renounced all literary ambition. A nice
interval of retirement! For ten years I gave no thought to writing. I
did other things, I earned my living, and I came home very tired in
the evenings. I read a great deal, though, and I did actually write a
few things, outlines or scripts of plays like *Le mystère d'Alceste, La
chute des masques,* and *La petite sirène,* the only three plays that were
entirely written in that period and that I have since left untouched.
I also translated Negro spirituals, because I enjoyed the work as
others enjoy watching television or going to the movies. I've never
felt that writing was a career that I needed to pursue actively, and
I've often felt that, had I not written, I could just as well have done
something else, or nothing at all.

G   Of course this was also the time when you moved to the United
    States. When did you actually arrive?
Y   In November 1939, during the "phony war," but it wasn't my first
    visit to America. I had spent several months there in the winter and
    spring of 1937—38, after which I returned to Italy, where I had a
    small house in Capri. It was there that I began *Coup de Grâce.* I
    finished it at Sorrento, shortly before the Munich crisis. From there
    I went to Germany and Austria, where I witnessed the frightful
    spectacle of nazism at close range, and then I returned to Greece,
    where I intended to live. My plan was to settle there permanently.
    For various reasons I had to return to France in August, however, so
    that I was there when war was declared.

I couldn't decide what to do. I even went to see Giraudoux, who had nothing to offer me in Greece, not even a lectureship or a minor cultural post, and I could no longer afford to return on my own. At that point, Grace Frick, who had just accepted an academic position in New York and whom I had known for nearly ten years, wrote to me saying, "Why don't you come here?" So I left for New York, planning to stay there for six months.

G   Did you meet any of the French writers who were already living in New York in exile?

Y   Of course! They were living then in suspended animation, like everyone else. I met Breton. I met Lévi-Strauss, still quite young. I saw Jules Romains once or twice. We ran into one another in cafés or at the homes of friends, especially Russian friends, who were very hospitable. At that time I was nostalgic for Europe or Asia or at least Mexico. In other words, I wanted to get out of the United States, because I felt bewildered there and at times found it difficult to earn living.

In the end I found a job, actually two jobs, both part-time. I taught French and comparative literature to extremely ill-prepared students, many of them lacking any basic notion of what literature is about. Fortunately, the teacher was quite free to select whatever theme or subject pleased her. Nothing penetrated very far below the surface, however. But thanks to my students I learned a fair amount. I learned, for example, that literary groups and society coteries bound together by political, religious, or other such ideas are like fortuitously gathered clumps of seaweed in that great ocean, life. I thought I knew something about life, but that was until I discovered the total anonymity of the great American city, the stark difference between life in the United States, at least as I experienced it, and life in Europe. Later I continued my education on the highways of the South and in New Mexico, and finally in this part of Maine, where I now live. All these experiences taught me how small one is compared with the immensity of mankind, how obsessed we all are nonetheless by our own worries, and how much we resemble one another at bottom. This has proved a very useful lesson.

G   In other words, until then you were a pure intellectual.

Y   No, I certainly was not a pure intellectual: sensations, fortune, people, dreams, if you like, all counted too much for me. But my knowledge of other people was nonetheless limited to comparatively few types. I used such words as poverty, misfortune, and suffering, but I remained confined within a society in which everyone knew certain things, everyone shared certain fashions and a certain culture, however superficial, and people amused themselves in similar ways. I discovered how hollow all of these things were. Or perhaps hollow is not the right word—such things may have been useful, even invaluable at times, for insuring the progress of certain aspects of human thought and sensibility. Elites are necessary, even if all too often they're not really elites. But in back of all that is an immense, undifferentiated mass. Even in Paris I could never leave a "cultural" gathering without treating myself to the pleasure of a conversation with the cab driver, the maid, the concierge, or the first passerby.

G   What did you learn from your students?
Y   How few are prepared for study, how many people never escape the status quo, and how brief the period of awakening is. Occasionally a teacher will come into contact with a student at the moment of awakening and cause something to happen to prolong the period of receptivity. Unaided, it seldom lasts long. Young people who show signs of intelligence or even brilliance at age eighteen or twenty for the most part don't live up to the expectations they arouse. Some can't sustain their enthusiasm, while others are overwhelmed by life.

I must say that I never liked teaching because I clung to my habit of allowing my thoughts to mature slowly: I liked to read without the immediate purpose of passing on to others the content of what I had read. I liked to make plans, to think about what I might write some day if allowed the time.

Besides, my work routine was difficult, particularly since I lived rather far from where I was teaching and had to spend two or three hours on buses and trains, crowded as they were during the war, to get back to New York. I was also very much aware of what was ersatz in American education.

Very little knowledge was conveyed to the students. I found that they came to so-called higher education so ill informed that everything they were taught remained vague, without moorings. I found myself discussing the Chinese theater when many of the students had not read Shakespeare or Shaw. I heard one professor say that the natural sciences were outdated, and another that astronomy was unimportant compared with nuclear physics (this, of course, was before the exploration of space). Many were so exclusively interested in the latest fashions that they were actually illiterate. The students, adolescents, lacked the firm basis of knowledge on which they might have built later on.

G   Had you been a teacher in Europe, do you think you would have been any happier?

Y   I don't know, because I'm not very familiar with European education. I'd probably have complained instead about excessively rigid curriculums and undue respect for intellectual prowess of a certain sort, not necessarily the best or most genuine kind. Whereas here, in the United States, a student who really wants to can study anything, can do more or less whatever he pleases.

I often made this point to my students, but they just weren't very venturesome. American students sin by turning their backs on the apparent freedom available to them and seeking out regimentation instead. If an American wants to learn cooking or flower arranging or the history of the Italian Renaissance, he runs down and signs up for a course. It did no good for me to say, "Why don't you try arranging flowers yourself? Then you'll find out what you like, what moves you. Or try trusting your own palate when you cook. Buy yourself a book on the Renaissance or borrow one from the library, and if you find it boring, look through the card catalogue to see if there's another one you might like better or that might teach you more. Just keep on until you begin to understand what cooking or the Renaissance is all about." They just didn't hear me. I know women in their sixties who have been stuck on fourth-year French for twenty years. They're delighted to be still in school.

As for freedom, many of my students in those years didn't know what to do with it. For want of passion. Want of passion is, I think, a very striking characteristic of Americans, not unrelated to their predilection for violence. For very few people truly have a passionate desire to achieve, and violence serves as a kind of substitute.

I taught both during and after the war, a war with which neither my female nor even my male students felt especially concerned.

This was only natural, after all: the war was being fought in far-off places which these young Americans had a hard time imagining. By contrast, students in the United States were very much aware of McCarthyism, with its attendant persecution of foreigners and foreign-born Americans. Many of the students in the school where I taught felt as threatened as I and other teachers did. It wasn't until the sixties, though, with the civil rights movement and the catastrophic war in Viet Nam and, later, with the growing awareness of ecological and other issues associated, rightly or wrongly, with various so-called sub-cultures, that young people here began, in my opinion, to understand youth for what it really is: the first bloom of adulthood, the first opportunity to make the choices that will determine what kind of life one leads. My rather intermittent experience as a teacher came to an end early in 1953, following a period of two years' absence in Europe, but I continued to feel closer to at least a portion of the younger generation of Americans than I did to their elders, with their implicit faith in the system and in their prosperity.

Earlier I mentioned some of the glaring defects of the American educational system. It is important, though, not to lose sight of the American aptitude for public service (far greater than our own), as well as the gift for charity work, enthusiasm for minority causes, and activism in the best sense of the word. I am constantly amazed to discover, here as elsewhere, that, despite the sometimes disastrous mistakes committed by politicians and governments and the prevalence of misguided prejudices and ersatz enthusiasms, there are in every generation a few people who exhibit genuine *human* virtues and merits (or are there a great many such people?—I haven't been counting). I noticed the same thing in Paris in 1968. But things are constantly in flux. Even as we speak in the year 1980, students are fiddling nervously with the dials of their radios and televisions, worried about the draft and the alarming news from Iran. I sometimes think that if I were twenty years old today, I wouldn't bear up as well as they do.

G   Let's get back to America in the forties. You were living near New York City at that time and no doubt had to make certain political decisions.

Y   Not so much decisions as spontaneous acts. I immediately signed up to support de Gaulle. I had visited Germany before the war and found it horrible and frightening. As a result, I never fell victim to the delusions that afflicted so many writers, Céline, for example, and Jaloux (to name two writers of very different sorts), along with various other French men and women of my acquaintance. Montherlant is another name I might mention.[1] I knew Germany too well to have any illusions on that score.

Most French people knew nothing of Germany. Just think how naïve their descriptions of Hitler's regime were: Hitler has reestablished order, they used to say, when the truth was that, as so often happens, appalling disorder coexisted with authoritarianism. Dictatorships in general are appallingly disorderly.

G   What did you feel when you learned, in the United States, that France had been completely occupied?

Y   Do you mean the fall of Paris in June 1940? I was already in the United States when that happened, and I collapsed in tears in the arms of Malinowski, the great Polish anthropologist. I happened to be at his home on the night in question. We were all aware that the future was now in doubt, one way or another, for a long time to come. I'm deliberately trying to avoid saying "forever," but in fact I feel very strongly that every event, whether good or ill, leaves behind an indelible trace, a scar if you will. What is really horrible is to think how little the world's wounds have healed in recent years, how many remain open and festering, arousing hatred, rancor, and cries for vengeance. Up to a point Hitler is responsible for what is happening now in the Middle East. Mussolini was responsible for Hitler. Napoleon together with the Holy Alliance was responsible for Mussolini. Political crimes and blunders inevitably snowball.

I could have returned to France after the Liberation, but I had a house here in Maine, I had friends, and I had a work in progress. I had no desire to change my whole life yet again. Then, too, many of the people to whom I'd been close in France were dead, or worse than dead. So I stayed in the United States. One must live somewhere, after all.

G   You published very little in this period, but the title of one of your

1. Louis-Ferdinand Céline, 1894–1961; Henry de Montherlant, 1886–1972, writer.

projects is intriguing. What was the *Canticle of the Soul and Its True Freedom?*

Y   It was a sort of paean to human freedom, freedom everywhere and in everything. Constraint is of course a part of freedom. The work was in prose but in reality it was a poem, of the same genre as *Fires*. In the end I couldn't see what could be done with it, so I threw it away. I couldn't imagine where I might publish it. You have to throw things away every so often.

G   But you didn't have much from this period to throw away, did you?

Y   No. Your question calls to mind a French friend of mine who said almost the same thing: "How can you not give more thought to your career as a writer?" I drew a small circle on a piece of paper and said, "Go ahead and divide this circle up into little slices, and we'll see what portion my literary career represents. A tenth, perhaps, or a twentieth. You mustn't forget the rest."

G   You were in the prime of life, though. You'd reached the stage at which a writer can give the most of him or herself. Didn't you feel any dissatisfaction or anxiety?

Y   On rare occasions. I was busy with other things. People rack their brains over Rimbaud: Why did he go away? I understand him quite well. He had written a certain number of things. Perhaps he didn't say to himself, I shall never write another word. What he did do was to involve himself in business and travel, first in Greece and later in Ethiopia. I can understand that. He was beginning a new chapter in his life. And I can also understand that Racine suddenly stopped writing tragedy and may well have stopped thinking about it altogether.

G   But you were a long way from having written all that you wanted to write.

Y   True, but I couldn't tell whether I would ever be capable of doing what I wanted to do. And then, really, one book more or less in a world that already enjoys a surfeit of masterpieces—I didn't think that way at the outset. As an adolescent, I had no idea what I was up against. You no doubt remember Goethe's most modest state-ment—and Goethe was a modest man—that "if I had known how many great books there are in the world, I would never have plunged into writing but would have found another way to occupy myself." How wrong he would have been, for we would have lost so much. Nevertheless, I think that he was sincere, and I think also that he was great precisely because, despite the ponderous and somewhat stately pride that coexisted with his modesty, he was fundamentally aware of what an insignificant thing literature is, and how little it is worth.

G   You speak somewhere of the "dark night of the soul" that you were going through at this time. What exactly did you mean by that? The war?

Y   I had left Europe, had more or less given up my work as a writer (even though I was still translating Negro spirituals and working, as I mentioned earlier, on several plays, I was no longer writing with the same intensity I had known earlier), and I was living among people I barely knew, many of whom didn't much interest me at first. It was like the *œuvre au noir,* the phase of dissolution in the alchemical process (if I may allude to the French title of the work of mine known in English as *The Abyss*), when everything begins to lose its shape. What I had written up to then ceased to occupy my thoughts. What I had done was, I thought, decent, good, solid work, but I almost never thought about it any more. Obviously, when I left Europe I had just published *Coup de Grâce,* and I didn't feel that it was a bad novel. During one of our last dinners together, Jaloux was kind enough to give me some advice: "Take a rest. The earth rests in winter." He was a wise, shrewd man, not what you might think from his works, which are rather insipid romances. "The earth rests in winter. You have just written a book that will last as long as the French language." That compliment gave me an enormous amount of pleasure, but at that moment I wasn't sure how long the French language was going to last—nor am I sure today, for that matter. In any case, it was a kind gesture on his part.

G   Winter lasted for ten years.

Y   Oh, no, not ten years! Two or three, perhaps. I sent articles or drafts of articles to Roger Caillois in Buenos Aires, who published them in *Les lettres françaises,* a favor for which I am still grateful. Fragments of my translations of Cavafy and my plays appeared in various magazines in Algiers and then, shortly after the end of the war, in Marseilles. Above all there was my new life, which was at times very happy, in spite of the war. I have memories of marvelous

springs in Virginia, then less spoiled than now by noise, construction, and traffic. There were also times, again, when things didn't
go very well for me, concerned as I constantly was by what was
happening in the world. It was difficult to measure the full extent
of the horror, since I was at once too close and too far away.
Distance is necessary in order to understand what is going on. In
reality, many things occurred of which we had no knowledge.

Many people living in France at the time knew nothing of the
concentration camps until 1945, when former inmates started
returning home. We exiles were no better informed. We were at
best only partly aware of what was going on in Europe. Awareness
came to each of us as an individual shock. In New York I was
friendly with a Jewish woman who was overwhelmed by the loss of
several close relatives. Her name was Rosa and through her I experienced the tragedy of the camps, though the facts were still partly
obscure, nothing was yet spelled out in black and white. And the
frightful carnage that took place in Asia was something of which I
became aware only much later. For many years now, not a day has
passed when my first thought upon awakening has not been about
the state of the world, as I try, for a moment at least, to immerse
myself in its terrible suffering. People do somehow manage to be
happy on occasion, in spite of it all; but the happiness is incommen-
surable with the suffering, it's of an entirely different order.

An Island
in America

MARGUERITE YOURCENAR:
I've always loved islands. I love Euboea, I love Aegina, and I love
Capri, which is not nearly as "touristy" as people say, especially when
one lives in an isolated section. Every island is a world unto itself, a
universe in miniature. Look how well I know my fellow islanders
here. If I lived in an apartment in New York City, I wouldn't know
a tenth as many people as I know here on this island in Maine. The
sea brings in fresh air. You feel that you're standing on the border
between the human world and the rest of the universe.

In rural America you can remain an outsider, a newcomer, for a
long, long time. The landscape doesn't accommodate itself very
readily to humans. Much is destroyed here. A man of means may
build himself a splendid mansion only to have his heirs unable to
settle the estate or pay the taxes on it, so that the house is eventually torn down. A year later, nothing is left. Where the house once
stood, there is only moss and brush. Nothing. It's impressive.

Houses are built of wood, which isn't very durable: many go up
in smoke, while others, somehow devoured by the weather,
crumble into dust. People here work on their houses constantly,
which is reminiscent of the Japanese custom of rebuilding Shinto
temples every twenty-five years.

MATTHIEU GALEY:
The American conception of the home must be quite different from
the French, which holds that a house is an immutable object, rooted
in the soil from which it springs.

Y Yes, it is quite different. Of course, houses everywhere serve as
shelters: that is why they are built. They mark a special place on the
surface of the earth, home. But that has nothing to do with
ownership; houses of the kind you're talking about in France can do
without us just as easily as we can do without them, and they die

just as we die. If disaster engulfed the population of Mount Desert Island, it wouldn't be long before no trace of human habitation remained.

G   When did you first come here?

Y   In 1942, I believe. Like so many others I was living in New York waiting for the moment when I might return to Europe. As the war dragged on, an American friend who had rented a large but sparsely furnished house in a nearby village invited Grace Frick and myself to spend a few weeks one summer on the island, which I had never heard of.

Compared to hellish New York, the spot seemed so beautiful that we started looking for a house. Grace, who was an excellent horsewoman, used to spend her vacations in the saddle. Though a mediocre rider myself, I have wonderful memories of touring the countryside on horseback. I should add that there was no other way of getting about in those days, given the shortage of gasoline, and Grace was known in the village as the "lady on horseback who's looking for a house." We finally found one in 1949, but it wasn't until much later that we actually moved in. But it was here that I finished *Hadrian*.

G   What attracted you about this village?

Y   The scenery, which is very beautiful and was even more beautiful back then. And then the village life. Here you see life reduced to the bare essentials, stripped of all literary embellishment. People kill each other here just as they do anywhere else. It's not uncommon, actually: I can think of six or seven murders or attempted murders. They also steal each other's wives. Vandals occasionally tear up gardens. Burglars who specialize in the theft of art works break into the summer homes of the wealthy. Scandals, big and small, keep the town buzzing, as they do everywhere. And every fall, throughout the area, there is the unbearable brutality of the hunting season (and hunting "accidents" which are often masks for people settling scores). But the island itself is an animal sanctuary where hunting is prohibited, though unfortunately it has its poachers, and at this time of year, hunting season, I refuse to set foot on the mainland. Fortunately there are also admirable people, honest and kind and utterly free of ideology of any kind.

G   Who are you to those people?

Y   Oh, someone—someone who isn't from the island, even after more
    than thirty years. We're "Down East" here, as they say, in the
    extreme northeastern corner of the United States, about eighty
    miles from the Canadian border. It's a region that's quite old-
    fashioned in its opinions and customs. It hasn't changed much since
    the nineteenth century. It's a very provincial section of the country,
    and the relationship between the "summer people" and the natives
    is symbiotic, if occasionally hostile—the natives live on the money
    they make from the summer people but don't really care for them.
    In my case I think that they've finally come to accept me. Of course
    in recent years, success, symbolized for the natives by the press and
    media attention I've received, may have helped me in overcoming
    the customary hostility to outsiders.

G   In what respects has your work been influenced by your envi-
    ronment?

Y   I think that had I remained in Europe, or even returned to Greece in
    1940, I would have become increasingly involved with the formal
    aspects of literature, because the circles in which I moved were
    extremely liteary, and I would have remained more closely bound
    to the past, because the places themselves were all associated with
    ancient legend. Coming here and being forced to confront a totally
    different reality, immense and at the same time amorphous, was a
    change that was quite useful to me, I think. I don't mean intimate,
    emotional, psychological reality but external reality, the sheer
    weight of the brutal outside world. Descartes found that he was
    quite capable of meditating on the docks of Amsterdam as the
    stevedores rolled their barrels to and fro. I'm not sure that rolling
    barrels would have done me much good. But here I've found the
    silence natural, broken as it is occasionally by the squawking of
    nocturnal birds or the foghorn of an approaching boat. In the pre-
    face to La petite sirène I wrote that that short play is a product of that
    period in my own development when geology began to overshadow
    history. This change in my outlook had very deep roots. It was here
    on Mount Desert Island that I began to take a greater interest in
    trees and animals, in the natural environment as a whole.

    But maybe I would have developed in the same way even if I'd
    lived somewhere else. Who knows? I have great respect for chance.
    I believe in making do with what life offers, and with the life that is

offered, which one must take as it comes. A writer to whom many people would deny the title of philosoher, Casanova, adverts frequently to his obedience to destiny, his *amor fati.* He doesn't, however, use that solemn phrase, later made famous by Nietzsche. He puts it much better: *sequere deum,* follow the god. So let me say simply that "the god" brought me to America. I say "the god" because I'm not sure which one it was. A Christian would say "grace," a Hindu "my karma." And things might change at any moment. Only God—"the god"—knows where we'll be in ten years, if we're still alive. . . .

G   Which doesn't prevent you from loving this house. It was originally a farmhouse, wasn't it?

Y   No one knows exactly when it was built. Probably around 1866, rather old for this island, which had few dwellings on it until the middle of the nineteenth century. Originally it was probably a very small house. The part that now contains the kitchen was added later. Apparently the wood that was used was cut on the mountain ten or fifteen miles from here and floated down on the sort of glacial fjord that cuts the island almost in two. The logs were then hauled up on the bank and left for the first owner to build his own house.

   I have a small photograph, from 1870 or so, showing the house as it was then. There was a large barn, unfortunately now gone, which must have burned down or collapsed. And there was also what people around here call a "summer kitchen," a large extra space attached to the kitchen that was used for canning and putting up preserves, which gave the luxury of additional space during the warm summer months.

   You've probably noticed that the rooms are quite small, which helped to conserve heat. When it's very, very cold, some of the rooms can be closed off. There are eight or ten rooms in all, haphazardly arranged. Each room had its own fireplace. Only three are left, but there must have been more originally. I may add some if there is a shortage of fuel oil. But I don't like to buy wood for heating either. I gather a lot of fallen wood and use the few trees that have to be cut down. I try to forego the use of wood sold commercially because we must save our forests. The ideal arrangement would be to build a small, solar-heated addition, but there is a stand of maple to the south that tends to cut off the sunlight.

The furniture is a hodgepodge, with a little of everything: pieces that survived two wars and a great deal of travel, along with others added by the friend with whom I bought the house.

Back then, the surrounding countryside was nothing like what you see today, a mixture of meadow and woodland, predominantly birch, fir, and maple. None of that was here; it was all heath. When the Scottish colonists first came here, they cut down trees right and left and tried to eke out a subsistence from the rocky fields. The trees gradually grew back. A few have grown up before my very eyes.

In the end I think this house has done the best it could. It is modest, small, yet practical in its own quiet way. Another room could be added—many people succumb to the temptation to expand these wooden houses, since it can be done so easily, merely by knocking out a wall, but that's precisely what I don't want to do. I don't even want to cut a blade of grass. I like to think of the house as a roadside stop. I don't like the idea of being encumbered by possessions. People always hold on to too much. The little land that goes with the house (just over two acres, I think) is quite enough. In the summer you can get lost on the property just as easily as you can in the densest forest.

No doubt if I were younger and had more energy to expend on material things, I would be tempted to own a farm large enough to keep some parts completely wild, so that I could really live in wood and pastureland. I would have a small house and live with a few friends in a sort of "commune." I had something of the sort in mind long before I moved to the United States. I used to talk about it quite often with Dutch friends of mine, and I had in mind a whole list of people with whom I might like to try such an experiment. They would have come from all over the world!

G You were something of a "hippie" before the fact, then?
Y Probably. There was something of that in it. I have respect for the hippies. They tried to renounce many things they had been forced to accept, including such false, noxious beliefs as the notion that one exists because one owns. Buy, buy, buy—

My own philosophy—if I may use so solemn a word—is that I never buy anything without asking myself if in fact I couldn't do without it. Why add to the surfeit of things already in this world? I could slip the key under the door and walk away from this place without any difficulty. I would miss the birds, I would miss Joseph the squirrel, and that's it. Wherever one dies, it's bound to be on this planet.

G The name of the island, for which you are not responsible, is somewhat deceptive, though, isn't it? Because it leads one to think that you live on a desert island.

Y The fault is Champlain's, for it was he who baptized this place. And he never even set foot on Mount Desert Island. He saw it from his ship after setting sail from Nova Scotia and was the first to sketch its shape. He has left an excellent description, couched in the beautiful language that, in the seventeenth century, was common to both spoken and written prose, of an island with a low profile featuring seven or eight mountains; since he saw no sign of life, no sign of any Indian encampment along the coast, he called the island Mount Desert—*désert* in the French sense, meaning an uninhabited place. According to the distinguished American historian Samuel Morison, he may have run aground on one of the nearby reefs and spent several days repairing his vessel. About ten years later a small group of French Jesuits attempted to establish a settlement. They too had run aground en route to Nova Scotia, but their camp was attacked by a pirate in the service of the king of England, and they were routed or killed. This anecdote figures as a brief episode in a story that I'm now writing.

Later, when Louis XIV was king and the marquis de Cadillac was governor of the region, French colonists settled here. In the early part of the nineteenth century there were people with a farm here who were actually descendants of Cadillac, but they grew old and rather poor and little by little sold off the vast property they once owned. They wound up as tenants of a Scottish farmer. In the midnineteenth century the population consisted chiefly of farmers, almost all of Scottish origin, whose entire consumption of manufactured goods had to be brought in by boat from Boston. These farmers lived quietly on what their small, rocky farms produced, with the help of a few water mills.

Then, around 1880, certain painters discovered the island and it became a fashionable resort. A fairly large number of fashionable Philadelphians and Bostonians built themselves horrid huge houses—it was a dreadful period for architecture—to which they came for periods of three to four months at a time with an entourage of twenty-five trunks and a dozen servants and horses in a splendid parade. It was a time when the wealthy took lengthy vacations each year at the same spot, and there was still no bridge to the mainland. These people traveled by ship from Boston.

It was the beginning of the Gay Nineties, when people gave balls or went riding in rustic carts wearing city gowns, flounced dresses I suppose, and the men wore top hats. They had fine lace table linen imported from Italy and silver from England. White-gloved butlers served elegant picnic lunches by lakeside or on mountaintops, rather like eighteenth-century paintings. This was the world of the young Edith Wharton and the young Henry James. Unfortunately it's no longer anything but a memory, and even that is faded almost to oblivion.

G   Who were these people who took such elegant vacations in the Gay Nineties?

Y   As I said a moment ago, fashionable society people from Boston, Philadelphia, and New York, and frequently each city's visitors formed a separate group. One notable visitor was old John D. Rockefeller, the founder of the Rockefeller clan, but he was an austere Baptist who I think never really belonged to this set. He owned an enormous house on the island, one of those that have been pulled down because they were too expensive to keep up. He was very fond of Mount Desert Island and came here often. He liked horses and laid out a number of bridle paths that are still in use. During the Depression he paid for the construction of bridges and roads in the mountains to keep the workers busy, but it didn't do much to make him popular. In appearance he was a gaunt, hard man. He died sometime in the 1950s at age eighty-five. I saw him occasionally. Anyone who wanted to see him could do so at the Seal Harbor village church, which in those days used to be packed with people eager to catch a glimpse of the old man.

G   In other words, life on the island was rather feudal, as in Europe of old, where certain families held sway over villages or even whole provinces.

Y   Except that the sympathy that existed in my village between what we called "the castle" and "the village" didn't exist here, as far as I

could see: the village people and the summer people didn't fra-
ternize much. And the summer people were just that, nothing
more.

G   Are you sure that the sympathy you just mentioned actually existed
    in Europe?
Y   At times, yes—so much is obvious if you listen to the interviews
    that were done for a radio program about Mont-Noir. The old
    village people were so gracious. They remembered having tea with
    me at the castle—for it was a castle of sorts. They remembered eat-
    ing apples in the garden. They remembered the family going to
    church on Sunday, and the first automobile that came to the village
    square, when everyone ran out of the church to see it, leaving the
    priest in the lurch. It's curious, even moving, to see the degree to
    which human sympathy will seek to express itself across the years,
    because I don't think that we did very much for them. We could
    have, we should have done so much!

G   That's easier to say from the castle than from the cottage.
Y   Obviously it's for the castle that I feel a pang of regret that we
    didn't fraternize more. What possibilities were lost. As for the
    situation here on Mount Desert Island, I'm not sure that the people
    here really envied the Rockefellers. I don't think they did. They
    respect wealth but not necessarily the wealthy. And over the years
    they became more familiar with the outsiders: the sons of yester-
    day's wealthy worked side by side with the local carpenters. That's
    one of America's good points, which it has along with its irritants,
    like the custom of always calling people by their first names; but
    customs are customs. It doesn't bother me that people here often
    call me "Marguerite." In this part of the world you exist as a
    person, an individual, whom people know and sometimes appreci-
    ate. When Allan, the fisherman, the man wearing the large boots
    whom you met earlier, comes to see me once a week, you could
    swear that we were close friends. I also like the friendly familiarity
    of the village women. There isn't much awareness of class or
    cultural differences.

G   Do wealthy people still spend their vacations here?
Y   Some do, but they spend less time than they used to. Nelson
    Rockefeller, the former governor of New York, had a very

110

beautiful house here which he almost never used, because the duties of office kept him away. There is also a family of Fords that has a house on a hilltop, and many others.

But the people who live here all year round are not wealthy. Many of them have a fairly hard time getting by. The winters are very long. It's like Brittany in France, I imagine, or any other place to which tourists come in summer: for a short time people earn good money, followed by long months of near penury. It's practically a tradition here. When the first French Jesuits settled on the island, they got on quite well with the Indians, recording their customs and the things they said. Among the things they have to tell us is the fact that the Indians called the month of February the month of hunger. In some ways it's still the month of hunger for many families on the island.

What I like about the island is the natural beauty of the setting and the company of plain folk. I don't attach a great deal of importance to the house itself, but it serves as an asylum, a cell for self-knowledge, as Saint Catherine of Siena might have said. I suppose that a sage, like one of the old Taoists, could circumnavigate the globe several times without leaving home, without ever stepping outside his cell. That would be the mark of a true sage.

G   He would dream his way out.

Y   Even more remarkable, he would think his way.

A Trunk and an Emperor
The History of a Book

MATTHIEU GALEY:
In 1948 a certain trunk came your way, quite by chance. Was it a
real trunk or a figurative one?
MARGUERITE YOURCENAR:
Oh, no, it was a real trunk, actually two or three trunks, with quite
an assortment of things inside. Of course the things of value had
somehow or other disappeared in transit, into someone's pocket,
and what was left was what nobody wanted, useless junk. I had
several days' fun throwing things away or tossing them into the
fire. I should add that Grace was away at the time. Had she been
here, she might have wanted to save some things, while I enjoy a
good bonfire. Among the odds and ends to be burned, I found an old
draft of the first few pages of *Hadrian,* which I had completely forgotten, it had been so long. Years had gone by, and so much had
happened in the interim: the war, the move first to New York and
then to Mount Desert Island, the charm of new acquaintances, visits
to various museums and historic sites. Much had happened in those
six or seven years. It's hardly surprising that I had forgotten all
about *Hadrian.*

G What happened then? Upon discovering that early sketch of
   Memoirs of Hadrian, did something click?
Y It was a bolt out of the blue! I found not only those first few pages
   but also, in the same trunk, a couple of books dealing with Hadrian's
   life. You know, I have an iron ruler that was forged by my father,
   and whenever I pick it up it brings back memories of my childhood.
   Well, when I picked up those books, the feeling was similar: I was
   immediately plunged back into the research that I had begun before
   the war. The books in the trunk were Henri Estienne's edition of
   Dio Cassius (at various points in my life I've been a bibliophile of
   sorts) and a modern edition of the *Historia Augusta. Hadrian* fairly
   leapt out of those pages.

113

   Most people, I think, have a mistaken impression about scholarship, or at any rate about the way in which a writer enters into the
world of scholarship (writers being, by definition, "creators," to
borrow the foolish term generally used in the United States—I
myself would prefer to say simply, as the Germans do, that writers
are poets, meaning that they rely on the imagination and the emotions). French readers especially conjure up the image of a writer
immersing himself in books from morning till night, like the
bookworms in Anatole France's novels. Americans will say, "Oh,
yes, you're doing research," and the image they have is of the
writer leaving home in the morning, briefcase in hand, and walking
briskly to the library for a full day's work, right up to closing time.

   But that's not the way it is. Anyone who loves life loves not only
the present but also the past, for the simple reason that the past, as I
can't remember which Greek poet once said, outweighs the
present, especially the narrow individual present that each one of us
knows. Thus it is only natural for a person who truly loves life to
read a great deal. I used to read Greek literature quite a bit, at times
with sustained intensity over long periods, at other times sporad-
ically, on my travels, for which I always prepared myself by putting
a small volume of some Greek philosoher or poet in my pocket
before leaving home. After a while I had reconstructed for myself
Hadrian's cultural universe: I knew more or less what he read, what
his points of reference were, and how, influenced by the philosophers he had read, he viewed various matters. I never sat down and
said to myself, You're going to write a book about Hadrian, so
you've got to find out what he thought. If you start out that way, I
don't think you'll ever succeed. The writer must soak up the subject
completely, as a plant soaks up water, until the ideas are ready to
sprout.

G   At that point doesn't chance also play a part?
Y   Of course. I'm an inveterate believer in chance, which has a large
hand in everything that happens. By "chance" I mean a
multifarious relationship of cause and effect which by its very complexity defies all attempts to circumscribe or calculate its nature
and which does not appear to be controlled by any agent outside
ourselves (how cautious I am—see how I say, "does not appear"!). I
certainly never foresaw the arrival of that trunk, but the accident
proved crucial. When I first touched those pages of manuscript and

those books, I was really setting my hands upon Hadrian and his world. In fact, my draft consisted of nothing more than the beginning of a letter, whose tone, as I immediately recognized, was much closer to that of a private diary than to anything a Roman might have written. Romans didn't keep intimate diaries. They might keep family records, or datebooks indicating appointments for business, political, or amorous purposes, or, as Marcus Aurelius did, they might record fragmentary reflections on various subjects; but they didn't keep diaries in our sense. I realized that if Hadrian's memoirs were supposed to represent the voice of a Roman, they would have to be cast in the form of a formal discourse; they would have to observe the rules of monologue and, like Seneca's *Essays,* be addressed to a particular person, even if a broader audience was envisioned beyond the ostensible recipient. The interest of Greco-Roman civilization in the formalities of discourse was, in my view, one of the major differences between it and other contemporary civilizations, such as the Celtic or African, which had their own, different subtleties and forms of wisdom.

If I may digress for a moment, the same thought occurred to me somewhat later, when I was translating the war songs of Tyrtaeus, fragments of which have survived. These fragments remind me of *La Marseillaise*—they have almost the same rhythm. How do they differ from the chants of African shamans and bards? In the fact that the Greek songs comprise a continuous discourse. The poet speaks to the soldiers: there are no cries, no incantations, but rational speech—the poet speaks.

Thus Hadrian, if he were to cast an eye on the life he had lived, would, as the consummate representative of Greco-Roman civilization, inevitably have made use of that civilization's instrument of lucidity par excellence: formal, almost impersonal discourse. I realized that monologue was the only possible form, and I deliberately refrained from including dialogue in the text because we have no idea how Romans spoke to one another. At a much later date I published, in the *Nouvelle revue française,* a long essay, soon to be reprinted in a volume of my works, in which I attempt to explain why it is so difficult to reproduce the dialogue of the ancients. True, we do have certain Latin comedies, which are themselves imitations of the Greek "new comedy" and which date from at least two and a half centuries before Hadrian. But their level of diction varies from street language, jeers and insults of the sort one finds in Plautus, to the artificially elevated, noble theatrical style of Terence, whose speakers are in any case almost invariably cast in a fixed set of standard situations. In all of this there is not a clue as to what precise tone Hadrian might have taken with Trajan or Antinous with Plotina.

G   There are also the tragedies.

Y   True, but the tragedies are written in a style all their own, not to say a language all their own, a language that was never spoken in the streets and houses of ancient Rome. How did they really talk? "Have a seat, Cinna." Fine, but Corneille, after that opening gambit, goes right back to the elevated style. We also have dialogues, of course—most importantly, perhaps, the dialogues of Plato—but their style is also very elevated and their tone very special, that of a group of people who have agreed among themselves to hold a conversation on some abstract subject. Realistic passages are rare. Plato gives us no idea whatsoever of what might have been said when someone entered a house or met someone on the street or when two or three people engaged in private conversation. We don't even have an example of an amorous dialogue, except in the poetic style of Theocritus's *Idylls,* for example. What we lack is naked, unadulterated evidence: true, we do know a few insults and terms of endearment that happened to be written on the walls of Pompeii, but those are scarcely adequate for reconstructing the conversations of a person of Hadrian's stature. Matters stand quite differently with respect to the Middle Ages or the Renaissance, for which abundant documentation of many kinds exists, including even "unretouched" records of conversations as they actually occurred, like the samples I took from the records of Campanella's trial. To get back to Hadrian, I quickly realized that in such a formal discourse, he could do no more than sketch the bare outlines of his life. Yet I was supremely fortunate in that he was both a man of letters and a man of action, a man with a depth of culture behind him and ideas about what he feared the future would, and what he hoped it might, bring. He was also a man old enough to know the shape his life had taken and therefore able to see it in perspective and to pass judgment on it. Had he been a man of twenty or even thirty, this would have been impossible.

G   Of all the Romans you might have chosen to bring to life, why did
    you choose Hadrian? For instance, Marcus Aurelius might have
    been a more logical choice.

Y   Marcus Aurelius's experience was deep but not sufficiently wide. It
    was the experience of a resigned moralist, a scrupulous servant of
    the state, yes, but also a discouraged man. It might make a fine
    story, but it wouldn't go far enough toward encompassing the
    variety of human existence. He himself said everything there was
    to say on the subject. He put himself back into harness every morn-
    ing and lay down his burdens, more or less, every evening. He took
    medication for his stomach ulcers. If what you're trying to do is
    portray a world, that just won't do, whereas Hadrian—*Varius
    multiplex.*

    What sparked the whole idea as far as I'm concerned was a visit I
    made when I was twenty to the villa Adriana. That visit also
    accounts for my interest in Piranesi, for among Piranesi's thousands
    of drawings of Rome are sixteen of the villa Adriana before it was
    pillaged by the archeologists. What stood then was a palace in
    ruins, encrusted with roots and brambles, rather like the castle of
    Sleeping Beauty, yet still fairly close to what it looked like in the
    last days of the Roman Empire, when Romans had ceased to live
    there. Piranesi's engravings exude a feeling of duration, of time's
    slow corrosion, which is similar in a curious way to a Chinese text
    that I used in the preface to my translation of Hortense Flexner:
    both emphasize the beauty of objects that have gradually been
    eroded by storm, encrusted by vegetation, buried in earth and mud,
    and yet have also been given, somehow, new shape and substance by
    these same forces of nature. The same is true of the Roman walls as
    depicted by Piranesi, which, new, would probably not have
    affected us as much as they do now, with all the beauty bestowed by
    time, by adversity, and by centuries of human feeling, beauty that
    seems to have permeated the very stone. Piranesi had feeling for
    that kind of beauty. It ceases almost to be history and becomes
    geology.

    But at the time I first conceived the idea of writing Hadrian's
    memoirs, I wasn't thinking of Piranesi. Being of studious bent, I
    scoured the works of historians who were Hadrian's contempo-
    raries or who came slightly later to find out what people had to say
    about him. In any case, had I written about Hadrian at that point, I

would have concentrated mainly on the artist, the great admirer and patron of the arts, and doubtless also on Hadrian as lover, but I would have missed Hadrian the statesman.

G   A letter from you, dated 1929 or 1930, has been found in the files of the publisher Grasset, proposing a "novel about Antinous."

Y   That's rather odd. It must have been one of my first attempts to deal with that subject. I wrote a number of drafts in which Antinous, identified with the genius of empire (which, incidentally, was the way Hadrian himself treated the young man) and involved in the Orphic tradition, played a major role. Distant glimpses were all one got of Hadrian. The problem with these drafts, as you can imagine, was that I succumbed to a certain aestheticism and even a sort of mysticism, inevitably quite vague given the state of my own education at the time. I quickly realized that these attempts were going nowhere. While the Hadrian of the final version remains to some degree open-minded on the subject of the occult, I had in the meantime gained twenty years of experience concerning what one can know and what one cannot.

G   In that regard, can you describe what you've called your "trancelike methods?"

Y   They're really methods of contemplation. It is true that, in writing *Hadrian,* I occasionally made use of various contemplative methods. I still use them, moreover. Some of them I've worked out for myself, while others came from my study of oriental philosophy, among other things.

In referring to a "trance," I'm speaking of what it looks like to someone observing from the outside. For the onlooker it's a trance; for the person involved it's the height of wisdom. The problem is that it runs counter to all our intellectual training, especially for someone of French background. To begin with, for a novelist, the essence of the method is to allow oneself to be totally invested by one's character. This involves totally shutting out all ideas, rooting out what one has learned, wiping the slate clean. I imagine that Descartes did something rather similar, though he uses a different vocabulary. Now, such a way of proceeding is so contrary to the way we usually live, write, and converse in France, where people like to embroider endlessly on their ideas, that it is very difficult to explain. In a trance of the sort I'm describing, one doesn't embroider at all. It's the same as in certain oriental methods of contemplation, where the object is to empty the mind completely in order to achieve a level of serenity in which objects are reflected as in the surface of a calm sea.

Generally speaking, one must try against considerable difficulty to achieve what Hindu sages describe as a state of "attentiveness," in which you get rid of three-quarters or nine-tenths of what you seem to think but really don't. Ordinarily, a person merely assembles bits and pieces of preexisting ideas. All of these must be eliminated and one's thought focused on nothing; the effect is quite salutary. Another procedure is to concentrate on a fixed spot without looking away for some period of time. It's extremely difficult to do. There are all sorts of tricks, a whole variety of ways, for arriving at this state of attentiveness, some of which I have Hadrian describe—but Hadrian, a Greco-Roman intellectual, tends to take a more intellectual approach to the whole question. In one way or another I think that meditation is absolutely essential. Only one must be careful not to confuse meditation with dreaming. Meditation is a daytime activity. At night one sleeps, and one has, or submits to, dreams.

Of course I also worked on Hadrian at night. At times I even tried automatic writing, only to burn what I had written the following morning. In writing about a character in a novel, I think that one has to know a great deal more than one actually says. In the case of Hadrian, there is his whole youth, the war years, the years of ambition during which he seeks to become an officer on Trajan's staff, consul, and governor. We know almost nothing about these periods in his life. Still, one must try to know everything, to use contemporary documents and the curriculum vitae of other high officials to reconstruct Hadrian's probable experiences. One must be capable of saying everything only to refrain from saying it because it isn't important. In *The Abyss* I used the same technique. In the case of Hadrian, I knew what positions he had held at various times and what ranks he had been awarded, but little else. Scholars knew the names of a few of his friends and a little about his group in Rome and his personal life. So I attempted to use the existing documents to put together a picture of his life, but above all to put some life back into that picture. As long as you don't put all your own intensity into a document, it remains dead, no matter what kind of document it may be.

G   Very little time elapsed between your decision to write the book
    and its publication in 1951.

Y   The writing took three years. Writing goes very quickly once
    you've made up your mind. It was three years of continuous work,
    exclusively on this one book, during which time I lived in a sym-
    biotic relationship with my character to such an extent that at times
    I understood that he was lying, and allowed him to get away with it.

    He arranged things, just as everyone does, wittingly or unwit-
    tingly. I think he lied quite a bit on the subject of his election, of his
    coming to power. He must have known a bit more about it than he
    told me. He wisely left the whole subject shrouded in uncertainty.

G   Having identified yourself with Hadrian, how did you bring your-
    self in your heart of hearts to accept the executions, crimes, and
    other deeds committed out of political necessity?

Y   Knowing the poker player that Hadrian was and adopting his point
    of view, one has no choice but to accept such deeds, for otherwise
    he wouldn't have been Hadrian and we'd never have heard of him.
    His crimes were hardly crimes at all compared with all that we
    have seen and are seeing still, but mere excesses of severity; and if
    to us he seems to speak of them rather coldly, we would do well to
    remember that for him these things already lay in the distant past
    and many other things had overlain them in his memory. Then, too,
    time plays tricks. The execution of the military party's four con-
    sulars when he took office must have seemed to him nothing more
    than a necessary settling of accounts. And it was just that. Three of
    the consulars in question were apparently politicians of dubious
    character and the fourth was a bandit. Later, when the execution of
    his aged brother-in-law is under consideration, Hadrian is already
    ill himself, and he must have felt, "One death more or less, my own
    included—what difference can it possibly make?" At that point he
    crossed a threshold. Any man of state—be he Lenin, Peter the
    Great, or Napoleon—is rather quickly and, I grant you, quite
    tragically, led to this kind of indifference. Well, perhaps not any
    man of state. I wouldn't presume to speak for all of them. But in
    Hadrian's case I think pragmatism won out.

G   How could you both assume the identity of your character and at
    the same time consider yourself, to some extent, as his amanuensis?

Y   Because, all things considered, the writer is his own amanuensis. When I write I am carrying out a task, writing under my own dictation, as it were. I am performing the difficult and exhausting labor of putting my own thought in order, straightening out my own dictation.

G   When you finished *Hadrian,* did you feel that you had written a book very different from your earlier ones?

Y   Something much more vast, at any rate, infinitely more vast than my other books. Its subject was an empire, as well as a man, dying at age sixty-two, who had seen and experienced a good many things. I didn't see it as a sharp break from my earlier works. Young Eric in *Coup de Grâce* might have grown up to be a Hadrian. In his own way he is just as hard and just as tender and just as clear-sighted. Hadrian, in the army, must have been rather like Eric. There are other echoes. "All happiness is a form of innocence," Alexis says. Whereas Hadrian says, "All happiness is a master-piece." The two statements are not quite the same, but they're of the same order. Between the one and the other, obviously, my own experience has intervened. In order to write *Memoirs of Hadrian* I had to know enough about the period and about the Roman world, and I had to have read the code in which many of Hadrian's decisions were written down. It couldn't be done in a day. But I also needed to have reflected sufficiently upon the conditions of life itself, conditions of which we cannot be sure whether they represent established order or chaos. At twenty, one has not yet pressed one's experience far enough. One has to be forty or more.

    It's a serious matter for a writer to die at forty. It would have been a disaster for Tolstoy, for Ibsen, even for Victor Hugo. Had Hugo died at forty, we would have had the Hugo of the Paris years under Louis-Philippe but not the Hugo of exile. A great deal of time is necessary. If you stop Hugo before *Les Misérables* and before *La légende des siècles,* you have a very good poet but not yet the unique visionary that he is in the history of poetry. I would be loath to give up the early Hugo, including the poet of *Odes et ballades.* That was a necessary stage, even if, as I believe, it reveals nothing of the great Hugo. You know, I'm so strongly aware of the need for time that I have Hadrian refer to it. When Lucius, his adopted son and onetime favorite, who gives the impression of having been above all a dissipated dandy—when Lucius dies, Hadrian says to himself, After all, if Caesar had died at that age, what would remain of him? The memory of a dissipated man, saddled with debt, who was involved in politics. And Hadrian acknowledges that ever since Lucius's death he has looked with greater pity on those who die before fully realizing their destinies. Of course forty is a median age, midway between zero and eighty. Forty-five would do just as well and thirty-eight wouldn't be bad either. It may not be life's apex, but in any case it's the middle. Alexander died younger, but he was a meteor. Jesus died younger, but he was divine. One can dream about what became in later years of the duc de Bourgogne, whom Saint-Simon describes in his youth, or of Rimbaud.

G Forty is also the age of political maturity, and that, too, must have played a part in the conception of your book. Isn't it true, for instance, that the establishment of the United Nations at the end of World War II had some influence?

Y The United Nations, at that time, counted for something, yes. It was possible to conceive of a political genius capable of restoring peace for the next forty or fifty years, and it hardly mattered whether it was a pax americana or a pax europeana. But no such genius arose. Only brilliant second-raters made their appearance. At the time, however, I was still naïve enough to believe in the possibility of such a thing. It was possible to convince oneself that a more intelligent person, one more skillful at navigating in difficult straits, had some chance of success. I now see that these hopes were illusory. This discovery explains why I moved on from *Hadrian* to *The Abyss*. But while I was writing *Hadrian* it was possible, during a very, very brief euphoric period of the sort that often follows the end of a war, to entertain hope. Thirty years later such a thing wouldn't have been possible. Just as, in Roman history, Marcus Aurelius, Hadrian's indirect heir and officially his grandson, dies in despair, confronted with the reality of the barbarians and the brutality of his successor.

G Your hopes were vested simply in a man, not a political system?

Y Systems are created and used by men. They are also rigid. Hadrian was flexible. And, by a stroke of good luck, the system in which he ruled was still fairly flexible, by which I mean that the empire had preserved some of the political features of the republic, including both the possibility that the emperor might ask the Senate for support and the possibility that he might take up arms against it. The emperor in Hadrian's day was still the supreme commander who received a fresh vote of confidence each year. He had not yet become, as he would in subsequent centuries, a monarch of the oriental type, though he had already ceased to be the sort of figure we associate with the final years of the republic, the politician constantly embattled in the public arena.

At the time I began writing my book, there was one statesman who may have inspired me in a very remote way: Churchill. For the simple reason that he had written his own memoirs, of which I read the first volume when I undertook to write *Hadrian*. In reading Churchill I said to myself that it was indeed possible, up to a certain point, for a political leader to explain his actions, even notwithstanding possible falsifications and omissions. I do not compare Hadrian to Churchill, though: their temperaments are very different. I think that Churchill enjoyed life more, and more crudely. He had his cigars. In any case it is impossible to compare ages and men so far apart from one another. What matters is the full realization of a man's destiny as statesman—and also, in the end, as a human being, for though few people know it, every human life is fundamentally divine.

G With the difference that Hadrian, as emperor, was by Roman law also a god.

Y He was one of the first to enjoy the position of divine emperor, because the practice of apotheosizing the emperor during his lifetime, which originated in the East, was not adopted in Rome until Hadrian's time or shortly thereafter. Augustus was not apotheosized until after his death. It is true, however, that Hadrian did, toward the end of his life, begin to arouse religious enthusiasm. One sees this quite clearly in contemporary documents. People believed in a form of power, or charisma, to use modern theological jargon. It's no easier to explain in Hadrian's case than in any other, whether it be a great actor or a musician or the Reverend Jim Jones leading his followers to their deaths. It's a gift, a very special gift, not necessarily to be confused with the gift that made Hitler der Führer, even if there was in Hitler something of the sorcerer.

Toward the end of Hadrian's life, the inspired man, or perhaps the man in the grip of a hallucination, seems to have gained the upper hand over the pragmatist.

One doesn't have the impression that Hadrian was particularly gifted at the outset. He was rather slow getting started, which is one of the things that interested me about him. Between the ages of fifteen and forty, he slowly makes his way over all the obstacles standing in his path. He learns Latin, of which his knowledge had been poor (he spoke with a Sevillian accent), he learns Greek, he teaches himself many things. He holds virtually every military and civilian office there is. He experiences life in the barbarian countries. He cautiously looks on when a crisis develops during the reign of Domitian, but does not take part because he is too young and is held back by prudent advisers. He also experiences fifteen years of war—Hadrian, the man of the pax romana. As soon as he becomes emperor, he puts a stop to the Parthian War. Later, of course, he is forced against his will to fight again in the war of Palestine, but that came only years later, owing to the perpetual misunderstandng that divides two civilizations whose exigencies differ. That's why I have him say that this war was one of his defeats.

G   Do you regard Hadrian as a genius?

Y   Certainly. Many present-day historians agree with me. Because he was a constant innovator and reformer and brought to these tasks a rare intelligence. When he came to power, the empire was on the brink of bankruptcy, and he restored the economy with admirable skill. He improved the conditions of the slaves without resorting to demagogic rhetoric. He "stabilized the earth," as the inscription on his coins read. He made "restitution" to the provinces without compromising the unity of the Roman Empire. His legislation was extraordinarily supple. Taking an admirably empirical approach, he put into practice the ideas of the Greek philosophers, without ever imposing his Hellenism by force. He inaugurated a new phase of development in Greek art, which actually ended with him. To be sure, he had no Praxiteles or Scopas in his employ, but we owe the survival of Greek art in our own time in part to his efforts. He was highly intelligent in everything. And if he spent a great deal of time and effort thinking about the past, he did not on that account neglect the future. He was far closer to us than the Roman emperors depicted in the works of Suetonius or in popular movies and novels; in a sense, he was a Renaissance man.

G   But his attention was focused on a much more ancient world, that of the Greeks.

Y   Certainly, and so was the attention of the men of the Renaissance. But I don't know any Greek politician who can be compared with him. They lack his scope. Greece squandered its energies in local squabbles. Of course Alexander was the one exception, but he was a shooting star.

    Hadrian wasn't flashy. That's one of the things I like about him. He was above all clear-headed and always open-minded about worlds different from his own, such as the barbarian civilizations, which may not have been so barbarous as we imagine. Making fun of Hadrian, Florus, a minor Latin poet, said, "The emperor loves to go walking in cold climates, in the snows of Scythia and the rains of Brittany." Hadrian's answer is roughly as follows: "Stay in Rome, then, and go to taverns and get yourself bitten by mosquitoes while talking literature." This feeling for the barbarian world and passionate taste for things Greek are new, though it should not be forgotten that love of Greece was typical of the best Romans in earlier times; in this respect Hadrian was merely reviving the tradition of the Scipios. Also new was the taste for the oriental world as well as the surge of religious fervor, which, though Hadrian was not its source, was contemporary with him.

G   Wasn't Hadrian's genius Antinous? Naturally I mean his unwitting stroke of genius.

Y   In meeting Antinous Hadrian may have encountered a person who embodied his human ideal, who combined both Greece and Asia. I was struck by something somebody said to me once, one of those things that is said almost by accident but afterward seems impossible to improve upon. The person who said it was Raïssa Calza, then director of the museum at Ostia. We were looking at effigies of Antinous. I was collecting images of Antinous at the time in the hope that by combining partial views I might compile a more complete likeness; Madame Calza, who was di Chirico's first wife and had been with the Ballets Russes before marrying him, looked at one of these and exclaimed, "Nijinsky!" That remark proved very useful in helping me to understand my character. Nijinsky was of course marvelously good at representing another man's aspirations, at realizing the visions of a great *metteur en scène,* and Hadrian was in a sense a great *metteur en scène.* Saying this does not diminish the passionate side of the relationship but explains its idolatrous aspect.

G   Without Antinous what would Hadrian be? An emperor like the rest—

Y   Certainly not. He would have been a great civil servant, a great man of letters, and a great prince. But it may well be that his posthumous cult of Antinous, which has been so widely decried right up to the present day, marvelously symbolized Hadrian's religious and emotional ideal. A touch of madness is, I think, almost always necessary for constructing a destiny.

G   All the same, contemporaries must have been quite surprised by the cult of Antinous and by the innumerable effigies of him that Hadrian had strewn about the empire. Yet there was apparently no resistance—

Y   There was most likely some passive resistance from the old-Roman camp, as the fact that there are no Roman coins of Antinous suggests. Decisions concerning the striking of coinage in Rome were the privilege of the Senate. Coins depicting Antinous are known from almost everywhere, from Asia Minor as well as all the Greek cities. But there is no Roman coin, even though Hadrian would certainly have wanted one. Apparently, however, authorization was never granted, supposing the Senate was even consulted in the matter. Admittedly, the evidence is of a negative kind, but bear in mind the long-standing mutual hostility between the Senate and Hadrian, which might have led the Senate to undo all of his work had he not so skillfully arranged his own succession.

G   How much of your account of Antinous's death is hypothetical, and how do you explain his suicide?

Y   I explained it to the extent that Hadrian was able to explain it to himself and, for that matter, to the extent that I was able to explain it to myself. In the first place Antinous must have believed in the value of his sacrifice. It may well be, moreover, that quasi-ritual suicide provided a way out of his situation as the emperor's favorite.

It offered an escape from the ravages of age, from the erosion of passion, and from the odiousness of court intrigue. The five years that Antinous's "reign" apparently lasted is in some respects a very long time. The letter that Hadrian is supposed to have written from Alexandria a few weeks before the death of his favorite is very Hadrian-like, even if it isn't altogether authentic: it has a rather grating lightness of tone. One has the impression that Hadrian is at this point letting himself go, that he is becoming a simple man of pleasure, if Hadrian could ever be simple. This suggests some reasons why Antinous might have chosen more or less voluntarily to do away with himself. The chronicles would have it either that Antinous sacrificed himself for Hadrian or, if the chronicler is hostile to Hadrian, that the emperor demanded the sacrifice of his protégé. But this version of events was not put forward until fifty years after the fact, and Hadrian does not give the impression of having been a bloodthirsty person. I would be greatly surprised to discover that he demanded the suicide of a friend for ignobly superstitious reasons, particularly since the death of Antinous plunged him into despair. Nor is it easy to imagine Antinous involved in a conspiracy of some sort. He was a Greek, or Greco-Asiatic, youth who strikes me as having been a melancholy as well as a voluptuous young man.

G   How was your book received when it came out?

Y   The reviews were enthusiastic and emphasized the portrait of Antinous, as doubtless I had done myself. Whatever else can be said, the relationship with Antinous was the high point of Hadrian's life, though to be sure it was preceded by forty-five years of hard work and followed by nine years of fatigue. But people weren't particularly eager to look at Hadrian's life as a whole. They wanted above all to see a success, an extraordinary triumph. They wanted to see a triumphant emperor at the height of his glory: it made them feel exalted. There are many things in the book that strike me as quite interesting but that the public has not been very quick to discern. One such is Lucius, the would-be heir, an elegant man who almost becomes a great prince but who dies instead without leaving a trace. To me the characters who "almost exist" are also fascinating.

It is curious, too, to watch Hadrian as he grows old. Each of us ages differently; as the years accumulate, each person follows his own path. Hadrian's lucidity grows with age to the point where in the end it becomes mistrust, heightened according to some historians by brief bouts of madness brought on by the bitter prospect of war in Palestine and the desperation of illness. But in each case he manages to recover his courage or at any rate his discipline.

G   In what respects did the success of *Memoirs of Hadrian* change your life? Did you expect it?

Y   Not at all. I didn't expect more than ten people to read the book. I never expect anyone to read my books, for the simple reason that I don't think that the things that concern me are of interest to most people.

So I was naturally quite surprised. I received some very moving letters, some that brought me pleasure and even a few that overwhelmed me—especially the anonymous ones. I wasted a great deal of time answering those letters and doing all the other things that one does when one enjoys great success for the first time. But finally I went to work on something else. Still, I must say that there are many people who like *Hadrian* and other books of mine without understanding them. It's like the parable in the Bible: there is soil in which the seed can flourish and soil in which it cannot. In the case of Hadrian, of course, the problem is that many readers tend to identify with the hero, particularly in the amorous episode we've been talking about. Few readers have looked at the book as a whole. People generally don't see the whole; they see whatever juts out toward them. In reading any book people always look at the facet that reflects their own life.

G   Did anything in the reactions of reviewers and readers really astonish you?

Y   Not really. I had the usual surprises, of course. For instance, I discovered that one critic, employed by a reasonably reputable newspaper, had not read a single word of my book, as his review showed quite plainly. Such things happen from time to time. In this case I was surprised, because one is always surprised to discover that a profession has its incompetents, and criticism is a profession. But most of the critics were kind, and some were remarkably generous.

I had written the story of a man who was both a prince and a supremely interesting individual, and for some reason it met with great success. It is always pleasant to give a figure from the past a new lease on life.

The Abyss

MATTHIEU GALEY:
How did you first conceive of the idea to write *The Abyss?*
MARGUERITE YOURCENAR:
To begin with, I was interested in the histories of the families and towns in the area where I had grown up. Then I realized that these histories might be combined so as to recreate a microcosm.

One of my discoveries was a book from my father's family library entitled *Mémoires anonymes sur les troubles des Pays-Bas* (Anonymous memoirs of the disturbances in the Low Countries), a nineteenth-century reprint of a work written in Old French. This became the basis of *The Abyss,* just as Dio Cassius served as the basis of *Memoirs of Hadrian.* I started taking notes when I was eighteen. At that time I also examined certain genealogical documents, some of which I still have while others were lost in 1944 or 1945. In these documents I ran across a person named Zeno, another named Vivine, and still another named Jacqueline Bell. These names, which were not uncommon in Flanders at that time, started me dreaming, but what I had in mind at that point seems to have been a series of character portraits spanning several generations; this would have included sketches of men and women who came and went quietly from this earth, the sort of people to whom Barrès used to refer as "cemetery fodder," as well as people who developed their gifts to the full.

Of course I also studied the illustrious and less illustrious writers of the Renaissance. Once again I formed an idea of the kind of world in which Zeno had lived, just as I had formed an idea of the world in which Hadrian had lived. Most likely the book, as I conceived of it in my youth, would have been a vast, fictionalized form of *Archives du Nord* in which Zeno's story would have been no more than an episode.

G   In order to bring Zeno to life, you must have studied Renaissance
    medicine, magic, and so forth.

Y   Some of that was necessary, of course, along with the theology and
    philosophy of what is so vaguely referred to as the Renaissance,
    whose timetable was quite different from one country to the next.
    Zeno, for his part, is a man of the northern Renaissance, by which I
    mean a man of the midsixteenth century. You are familiar with the
    citation from Pico della Mirandola that I chose to use as an epigraph
    to the first section of *The Abyss.* Here it is in full:

> I have given you, O Adam, no fixed abode, and no visage of your
> own, nor any special gift, in order that whatever place or aspect
> or talents you yourself will have desired, you may have and
> possess them wholly in accord with your desire and your own
> decision. Other species are confined to a prescribed nature, under
> laws of my making. No limits have been imposed upon you,
> however; you determine your nature by your own free will, in
> the hands of which I have placed you. I have placed you at the
> world's very center, that you may the better behold from this
> point whatever is in the world. And I have made you neither
> celestial nor terrestrial, neither mortal nor immortal, so that, like
> a free and able sculptor and painter of yourself, you may mold
> yourself wholly in the form of your choice.

This passage is important because it reflects the spirit of the young
Renaissance, the period when faith in human dignity and man's
infinite powers was still enormous. In other words, as a theologian
once pointed out to me, it is a passage composed at a time when
man's idea of the world was not yet Copernican. Man is still at the
center of things, on an earth that is still at the center of the
universe.

Contrast this with the epigraph of the third section, from
Giuliano de' Medici, which reflects the disillusioned climate of the
later Renaissance, a period when man's dignity consisted in
enduring disaster:

> It is no villainy, nor from villainy proceeding,
> If to avoid a crueler fate someone
> Hates his own life and seeks for death.

Better to die, for one of noble soul,
Than to support the inevitable ill
That makes him change both heart and bearing.
How many has death already saved from anguish!
But those who hold the call to death as vile
Do not yet know how sweet sometimes it is.

After Rome fell to Charles V's reiters in 1525 (a watershed date like 1914), the outsized hopes of the early humanists gave way to discouragement. We have experienced similar breaks in continuity with the past, not only in 1914 (which I experienced as a child) but also in the period of increasing violence that followed the euphoric interlude of the twenties, violence whose spread has not abated since. Nineteen forty-five, the year of Hiroshima, must be added to this list of ominous dates.

To return to the Renaissance, Giuliano de' Medici's melancholy pride echoes the accents of distress that Michelangelo has given to his statue *Night*. A change of climate had occurred. A similar change of climate has occurred in our own time, and, for that reason, had I written *Hadrian* ten years later, the book wouldn't have been the same. Today I don't think I could even conceive of writing it. Just after the end of the war, in 1945, I still held out hope for some kind of reorganization of the world, but this is a hope that most of us have lost, even if, out of discipline and courage, we continue to act as if we still believed in it. Between the *Memoirs of Hadrian,* in which a powerful mind attempts to rebuild the world, to "stabilize the Earth," after years of war, and *The Abyss,* in which Zeno sinks ever deeper into an inferno of ignorance, savagery, and imbecilic rivalry, fifteen years of our own experience had unfortunately elapsed.

It was 1956, a very bad year, when I resumed work on the book. Think back to that time: Suez, Budapest, Algeria. . . . I realized how easy it would be to evoke the disorder of the sixteenth century, the iron curtain that separated Catholic Europe from Protestant Europe, and the tragedy of those who were at home in neither and forced to flee from one to the other.

At the time of the Suez crisis I was staying in Holland. And when I visited the Brussels museum I looked at the Brueghel paintings, with their images of war and destruction.

G Oddly enough, your book was published in 1968, yet another note-
   worthy date. Would it be correct to characterize *The Abyss* as a
   book of protest?

Y If by "protest" you mean anti-institutional, then, yes, certainly.
   Because Zeno is against everything: the universities, when he is
   young; the family, in whose eyes he is a bastard and whose vulgar
   riches he disdains; Don Blas de Vela's Spanish monastery, which he
   hates so much that he abandons the old Marrano who is being
   pursued by its monks, to his later regret; the professors at Montpellier, where he studies anatomy and medicine; the authorities;
   princes; and so forth. He rejects the ideology and intellectual
   endeavor of his age as nothing but a magma of words. Though he
   has experienced various forms of carnal pleasure, in the end he even
   rejects sensuality, up to a point. He naturally rejects Christian
   thought, though he gets on best with certain ecclesiastics, like the
   Prior of the Cordeliers. He looks on, disdainfully, at the collapse of
   Protestantism's left wing and finds scandalous the counterreforma-
   tion alliance of the Church with monarchy. As the world crumbles
   around him, he realizes that it is the human condition itself that is at
   issue. This can be seen, in particular, in his encounter with three
   Calvinists and two Catholics, who are fleeing to England or Holland. Some of them blame religious intolerance or Spanish policy or
   the duke of Alba for their troubles, but Zeno thinks that the world's
   problems are more persistent than they recognize. His observation
   is valid, incidentally, for all time.

   Consequently, for me *The Abyss* became a kind of mirror, which
   concentrated the human condition itself in the series of events that
   we call history.

G In developing the character Zeno, did you have any historical
   models in mind?

Y I had various people in mind at different stages of the writing, but
   they weren't exactly models. I never said to myself in so many
   words that I was going to base Zeno, or even some episode in
   Zeno's life, on such and such a historical figure. But while I was
   writing about Zeno and thinking about him, as I do about most of
   the characters in my books, over a period of many years, I was constantly on the lookout in whatever I read for ideas or for confir-
   mations of decisions already made. It may be that Zeno held certain

134

opinions because Campanella held them or because Giordano Bruno died for them. When I instinctively chose to make Zeno a man of the cloth, a bastard whom his family had originally intended for an ecclesiastical career, I said to myself, Well, after all, that's how Erasmus began his career. As for his physical appearance, I'm not sure but I think I always saw him as he is, nervous and long-suffering, fire and flame; for physical form is nothing but temperament made visible. I picture him as a young man of pale complexion in his student years, bronzed by the sun and the wind of the open road later on. Mainly I imagine him as thin, indestructible, sharp, and high-spirited. Oddly enough, he didn't change much over the years. I pictured him in the same way when I was twenty. I looked for people who resembled him in portraits of the time. A few come rather close to the way I picture him, one bust by Donatello in particular. When I went back to the Bargello to see it, I said to myself, Well, now, in a pinch, that Italian could be Zeno.

By contrast, the prior is a scholar, a humanist, a courtier, a diplomat, and a contented husband who, little by little, as he loses his wife and sheds his illusions, finds his way back to God. But he is not a man of science or a bold intellect, at least not at the outset.[1] And perhaps never, because his duty as he sees it is to raise a discreet voice of protest without breaking with the church to which he had devoted his life. He is a hero in that he keeps his faith in spite of everything. His fervor is neither revolutionary nor fanatical. He is no Savonarola. He is a man who suffers but who leaves judgment to God.

Zeno, I think, is rather closer to some of the lost youth of our time, though few that I've known have his passion. Most suffer from a rather feeble brand of nihilism, comprehensible enough in an age even more chaotic than Zeno's was. They want to escape what they see as complacency, but their escape becomes in turn complacency of another kind. Zeno's quest is not an escape. He goes off initially to study with Don Blas de Vela. Then he goes to Montpellier, and after that comes a period I didn't describe but only alluded to, the years of practicing medicine at Pont-Saint-Esprit and at the legate's court in Avignon.

1. Neither is Zeno a humanist in the strict sense of the word, or even a man of letters. He has about him something of the empiricist and the autodidact, rather like Paracelsus and even Leonardo.

After that, he travels to the East, and again I don't describe his adventures there in detail, but the reader can guess what they were: the Hungarian campaign, the horrors of war, and then the years of wandering in Italy and Germany, which are also partly years of professional labor, of practice as an itinerant physician, traveling from town to town. I didn't dwell at length on this part of his life because the details didn't interest me much. What did interest me was the character of fire and ice who endured it all. We sense that he was tempered by his experience much as a sword is tempered, but the details are not very important. As far as he is concerned, his life, by the time we meet him again back at Innsbruck following the plague, has already been used up, consumed, burned—the word "burned" is very important in *The Abyss*—and reduced to ashes.

G   At what point did you settle on the French title of *The Abyss* (*L'œuvre au noir*)?

Y   In 1957 or 1958. By that time I must already have written a hundred pages or so. I was looking for a title but hadn't come up with anything satisfactory. *La nuit obscure* too strongly suggested a mystical and Christian subject matter. The phrase "oeuvre au noir" appears as early as 1956–57 in my study of Thomas Mann, however. In some vague way it was floating around in my mind. I say "in some vague way" because initially I wanted to see what would happen to Zeno. I had gotten off to a bad start at age twenty—one always gets off to a bad start at that age—by making Zeno's character too schematic: he was a typical free thinker as an old-fashioned radical might have imagined him around 1920. I realized that this was a distorted picture, that the character was actually much more complex, that his intentions and his experiences contradict one another, or at any rate appear to do so, and that past a certain point in the story the various strands in his character ravel and unravel at the same time. At the end of his life, for example, Zeno, even though he has not shed a single one of the opinions that make him, according to the official precepts of the Christian religion, an atheist, he is far closer to the bishop who condemns him than he would have been at twenty. The naïve nihilism of his school notebooks, which shocks the theologians who sit in judgment of him, bores the bishop, an intelligent man, just as it bores Zeno, who muses, "To think that I went to the trouble of writing down such commonplaces."

G   Didn't you find yourself hampered by the elliptical structure of the
    work in your effort to breathe life into Zeno and the four hundred
    characters who accompany him?

Y   Not at all. On the contrary, they are alive precisely because they
    change. The same can be said of the *Memoirs of Hadrian*. We see very
    little of Hadrian in the army and very little of the tragic winters he
    spent campaigning against the Scythians, which must have marked
    him for life. Can any of us remember everything about our lives?
    We retain only an infinitesimal portion of what we experience.

    People vanish from Zeno's memory; they simply dissolve. Some
    stand out more clearly than others, though. The same is true for any
    one of us. For instance, Zeno's jailer, Gilles, is sketched fairly close-
    ly, because Zeno found this crude, wily fellow rather amusing and
    besides, he was one of Zeno's last companions in life. Other figures
    flit through his memory as rapidly as they flitted through his life.
    Each one leaves some trace, and what Zeno remembers is this trace,
    this scar that others leave behind, not the person himself in his
    routine existence. The time of memory is very fleeting.

    On the other hand, in the abyss, as Zeno says, memory is fixed.
    Don Blas de Vela is still there, Henry Maximilian is still there, the
    Lady of Froso is still there, and so is the surgeon-barber Jan Myers.
    In the chapter entitled "The Abyss" we see the residue of a life, and
    the characters in the distance become confounded with one
    another, the different phases of a single solid: man. Doubtless this
    has something to do with Zeno's temperament: other people exist
    for him as more or less temporary manifestations.

    In the typical novel the succession of characters and events is
    taken to be a solid reality; that is as far as the novelist can see. But
    Zeno stands behind the tapestry. Not at the beginning, however.
    When he meets Vivine, the young woman who is something of a
    fiancée to him, and they speak to each other in terms reminiscent of
    the stanzas of a ballad, and when he later refuses on the one hand to
    serve as secretary to Margaret of Austria and on the other hand to
    join the rebellious workers, he is still quite sure of what he wants
    and what he does not want, still quite firmly in possession of the
    moment. He has not yet left home: he is merely a young man who
    refuses and believes himself free to do so. As I said before, he then
    spends the rest of his life trying to acquire the freedom he thought
    he possessed at age twenty.

When I began I had no precise plan. It was when I reread, with some distaste, the draft of the Zeno novel written when I was twenty that I said to myself, The workers' rebellion can be reused. It's a very important episode, almost a historical document. The meeting of the two cousins can also be reused, for it has in it something of the warmth of youth. Or else the story of the Franciscans of Bruges, which was summed up in a few lines by a chronicler, could now serve as the kernel, or rather the framework, of the whole second part of the book. And then, of course, Zeno will travel, as all philosophers did in those days.

Beyond that, however, I wasn't sure what I would do. In general I have very few fixed ideas when I begin a book. I checked constantly to see what was possible and what was impossible for Zeno, what could be said and what could not. But in order to know what form chance will ultimately take, events must be allowed to run their course, and in a long life there is plenty of opportunity for chance to intervene.

I've said in the past, and reiterated in *Archives du Nord* and again to you earlier, that people don't like to discover how much their lives depend on chance. It embarrasses them. They like to feel that they are largely in control or, if not in control, then at least that their passions, their loves, even their errors are ultimately what decides. Most people find it more beautiful and more interesting to believe that this is so. But the notion that everything depends on what bus you happen to get on—

G   That isn't the impression one gets from reading the novel, though; what I mean to say is that if chance decides, it's chance of a highly directed sort.

Y   Perhaps, but that takes you into the realm of metaphysics or magic. In his conversations with the bishop, Zeno indicates that everything is magic. This is related, first of all, to the fact that everything exerts some kind of influence and, second, to circumstances' being so complicated that it is not always possible to provide a rational explanation. Nothing prevents our saying that everthing is predetermined, that events have been arranged according to some extremely clever plan of which we glimpse only a small portion. But we can equally well say that everything is chaos—there is no escaping this dilemma. Hadrian, too, had to confront it, and it is treated at length in the first part of the *Memoirs,* at the end of the chapter entitled "Animula Vagula Blandula." Actually, I surprised myself as the writing of *The Abyss* progressed. Right up to the end, Zeno remains in a state of bewilderment and uncertainty. He might choose to betray his own philosophy. Right up to the final moment he might decide to inform one of his guards that he is ready to engage in public self-criticism. He might also decide to resign himself to being burned alive, consoling himself with the thought that in that event his death would be no more extraordinary than if his clothing had caught fire while he was working in front of his alchemist's furnace. He can also elect to die in relative tranquility, in prison. I didn't make the choice for him. I had to let him choose, right up to the end.

What is more, the book took a turn that came as a surprise to me as well as to Zeno, thanks to his meeting the Prior of the Cordeliers. Originally the prior was only a minor character, which shows how little difference there is at first between a major character and a secondary one. Before leaving the United States for a trip to Poland in 1964, I had finished a chapter: Zeno looks at himself in a mirror and sees dozens of faces (the mirror is a small one with many facets—I had seen one like it in a house in Lübeck); he then departs. That image is almost a symbol of all the Zenos still possible at his age, fifty. Immediately thereafter I began work on the following chapter, in which someone in Senlis offers Zeno a place in the prior's carriage, which is carrying the prior home from a visit to one of the chapters of his order. When I began I simply said to myself, He'll get to Bruges one way or another and lose himself there. I had no idea that he would see the prior again and attach himself to his person.

Somewhat fatigued after these exertions, I went to Poland and took a short side trip to Russia, leaving Zeno behind, as it were. On my way back I stopped in Austria and suddenly realized that I wanted to visit the very beautiful Franciscan church in Salzburg. I sat in the church and attended high mass. And I literally saw the Prior of the Cordeliers enter the scene, in my thoughts of course, or perhaps I should say in my mind's eye. Suddenly this character was there, vibrantly alive, even though he did not yet exist in a single sentence of the book; he had a great deal to tell me, moreover. And so the book, rather than come to an end in ten pages, went on for another two hundred.

The ending forced itself on me. I saw that the prior and Zeno were complementary characters: the prior with his inner rebellion and Zeno a rebel almost by intuition in everything he ever did. Both men are extremely intelligent, kindred spirits, but the prior is ruled by pity, which he extends to every human being, whereas Zeno, whose passion to serve his fellow man insures that he too is no stranger to pity, preserves "his physician's cold compassion" to the bitter end.

. . . and Its Aftermath

MATTHIEU GALEY:
I imagine that the character Cyprian wasn't particularly important
initially.
MARGUERITE YOURCENAR:
He didn't even exist, frankly. He came into being when I remembered having read, thirty years earlier in some documents of the
time, that arrests had been made for "crimes against morals" among
the Franciscans of Ghent and Bruges, and I realized that this episode
could be used to show Zeno caught in a trap. Eventually I had to
give faces to the people involved; only one of them is identified in
the chronicles, described physically, and linked to certain incidents:
that was Pierre de Hamaere. This wasn't enough, so quite obviously
I had to imagine a young monk who might have worked with Zeno
in the hospice. Cyprian was born on that day.[1]

His role is somewhat that of a dangerous, if familiar, spirit, Zeno,
who has all but lost his yen for adventures of the flesh, is indulgent
toward Cyprian, because he realizes that at his age he himself might
have been compromised in a similar situation. Yet he is afraid of
being implicated—the consequences in his case might well be
severe—and the childish superstitions of the group of "Angels"
exasperate him. On the night that Cyprian calls him to the Sabbath,
however, he does experience a moment of desire, almost another
optical illusion. In the end, when he offers the boy money to flee
and Cyprian refuses because he doesn't want to abandon the girl he
loves, Zeno quite simly feels an immense, almost impersonal pity
for him.

G   Still, it's because of Cyprian that he is compromised, and as Zeno
himself points out to the canon, the only sins severely condemned
by the Church have always been sins of the flesh.

1. In a similar way I created two female characters, the demoiselle of Loos
and la Moricaude, in order to introduce female figures into the episode.

Y   That's still true today, almost. The pope worries a great deal about
contraception, but publicly at any rate condemns the Belfast terror-
ists only in the vaguest of terms. But to get back to Zeno, if there
had been no amorous games in the bathhouse, no one would have
cared what went on in the hospice. As Zeno says, "one always falls
into some kind of trap." As well this one as any other. Like
Hadrian, for whom the problem did not arise, Zeno was not what
we would today call a homosexual but a man who from time to
time had adventures with other men. The few, almost paradoxical
statements he makes on this subject, at Innsbruck, are readily un-
derstandable. He prefers someone who resembles him, whom he
can approach as it were on a footing of equality, a lover who is also
a traveling companion and a comrade in time of danger. Many men
would make the same argument even today, and in Zeno's time the
position of women made it even more difficult to treat a woman as
anything other than a wife or a mistress, never as a companion.
What possibilities were open to him? An assignation with a bourgeoise behind a cask in her husband's wine cellar, as in the *fabliaux*?
Courtesans? Prostitutes didn't interest him. Women of the aristocratic classes? They were almost inaccessible, and in any case it is
hard to imagine Zeno as a gentleman-in-waiting.

   Hadrian, according to one chronicler, had an "amorous friendship" with Plotina. Zeno had a single encounter with the Lady of
Froso, a brief interval of tenderness and sensuality for which he
always remained grateful, for this woman, as he puts it, might have
been a companion, a colleague, an ideal physician's assistant, and
not merely a lover, though she was that too.

G   In your other works there are a number of homosexual characters,
from Alexis to Hadrian, but the choice always seems to have been
dictated by the subject or by history. In *The Abyss* that isn't the case.
Y   On the contrary. The problem was to show where repression
always leads. My intention was to show Zeno as a free man, that is,
a man who by and large makes his own choices; chance played a
part, naturally, and so did the subversive side of adventure, perhaps,
which tempted Zeno as it could not have tempted Hadrian, for
whom it didn't exist. The choice was in some sense a philosophical
one, to reunite mind and body. Incidentally, both characters are
more bisexual than homosexual. Of course there are homosexual

elements in Hadrian's character; he prefers to seek his lovers outside the rather hermetic world of women, which he thinks of as frivolous and hopelessly domestic, particularly after his unfortunate marriage to a sullen woman whom he does not love. This doesn't however prevent him from having mistresses, some of whom leave him charmed memories, as I've tried to show.

There are very few examples of pure homosexuality in antiquity. In fact, it was such a rare thing that I can't cite a single example, at least not from the Greek world. From the Latin world in the period of decadence, perhaps. Men married and had mistresses. They felt they had freedom of choice; their homosexuality had nothing of an obsessive or compulsive quality about it, unlike today's homo-sexuality, in which one occasionally observes a tendency for men of "minority" tastes to create around themselves a mythology of hostility toward women or fear of women. This is very striking nowadays. But it cannot be emphasized too strongly that whenever minorities are placed in a position of inferiority and discriminated against for reasons of race, ideological adherence, or sexual prefer-ence, the suffering caused by their inferior status eventually results in certain intellectual or moral peculiarities. This is true of blacks in the United States and of Jews living in anti-Semitic countries. A kind of psychosis develops for which there would be no reason if there were no racial, religious, or sexual discrimination.

G   There are hardly any examples of female homosexuality in your works.
Y   There is Margaret of Austria in *The Abyss,* as Brantome suggests. But you're quite right, there are none in *Hadrian*. If Plotina had such leanings, or any other leanings for the matter, we see nothing of them, and Hadrian describes her as "chaste, by reason of disgust with the merely facile." If I may consider the past for a moment, particularly the Greek poets, since I've been working recently on an anthology, the only example we find is Sappho, a unique case, or *hapax,* as a pedant of ancient grammar might say, which tells us nothing about ordinary life. Throughout much of history female homosexuality must have been all but invisible, I imagine, since it would normally have involved the mistress of the house and female domestics, cousins and friends in the gynaeceum, or again, young

courtesans, as we see in Lucian and in Valery Larbaud's delightful short story *Amants, heureux amants.*

In the ancient world and even in the Middle Ages, the rule, of course, was silence. Brantome refers to a female friend of Margaret of Austria only because Margaret was a princess and only after the death of her young husband, whom she loved passionately. She, too, would be defined as bisexual.

G   Female homosexuality was quite common at the end of the last century and the beginning of this one.

Y   There was, I think—and you have to go a little father back in time, to the eighteenth century—a prurient interest on the part of certain men in women who love other women, and many women took advantage of this fashion, or made themselves fashionable. I wouldn't go so far as to say that this was the main reason, but there was an affectation or mode of this sort among high-society women. Back in the eighteenth century, we see that Casanova was delighted to have his lovers climb into bed with one another, and so was the duke of Morny a century later. Think of Courbet's paintings; they reflect the same taste. Even Ingres, in *The Turkish Bath,* becomes aroused at the sight of what he felt to be an audacious form of sensuality; and obviously it enabled him to double, indeed to multiply at will, the attitudes of abandonment in which he depicted the feminine objects that stood before his eyes and stimulated his desire. All of this was foreign to the Greeks. Perhaps they weren't sufficiently interested in what went on in the gynaeceum to wonder what the women were doing when they were absent.

G   In your opinion, then, is the whole issue a false problem in this day and age?

Y   Tremendously false. Greater freedom should one day—soon perhaps—resolve the issue if all goes well. On the other hand, certain Islamic countries such as Pakistan and Iran have clearly regressed on all fronts, reinstating medieval codes with even harsher than medieval punishments in the case of Iran, On moral questions we can expect unreason to rear its head again and again.

G   What position should one adopt?

Y   Fight against it.

G   *The Abyss* has something else in common with out own time,
    namely, the sects. There are quite a few rather bizarre sects around
    these days—

Y   The Anabaptists, among others; what was involved seems to have
    been a revolt against the rigidity of the Church's teaching. It was
    also a form of protest. People like the Anabaptists fought with the
    intellectual weapons they had at their disposal, weapons that had
    been handed to them. In the modern world, especially in the United
    States, the spiritual influence of religion is still very great, but too
    many Protestants seem emotionally to require something more than
    the ethical teachings they find in their religion and are beginning to
    search for something else.

    The Jim Jones affair, for instance, shows the degree to which a
    society like our own is fragile because it drives isolated individuals,
    frightened by new dangers, to seek refuge in sectarian catacombs
    or, ultimately, in death orgies of the sort that occurred in Jones-
    town. The facts of the Jonestown affair are not very clear, but
    Jones's disciples must have looked upon death as a remedy for their
    dissatisfaction, which is hardly surprising. People must either rise
    above their circumstances or else plunge headlong into drugs,
    alcohol, or sectarian madness. The more overwhelming, the more
    dehumanized things seem to be, the more people will look for such
    ways out.

    Obviously, a completely free society would have neither sects
    nor fanatics. But no such society has ever been seen on the face of
    the earth. We usually think of the eighteenth century as a period of
    liberation and enlightenment, as indeed it was in the upper reaches
    of the cultural hierarchy; but I would point out that, lower down,
    one finds innumerable sects, such as the so-called convulsionaries
    (who gathered in Paris, in the cemetery of Saint-Médard—
    TRANS.). Nowadays, the issue is not so much religious doctrine as
    morals; there is disagreement over the very shape that society ought
    to take. This aspect of the question has been marvelously well
    described, I think, by the well-known American anthropologist
    Ruth Benedict in her classic book, *The Chrysanthemum and the Sword*.
    Her research focused on Japan, but the results apply to other
    countries as well. According to Benedict, there are two kinds of
    constraint, that of sin, which has practically disappeared today, and
    that of shame, which is now prevalent and which originates when

an individual feels that he or she does not correspond to the society's ideal prototype. Benedict shows that we believe we are freer now that we used to be because we are no longer subject to the Christian category of sin, whereas in fact the guilt associated with sin has been supplanted by anxiety over our failure to conform exactly to some norm, whether Freudian or Fordian or Marxian. For the "abnormal" individual the sect provides a comforting environment, which may involve the use of drugs or superstition.

G   Do you think that an individual might possibly find something of value in one of these sects?

Y   It's as if you asked me, Can an individual find something of value in debauch, or in poetry regarded as individual exaltation, or in anything else that gratifies his intimate needs of the moment? Yes, certainly, he can find gratification, and in the first place the gratification of being a member of a group with which he can share his enthusiasm. A very similar observation occurs in my discussion of medieval and seventeenth-century sorcerers in *Archives du Nord*. For the peasant leading a harsh life, what must attending a Sabbath have meant? "Painting the town red," as they say in English—in other words, having a good time, with the excitement of danger thrown in for good measure. The Sabbath was the peasant's discothèque, a place of sensual abandonment, drunkenness, and debauch, as in a bordello. If people want to make sects less attractive to youngsters, there are better ways than to hold congressional investigations or stage police raids. What young people need is a more satisfactory alternative which offers a chance to experience the sacred, to experience beauty, and to experience happiness. Unhappiness would of course continue to exist, but it would no longer be unalterable unhappiness, unhappiness inscribed in the natural order.

G   Wasn't magic also a form of the will to power?

Y   Power was always a temptation. I'm not speaking of the really great magicians, like Agrippa, who crossed the dividing line between magic and psychological research at the very highest level, but of ordinary magicians, who did respond not only to man's very urgent need for power but also to his need for access to forbidden worlds. At a very low level, though, I'm really afraid that the role of magic has today been usurped by various gadgets, like the auto-

146

mobile and the computer, which deceive people into thinking that they can increase their powers and skills simply by acquiring a faster or better machine. Such material objects do afford a certain power over the world as long as the complex society of production and exploitation from which they derive continues to function, but without it they would disappear, and nobody seems to notice that these very same machines are slowly destroying the intellectual and physical capacities of those they serve. People too fond of driving forget how to walk; students who use computers forget how to count. Oddly enough, my criticism parallels the criticism of magic by various theologians and mystics, who argued that the danger of magic was that the support it provided for the soul and mind, and indeed the will, was deceptive, not really solid at all.

In his own way modern man believes in alchemy, as when he exhibits naïve faith in the efficacy of certain chemicals that often do him more harm than good. Because magic, in a word, is external. A man in love with a woman who doesn't return his love may buy a potion that is supposed to make her fall in love with him or a sleeping draught so that he might rape her. What is sought is always power over objects or people. That is why most people whose minds are at all above the ordinary will flirt with magic for a time but generally reject it in the end.

Zeno was no stranger to the will to power you just mentioned. But he managed to overcome it completely and turn instead to pure knowledge, which is something of another order entirely. All mystics do this, no matter what religion they espouse. Buddhists, for example, tell the story of an ascetic who boasts to Buddha that he can walk on water. Buddha says, "How long did it take you to develop this talent?" "Ten years," the man answers. "What a pity," says Buddha. "For a few coins you could have taken the ferry."

G   Does this "pure knowledge" reach its zenith at the end of the book, in the famous line, "And this is as far as one can go in the death of Zeno"? Is this an opening toward metaphysics, or are you slamming the door shut?

Y   The door is opening, but we don't know what lies beyond. Possibly a world in which Zeno no longer has to be Zeno, a world in which he might not even remember having been Zeno, or at any rate would not go on remembering. A return to the universal. Or, rather, a transition, which is not easy: Zeno's sufferings were, I imagine, harsh. It's very painful to die by opening one's veins. There is a risk of horrible cramps. You lack oxygen, and the doctors I consulted (naturally I spoke to doctors before attempting to describe Zeno's death) tell me that people sometimes experience pain like that of angina. It's only in novels written "in the manner of the ancients" that people who've slit their wrists die peacefully, crowned with roses, in an almost voluptuous swoon.

Horrible deaths were not unknown; Seneca's was one. He just wouldn't die. In Zeno's case death comes relatively quickly. I liked him too much to allow him to suffer. Still, there is one moment that must have been very hard, when he regains consciousness in the final agony and his whole body stampedes toward death, just prior to the ultimate vertigo, at which point, in Zeno's case, serenity, indeed a kind of tragic joy, begins to take hold: the return to the universal is indicated by the sound of torrents and by the sun bleeding into the sea.

G   What was your feeling when you finished *The Abyss*?

Y   A kind of intoxication. It was the middle of the summer. Quite often, as Jean-Jacques Rousseau remarked long ago, a writer situates characters or events in a season opposite to the one he is writing in. I finished *Memoirs of Hadrian,* whose hero dies in the heat of an Italian summer, during a very cold winter, and *The Abyss* in midsummer, even though Zeno kills himself on 17 February. I remember the very last moment of the work. I was lying in a hammock, in the garden—I should mention, perhaps, that both *The Abyss* and *Hadrian* were completed here in Maine—and I remember repeating, almost without being aware of it, what Colette (who had observed similar things in the faubourgs of Paris) would have called a magical incantation: still lying on my hammock with my just-finished manuscript still in hand, I repeated Zeno's name over and over again, perhaps as many as three hundred times or more, trying to bring him closer to me, to secure his presence in that moment, which in some sense was his last.

G   But what does the writer feel when confronted with the completed work?

Y   One feels, first of all, that the job is done, that the long and arduous task one set for oneself at the outset has been accomplished and that, by good fortune, nothing has happened to keep one from reaching the goal. Good, it's finished. That, I think, is one's simplest feeling. After that one feels a sense of emptiness, of very deep emptiness, obviously. But Zeno existed. He still exists.

G   Is it true to say that Zeno is the antithesis of Hadrian?

Y   Not at all. They resemble one another intellectually and in certain other respects. It is possible to conceive of a Hadrian who was not an emperor but a physician and persecuted intellectual living in difficult times. Zeno and Hadrian are kindred intellects. They differ in their temperaments. Hadrian is far more sanguine, far more influenced by his immediate emotions, and far more likely to crumble in adversity. At various times in his life Hadrian's spirits plummet abruptly. Nothing of the kind happens to Zeno; one feels that he is indestructible. If he hadn't killed himself, he would have lived twenty or thirty years longer. He is a far more somber figure than Hadrian, however, and his destiny is also more somber. I wouldn't say that all the cards were stacked in Hadrian's favor—if they had been, his story wouldn't have been very interesting—but he had a lot going for him. He was related to the reigning emperor. He progressed in his career, slowly to be sure, somewhat indecisively, but he did progress. He reached the final goal late, but he did reach it. And he ruled for twenty years, during which time he felt, rightly, that he would be able to do a great deal for Rome, Greece, and the world. Whereas Zeno was constantly in danger and had to build and rebuild his life surreptitiously in order not to arouse suspicion. What is more, he fools himself into thinking he is safe, tranquil at last, because Flanders is in such political turmoil that surely no one will bother about him: it is at that moment that he falls into a trap.

G   It seems to me that, beyond this, there is in *The Abyss* something more intense, something indeed blacker than one finds in *Hadrian,* and that this something must reflect a harsher, starker view or experience of life.

Y   The times had changed. Zeno's age is much closer to our own. To begin with, Zeno's was a Christian age, whereas Hadrian's retains something of the Greek feeling for uncomplicated happiness. No matter how desperate things got, the Greeks always loved life. Happiness is something important to Hadrian. It is not something important to Zeno. If one is happy for a time, so much the better; if not, it matters little. For Hadrian, however, there is a very clear relationship between greatness and happiness. The best moments, the greatest moments, are also the happiest. Zeno has no comparable sentiment. Despite the sensual part of his nature, which he has in common with everyone else, Zeno is by nature an ascetic, whereas Hadrian merely has the ascetic experience of the military together with a few later attempts at ritual purification and abstinence, really quite minor episodes in his life.

An astrologer—and please note that I am no believer in astrology—might say that the two men were born under very different stars, meaning that they exhibit two quite different human constellations: Hadrian, with his generosity and what I might call his abundance, is an Aquarius, whereas Zeno is a Pisces.

G You gave him a precise date of birth?

Y Of course: 27 February, and I had his chart cast. The forecast was a silent slide into the abyss.

G But to do an astrological calculation you also need to know the time of birth.

Y The novelist was free to choose. It was a nighttime birth, because the women bathe and swaddle the infant "in the (prophetic) glow of embers on the hearth." I wasn't very precise, though; like Zeno, I don't take astrology very seriously. Remember that when he served as astrologer to the king of Sweden and Prince Erik was not there to work with him on the horoscopes, he redid the calculations so that the results were more favorable to the royal family, with a shrug of his shoulders. A committed believer in astrology would not have been so nonchalant. In any case there is no doubt that the emperor was by nature a creature of the sun, whereas Zeno was by nature nocturnal. They represent two complementary poles of the human sphere as I imagine it.

Beyond the Novels

MATTHIEU GALEY:
Given that you have lived for so long in the United States, why is it that America never appears in your work?
MARGUERITE YOURCENAR:
A little of it does appear in the form of an enslaved and mistreated race in my translations of Negro spirituals. As for the United States itself, I still don't know the country well enough, even after forty years, to hazard a judgment. I am constantly struck by the immensity of this shapeless, ever-changing country. I know Mount Desert Island quite well, but I don't write regional novels. In any case, the job has already been done spendidly for New England, most notably by Edith Wharton. Many writers have said all that needed to be said about small-town America: what would be the point of doing it again? My concerns were different; I wrote essays on other subjects. But the essay that precedes my play *La petite sirène* (The little siren) is a quite detailed study of the city of Hartford, Connecticut, in the 1940s, and the preface to *Fleuve profond* is a lengthy consideration of the condition of blacks in the United States.

G Was the decision to write essays made by chance, or did you want to rest your mind between two purely creative works?
Y Nothing is more tiring than writing an essay. Not only do you have to do research, but you have to transform yourself into a prosecuting attorney or judge. There's also something discouraging about the work. No matter what you set out to do, it quickly becomes clear that you'll never succeed. It's rather like doing a translation, in that absolute accuracy is impossible. One does the best one can to capture the sound of another spirit and to avoid misrepresentation, but to keep from making Thomas Mann sound too much like oneself the essayist has to reread *Doctor Faustus* ten times over and find the thread. It's exhausting. I rewrote my essay on Mann two or three times. It started out as a short article for a *Fest-*

schrift, developed into a longer piece for an American magazine, and then came the final version. Writing the forty pages for my preface to *La couronne et la lyre* took me nearly a year. So you see that one must deliberate a great deal before committing oneself.

G   Not to mention the fact that you also needed forty years of experience and knowledge of Greek poetry. But does one really need that much time to write a piece of this sort, when one knows the subject as you do?

Y   Everything must be checked, and every work must be reread as if one knew nothing. One's knowledge is never thorough enough. When it exists at all—in order to write my essay on Chenonceaux, for example, I had to immerse myself in archives of which I knew absolutely nothing when I began. That also took me a year, and if I decide to write my planned essay on Mishima, I'll need at least that much time, to say nothing of a trip to Japan, which up to now I've always been obliged to postpone.

G   Why were you interested in Chenonceaux?

Y   My interest grew out of a rather silly commission from an American magazine, which offered to pay a large sum of money provided I came up with a romantic account of Chenonceaux, "Castle of Love." I knew the castle only casually and decided to find out whether life there had or had not been romantic. The answer, I quickly realized, was that life at Chenonceaux had not been romantic in the least, dominated as it was by political crises, wrangles over inheritance, and worries about money. Accordingly, I notified the magazine that my article would not be the "glamour" piece they had commissioned, and they cancelled it; but having become fascinated by the subject, I continued my investigations anyway. To me Chenonceaux stood for all that was unstable in those ancient palaces that to us seem so sumptuous and peaceful, whereas the magazine's editors had hoped for fairy tales about the loves of Diane de Poitiers and Henri II.

G   All your works are written with minute care, but what is it that ties together the essays collected in *Sous bénéfice d'inventaire*?

Y   Nothing other than my interest in the various subjects they treat. Cavafy and Selma Lagerlöf are both great writers, but that's all they have in common. As for the widows of Chenonceaux and the engravings of Piranesi, both illustrate aspects of life at a given moment of history. Life ties them together.

G   Do you regard these as minor works?

Y   They're related to the others. They are the form taken by the work *before* inspiration makes it into a poem or novel. In the essay one must beware of imagination. Like it or not, imagination distorts, it pushes you in a certain direction, which is not always the right one.

G   Another danger of the essay is identification with one's subject. In Thomas Mann you discovered ideas similar to those that you yourself hold dear, in particular his way of locating himself in the universe, and much of what you say about him might be said about you as well.

Y   Only up to a certain point. Many aspects of Mann's personality are not attractive to me. I discovered his work rather late in life and was naturally greatly struck by the fact that, though we began with very different views, our working methods were quite similar. But some of Mann's tricks and some of his observations are foreign to me, just as Cavafy's methods, and for that matter his sensibility, are very different from my own.

G   Are you sure that there's no "autosuggestion" in your conception of Thomas Mann's work?

Y   How could I possibly maintain that I'm "sure"? I saw his work from my own angle, but that is a truism, no truer in Mann's case than in Selma Lagerlöf's or Piranesi's. In each artist one looks for the vital core of the work, which is different every time. The core of Lagerlöf's work, for example, is the epic, the epic tale. In Mann's case it's harder to pin down: perhaps it's the desire to *comprehend* the world through a very German sensibility.

G   Have you ever been interested in authors who were totally alien to you?

Y   Yes, of course, although it isn't easy to say that any author is totally alien. Dickens, whom I like very much, comes to mind, for at times it seems to me that he and I are quite remote from one another; but are we really? His feeling for the poverty and wretchedness of London has much in it that corresponds to my own idea of charity.

Whenever we choose to be interested in an author, there has to be some basis for the deep bond or kinship that we feel—not necessarily the essence of the man, but something sufficient to account for the closeness of the tie.

G   How did you come to write plays? We haven't spoken of your plays up to now, perhaps because they're rarely performed.

Y   Performance isn't what matters to me. Quite often I will allow an amateur troupe or a suburban summer theater to try its hand at one of my plays, knowing full well that many of my intentions will go unnoticed and that some of the ideas will be lost. But I tell myself that the text remains and that it's not a bad thing for young actors to practice by *playing* with it. I follow the work only from a distance and generally don't expect any kind of success.

G   Because the theater is just a secondary occupation for you?

Y   Quantitatively speaking, yes. Qualitatively it remains to be seen. I sometimes enjoy myself in my plays as I might in a private preserve still largely free of intruders. Like the prose poems in *Fires* and *Nouvelles orientales,* the plays are more playful though just as truthful as my other works; the form itself often gives the impression of being a game. What I think about my plays is, if I may make so ambitious a comparison, not unlike what I've said about some of Mann's late novellas, such as *Felix Krull* and *The Transposed Heads:* namely, that these works contain Mann's ideas (the same ideas as *The Magic Mountain* or *Doctor Faustus*) but expressed with the freedom of a masquerade ball.

G   None of this explains, however, why a novelist or essayist should take a somewhat dilettantish interest in the theater.

Y   But the trajectory is obvious. I've always attached a considerable importance to voices. I referred once to *Alexis* as "the portrait of a voice." The monologues in *Fires* are voices raised to a fever pitch. The long discourse that I call *Memoirs of Hadrian* is again a solitary monologue, as the meditations of a man who stands at the summit of the world must inevitably be. In the polyphonic late medieval and Renaissance world that is Zeno's, voices again occupy center stage: the shrill voice of Hilzonda praying In Münster, or Zeno's rather severe voice set in antiphon to the emotional voice of the Prior of the Cordeliers, or again to the fine, deep voice of that hardened but literate old soldier, Henry Maximilian. There are also the voices of the judges and the somewhat unctuous voice of Gilles Rombaut, former peddler now promoted to prison guard: these minor voices must be picked out of the third-person narrative by the reader. And then there is the "public voice," which of course distorts everything. In *A Coin in Nine Hands* nothing was more important to me than the voice of Marcella, a sort of loose vernacular, speaking French with Italian turns of phrase; or the grumpy voice of old Clement Roux in the midst of Rome's crowds or wandering its empty streets; or again, the youthful voice of Massimo speaking to Clement Roux, heedless and unheeded, the youth of the one as solitary as the old age of the other, all at once making Rome's deserted nighttime streets reverberate with the sound of three words of church Slavonic. In still another part of that book, love and pain are mimicked in silence by the little siren who has sacrificed her voice. So it was natural for me to try my hand at theater now and then, the intention being not so much to write a play that one would want to see produced on stage as to create a labyrinth of monologues or dialogues in their pure state.

Few people to date have noticed the links between my plays and my other, better-known works. The differences between them are differences of form only, not of substance, though hardly anyone has noticed this. *Electre ou la chute des masques* is *Coup de Grâce:* three people, or rather four, bound together by love, hate, and danger. Admittedly, the respective positions of the characters are different: Electre is a sister and not a lover, whereas Sophie is far more a lover than a sister; Electre is odious, whereas Sophie is good. But the sum total is the same, and it was in no way paradoxical for me to transform the honest Chopin of *Coup de Grâce* into the honest Theodore of *Electre.* The same triangle occurs again in *Fires* with Lena, or again in *A Coin in Nine Hands,* in which Marcella's love wavers between two men, while her deepest devotion is reserved for a dead partisan whom she hopes to avenge, just as Electre hopes to avenge her murdered father.

Nor has anyone noticed that the humble prayer of little Father Chica in *Rendre à Cesar* echoes the prior's tragic meditations in *The Abyss,* overwhelmed as both men are by the world's suffering.

In fact, it may well be that, taking advantage of the freedom afforded by the dream, I recorded the view of the world that underlies all my work in *Qui n'a pas son Minotaure?,* from the prisoners of the ship's hold who accept, reject, deny, or simply ignore their destiny, to Ariadne, the ascending soul. Theseus, a caricature of the average man, who is constantly lying to himself, becomes bearable only when he admits that he is "a poor man." In the dialogue between Ariadne and Bacchus (God), I deliver my most considered thoughts on a subject that surpasses language.[1] I'm afraid that no one sensed what I tried to express in this conversation at the outer limits of speech, just as no one has noticed that, in *Le mystère d'Alceste,* the two supposedly fictional characters, weak Admète and moaning Alceste, are there only to set off those simple but wise characters, the rough-hewn Hercules, "son of God," and old Georgine, who embodies a sort of sacred common sense. Nor has anyone noticed that Hercule's confrontation with the temptations and terrors of Death is similar, detail for detail, to the meditations of both Hadrian and Zeno on the wish to die and the fear of death.

In the preface to *La petite sirène* (and to date, by the way, the prefaces of the plays, along with that of *Fires,* are by far the most autobiographical part of my work), I dwelt at length on the importance that this spark from Hans-Christian Andersen's delightful story held for me. It was the parting of the waters, so to speak, between my life before 1940, which revolved around the human, and my life thereafter, in which changing humanity is always set against the changeless universe. The little mermaid who for love renounces her underwater estates and then, sacrificing both love and vengeance, rises from the sea to the sky, foreshadows the vistas of water and sky wherein Zeno accomplishes his renunciation. The angel-birds with shrill, celestial voices are also the gulls that Zeno sees on the beach, which have, "more than the Seraphim and the Trones, palpable existence." The themes are always the same.

1. I did the same in the most recent story in *Nouvelles orientales,* which was not included in the collection until 1978. But no one noticed that the handsome Bacchus (God) of the play and the little pot-bellied old man of the story are the same person, or, if you prefer, the same thing, for which there is no name.

The Art of Translating

MATTHIEU GALEY:

Many people are not aware that you are the translator of Virginia
Woolf, Henry James, Hortense Flexner, and Cavafy as well as of
the anonymous authors of the Negro spirituals collected in your
Fleuve profond, sombre rivière. How did you come to do that rather
surprising piece of work?

MARGUERITE YOURCENAR:

Negro spirituals are an old passion of mine. I came to the United
States for a brief visit in 1937, and it must have been in that year
that I went for the first time to South Carolina. While there, I saw
blacks and heard them sing, and their songs impressed me a great
deal. Shortly thereafter, when I returned to New York during the
"phony war," I, like everyone else, had black domestic help. The
doorman of the apartment building was black and I knew a number
of other blacks. There was also Father Divine, a sort of prophet,
who was well known at the time. My American friend and I sometimes ventured up to Harlem to hear him. Or rather to watch him,
because he didn't talk, he ate. He used to sit at a very large table,
but the meal he ate was quite modest, consisting of chicken necks
and feet, potatoes, and various other low-cost items, served by
magnificent black women dressed in white synthetic satin. Each
dish was set before Father Divine, who stared at the food with a
vacant look while continuing to eat. The people, the blacks, who
were there, quite a large crowd, pressed up against the table and
said, "Bless us, Father, touch us, Father." It was quite moving. I
made use of this scene in my attempt to portray the prophets'
banquet at Münster in *The Abyss.* I tried to capture the almost
sensual enthusiasm of the crowd at Father Divine's dinners.

When we returned home to our tiny apartment on Riverside
Drive, which was not then the dangerous neighborhood that people
tell me it has since become, the doorman came up to us with a
worried look and said, "What! You mean to say you went to Father

Divine's? That wasn't very smart, he's probably cast a spell over
you."

Subsequently, I read practically all there is to read on the subject
of Negro spirituals, which is a highly complicated one because most
of the spirituals that one hears have been reworked, and often made
more conventional, to suit the singer's taste. Still, the lyrics of some
very old songs have been collected, and they are the most reward-
ing to study. Some, from the time of the Civil War, were written in
an often thick dialect. For many spirituals dozens of different
versions exist, and the anthologist has to decide which is earlier or
more authentic.

G What lesson did you draw from your work on spirituals?
Y For one thing, I discovered the profound unity of the human race in
the face of suffering. Many blacks today don't share our enthusiasm
for Negro spirituals, and of course I understand their reasons. The
spirituals are disturbing reminders of the era of slavery, reflecting
attitudes of patience and resignation that blacks no longer accept.
The black reaction to spirituals is thus reminiscent of adolescent
feelings about religion: when one has been brought up in a religion,
no matter which, there comes a time when one rebels against it—
it's a natural and very healthy sort of reaction.

But blacks who react in this way are wrong, because, all things
considered, these spirituals, profoundly Christian as they are, are an
admirable part of the black heritage; what is more, gospel music,
the latest form of black religious music, is intimately related to the
older spirituals. The spirituals were written by people who had
been plucked from their own worlds, who came from different
tribes and spoke different languages and who, after learning to
speak rudimentary English, somehow managed to express in their
new idiom suffering, death, pity, and religious exaltation; and into
all this they somehow instilled ancient memories of African initiations, the profound individualism of the black man who sets off into
the mountains to seek his God. All of this makes for magnificent
music. In the atrocious conditions of slavery, this kind of fervor
was, in a sense, a gift from God. I myself rank the Negro spirituals
along with the German lieder, the songs of the French troubadours
of the Middle Ages, and Italian mystical poetry of the twelfth
century. Spirituals are, I think, an important aspect of the history of
human emotion. I confess that I would assign a somewhat less

158

exalted rank to the more modern gospel music and "freedom songs," which thanks to the warmth of the black voice can be beautiful and even overwhelming to listen to but which are musically less original and frequently expressive of fairly commonplace feelings. Yet all these musical forms have in common the fact that the voice is allowed to range, very freely indeed, from murmur to shout, from stammer to lament; now it seems to limp along, then suddenly it will leap without fetters. Rather than the voice submitting to the rhythm, the rhythm insinuates itself into the voice.

G   How were you able to translate these Negro spirituals in a manner that captured some of the qualities of the original language?

Y   I had first to find a vernacular form that was not Limousin or Flemish or Norman or Provençal or Breton but that somehow gave the impression of being derived directly from popular speech. This was a fascinating metrical exercise, by the way, because of the extraordinary poetic freedom it opened up to me: half the words could be swallowed and there could be as many false rhymes as one wished. In doing this kind of work one sometimes wonders if perhaps French poetry has gone dead from having lost touch with popular forms. What I was looking for was something of the liveliness of poetry in its childhood. In translating Negro spirituals there is obviously one quality that can never entirely be captured, and that is the power of the black voice. Listen to "We Shall Overcome" sung by blacks and then try to say *nous triompherons* or some such thing in French. There's no getting around the fact that the dazzle has been dulled.

G   Isn't your task hopeless, then?

Y   No. Obviously one is aware that one can never completely succeed. Readers will always be entitled to criticize, and though their objections will often fail to take account of the complexity of the problem, some will be justified. Still, one can at least take satisfaction from having helped make these great poems available to a new group of readers—an indispensable service. After all, three-quarters of what we read is translation. We read the Bible in translation, the Chinese poets, the Japanese poets, the Hindu poets, Shakespeare (if we don't know English), Goethe (if we don't know German). We would be greatly hampered if no translations were available. At the same time, this state of affairs imposes a solemn responsibility on the translator: another person's work is placed in my hands, and I know only too well that I will never be able to convey all of it, to render everything that is there. Some time ago I wrote to the person who proofread my anthology of Greek poets that a translator (and particularly a translator of poetry) is like a person packing a suitcase. The suitcase lies open in front of him. He puts in one item, then wonders if perhaps another wouldn't be more useful and so removes the first, only to put it back in after a moment's thought since it does seem clearly indispensable. The truth is that there are always things that translation won't let transpire, though the translator's art is presumably to allow nothing to be lost. So one is never really satisfied. But that is true also of one's own books, which, as Valéry might have said, are translations of the language "self" (a word that Valéry loved [in English in the original]) into a tongue accessible to all.

G   Are you more satisfied with your translations of Virginia Woolf or Cavafy?

Y   Less so with the Cavafy, even though I translated him into prose, in the first place because his prosody is not what is most important about his work, and in the second place because, had I translated his poems with their deliberately banal settings into French verse, the result would have been reminiscent of a François Coppée[1] in the grip of eroticism. But Cavafy is inimitable. At once more supple and more incisive than French, Greek lends itself better to the expression of a mind like Cavafy's and to effects of the sort he produces, carefully calculated yet seemingly "made of nothing at all." The constant juxtaposition in his work of present and past (the historical past as well as his own) is very striking, but his temperament is so different from mine that I was frequently tempted, quite wrongly, to accuse him of stinginess. His total production amounts to some 150 poems, all very short, which with his tremendous concern for perfection he revised throughout his life, though little seems to have been added or changed. He was an old man who had assumed responsibility for a younger poet. For him it was a particular hour of a particular day of a particular year that counted, some

1. Francois Coppée, 1824–1908, poet, member of the group known as the Parnassians.—Trans.

unforgotten moment of love or pleasure from the year 1909 or 1911 or 1912. Nothing else mattered, except perhaps the Greek setting, which is discreetly but brilliantly described. From this intensity derive his unique qualities of spareness and ardor, as well as certain of his limitations. He kept almost maniacally precise accounts of his poetic labors, recording the number of lines he wrote, rejected, or reworked each day and each month. This method of working is totally alien to me, but for that very reason I learned a great deal from it. The more I have seen of how much those 150 poems have meant to so many people (some of whom have read them in my translations), the more I've appreciated the unique greatness of this poet of contemplation and desire.

G   What brought you together?

Y   A feeling for the link between the present and the past, and a burning ardor like a Greek summer's night. And then there was chance. I discovered him at the time of his death, when a poet somehow sets himself free. Often poets must die before people begin to speak well of them. It was around 1936, during my second stay in Athens. A friend of mine was a bookseller. Incidentally, he was also the person who helped me over the difficulties of modern Greek, not to mention Cavafy's Alexandrian slang. One day, when his bookshop was closed and his employees away on holiday, we had dinner in a tavern, after which my friend decided that I simply had to be introduced to Cavafy. But he didn't have the key to the bookshop with him, so we had to break the front window. (Did we really? It was so long ago I can't be sure, but my impression is that we behaved like burglars.) Anyway, we managed to ferret out the precious volume of Cavafy and read it right then and there. Two or three years later I decided to translate it; there you have it.

G   How did the Virginia Woolf translation come about?

Y   In a way I did it to eat: I was thirty-years old and at that point had no money. The offer to do the translation seemed wonderful to me, even though translators are never very well paid. But I had the pleasure of meeting the author. As a conscientious translator, I said to myself, Go and ask her what she wants me to do, ask how she would like me to translate her book. The book in question was *The Waves,* which is still my favorite of her novels. In fact she had no opinion on the question. She said, "Do whatever you like." That didn't get me very far, but at least I had seen her. Even at that early date she seemed very threatened, very fragile.

G   Are you that indifferent about translations of your own works?

Y   Oh, no, not at all. I follow the progress of the work from beginning to end, as closely as possible. But obviously that depends on what language the book is being translated into. When it's Italian, Spanish, or English, I panic at the thought of the slightest error. When the translation is into Japanese or Hebrew, I have to trust in others.

G   With the Greek poets, whom you've been translating for years, what method did you use to go from one language to another without killing the rhythm?

Y   With the ancient Greek poets I tried to choose a meter as close as possible to that used in the original, which is not easy to do in French. Greek prosody is infinitely more complex than our own has ever been, even in periods of the greatest poetic sophistication such as the seventeenth century. For narrative poetry I therefore tried to maintain a continuous melody, a rhythm in which the lines create the illusion of sliding into one another, with varied caesuras. In this way the rhythm of the line itself, or rhythm in the usual sense, becomes intertwined with the rhythm of the phrase. Adopting this approach enabled me to get away from French habits while providing an orderly form for translating poets who used regular and sophisticated meters. The rhythms contradict or sustain the music of the words, though actually we know nothing about the music of the ancient Greeks. Only two or three written measures have survived, and much of what scholars believe they can detect of Greek survivals in more recent religious and popular music is hypothetical. The same is true of the tone of the style and the sound of the words, whose pronunciation has changed frequently over the course of twenty-five centuries. In any case, what we do know is that ancient Greek prosody was based on quantity and that scholars have had little success trying to bring French prosody into line with that system. When metricians attempt to analyze "La fille de Minos et de Pasiphäé" as a line of dactyls or spondees or iambs or what have you, each one scans the line in his own way, and three professors will have three different opinions. Notwithstanding the noble efforts made by Baïf[2] during the Renaissance, literal imitation of the metrical system of the ancients does not get one very far in French. To some extent I tried to replace quantity by rhyme, since rhyme is a system that has long been accepted in Western languages and in French in particular. Only my rhymes are not arranged two by two or four by four but echo across as many as thirty lines. There may be five in a row, but you will find places where a rhyme is repeated no more than three or four times in sixty lines. I wanted to give some idea of the variety of Greek prosodic devices, without limiting myself to mere artificial imitation. In any event, I tried. What I've just said, incidentally, applies only to the narrative poems, the odes and the fragments of tragedies. For the epigrams, written as they are in a less ornate, less complex style, I adopted the custom of our eighteenth-century poets such as André Chénier, which was to translate them into alexandrines. (Voltaire, however, deliberately translated them into octets.) Here the important thing was to obtain an accurate and limpid rendering.

G   But why did you look to poets rather than, say, philosophers? Do you consider yourself a poet?

Y   As I understand the word, yes. For me a poet is someone who is "in contact." Someone through whom a current is passing. When all is said and done, poetry and prose are quite similar. Prose is full of underlying rhythms, as one sees very quickly if one is paying attention. The main difference is that poetry—and in this respect I think modern poets have been off the mark—depends on repetitive effects, which are capable of playing an incantatory role or in any case of imposing themselves upon the subconscious. A poetry without immediately perceptible rhythms doesn't establish the necessary contact with the reader.

G   In short it's a form of magic.

Y   An incantation. If one tries to arrange lines of prose to mimic unequal verses, the reader can no longer follow the movement of the poem and the poetic current ceases to flow.

2. Jean Antoine de Baïf, 1532–1589, poet, member of the group known as the Pléïde—Trans.

G   Don't you run that kind of risk with your translations?

Y   No, I don't, precisely because I decided to make rhythmical translations. I would point out that my translations of Negro spirituals
are also in verse, popular verse like the originals, with the difference, of course, that the coloration of the voice isn't the same. My
translations from the Greek are also in verse, and I've tried to make
them conform as faithfully as possible to the originals. I don't
flatter myself that I was successful in every case. There are times
when it is impossible to obtain quite the same effects. Ultimately,
though, a poem is rhythmical in order to remind the reader that it is
a kind of incantation and a song which relies on the number of feet
in the line and on the repetition of groups of sounds.

G   Apart from *Les charités d'Alcippe* and your two youthful collections,
which of your works could be said to be poems?

Y   All of them. Allowing, of course, for the fact that prosody creates a
kind of sacred psalmody that doesn't exist in prose. Prose always
leaves the reader's mind much freer to escape from the magic
circle, to judge. But the music is no less present. Beyond a certain
threshold one speaks poetically whether one wishes to or not. Just
listen to the voices of people who are angry, in love, or in moments
of idle relaxation: they speak with the rhythms of poetry.

G   But how do you experience that "music" when you write?

Y   I have the feeling that a current is passing through me, the current
we were discussing a moment ago. Living prose has a rhythm of its
own. The error committed by writers who attempted to write
poetic prose was to use prosodic forms that stood out too much,
that could be separated from the prose itself. Maeterlinck, for
example, put alexandrines into his prose; the result was horrible. It
was obviously a fake veneer. Prose, as Maeterlinck's errors demon-
strate, should be infinitely varied. When laden with strict, repetitive
rhythms, it becomes horribly monotonous.

G   But how can a writer follow the dictates of his thought at the same
time as he is trying to maintain a musical tempo? Isn't there some
contradiction in what you're saying?

Y   I don't think so, insofar as music unifies form and content. The form
emanates from the content. In prose, however, the author doesn't
insist that the reader scan the line in a certain way. The reader does

what he wants, he is free. If you and I were to read the same paragraph of prose without comparing notes, we would scan it differently, because we wouldn't ascribe the same importance to each word. In a poem, the scansion is more or less prepared beforehand by the poet, who thus discharges his role as musician and magician: he imposes on you a certain way of construing the sounds, a certain illusion, a certain reality. In prose the reader chooses. The prose writer, too, has his own ways of scanning, his own choices to make. The upshot is that a sentence considered essential by its author can pass practically unnoticed by the reader who fails to read it with the emphasis or musical quality the writer had in mind.

G   In this respect, then, prose is inferior to poetry.

Y   Indeed, if the writer's purpose is to impose a vision, a mirage. But prose offers matchless possibilities of its own. Like life, it offers any number of routes and allows each reader to choose his own. It makes available a far wider range of resources.

G   Be that as it may, it hasn't stopped you from varying your means of expression as much as possible in your verse translations of the Greek poets, for instance.

Y   True, but I hope that my technical experiments won't even be noticed. If one notices that the dancers are always counting their steps, then one mustn't be very taken with the dance.

In Search of
the Sources of
the Self

MATTHIEU GALEY:
How are *Souvenirs pieux* and *Archives du Nord* related to the rest of
your work?
MARGUERITE YOURCENAR:
When I was twenty, I sketched out, as I mentioned earlier, the plan
of a vast historical novel, which would have incorporated all the
generations of my family, albeit in a manner highly transformed by
my imagination. Though I soon gave up the idea of writing this
book, it did nevertheless provide the core of *The Abyss* and the first
version of *La mort conduit l'attelage,* two works that for me have been
like grains of seed long buried in the earth, needing a very long time
to mature and germinate. In thinking about this early plan, whose
outsized ambition is a mark of my adolescence, I consulted various
family documents in some detail. During subsequent years (the
years of *Alexis, Fires, A Coin in Nine Hands, Coup de Grâce,* and
Hadrian), I ceased thinking about the social and physical landscape
of the region that now comprises northern France, Belgium, and
the Netherlands. My imagination reoriented itself in another direction. But my thoughts turned back to this part of the world when I
began writing *The Abyss,* and when I scanned those old documents
once more in search of a name for a place or a minor character I
was reminded of other aspects of my youthful projects. Thus, in a
sense, *Souvenirs pieux* and *Archives du Nord* came into being as a result
of my return to Flanders in the company of Zeno.

G   But how do you explain the need to bring back to life a mother
     about whom you had concerned yourself very little until then?
Y   Because she existed.

G   Why did certain characters gradually come to stand out from the
     others?

Y   They stood out of their own accord. They were the ones who seemed most interesting to me, the ones about whom I had the most detailed information.

G   In writing this kind of book, is your approach the same as when you write a novel?

Y   Yes and no. It depends on what novelist you have in mind when you say "you." The novelist who wrote *Hadrian* had to base her conclusion on what the documents had to offer; she had whenever possible to blend and reconcile two different traditions. I reconstructed, say, a day that Hadrian spent in Palestine with the same concern for the truth as in writing about a day in the life of the Cartiers or the Crayencours. In *The Abyss,* whose characters were invented, the novelist had a freer hand, but still the palette was restricted to the colors of the sixteenth century.

In *Souvenirs pieux* and *Archives du Nord* I also relied on my imagination, when I described, for example, my grandmother Mathilde's return from church and the happiness she felt walking in the meadow on that summer day, or when I conjured up the final thoughts of my grandfather Michel-Charles. Yet the nature of my project required me to make sure that *all* the details were authentic, even if they were ultimately assembled into a form rather like a novel.

From time to time, of course, I allow my imagination (or my sympathy, which is the same thing) to run free, which is legitimate provided that it's done in such a way that the reader cannot mistake what is happening. The chapters on Octave Pirmez are a veritable mosaic of citations from his work, but suddenly in the midst of all this are the pages in which Zeno, a man of the sixteenth century, emerges naked from his ritual swim in the ocean and walks across the beach at Heyst, crossing the path of a nineteenth-century gentleman wearing a straw hat and a suit of white linen who happens to be strolling there, and of course neither man sees the other.

G   But how is it possible to relate individual destinies to the context of history, to life's ebb and flow?

Y   How is it possible not to? You seem to be making an idol of history, as the Marxists do. History consists of individual lives, a few of them illustrious, most of them obscure. There is no such thing as the history of France as distinct from the history of the French, of each individual French man and woman.

G   What part do personal memories play in this world you never knew?

Y   Obviously, since both *Archives du Nord* and *Souvenirs pieux* end when I am approximately six weeks old, "personal memories" play a negligible part, except for occasional digressions such as my visit to the Suarlee cemetery at the age of fifty. It is true that when I actually knew, in subsequent years, the characters about whom I'm writing, I give their portraits as they were when I was six or seven (as in the case of Uncle Octave and Aunt Georgine). And the portrait of Michel (Marguerite Yourcenar's father—TRANS.) is of course authenticated and enriched by memories accumulated over a period of more than twenty years.

G   After *Souvenirs pieux* it was natural for you to turn to your father's side of the family, which completes the picture; but *Archives du Nord* begins with a notable "broadening of the horizon." Why did you do this in that particular place? Have readers failed to understand what you were attempting?

Y   What interested me in both books was to work from almost the present day back toward the past of the human race as a whole. I made a start in *Souvenirs pieux* by describing the day when mementos of Trajan's contemporary, the veteran of Flémalle, are fished out of the Meuse, or again, the flight from the barbarian invasions, which anticipated the evacuations of 1914 and 1940 and even followed the same routes. *Archives du Nord* is merely a further development and orchestration of the same theme.

G   What, specifically, were the sources you used in writing *Archives du Nord?*

Y   Innumerable documents from family and local archives, which I studied very closely. I am struck by most people's paucity of genealogical imagination. You will object that few have family archives to consult, but even those who do generally limit themselves to tracing the paternal line, as they say "from father to son." How many of them ever think of what their father's great-grandmother's father might have been? People are generally ignorant of such things unless some ancestor happened to make "a name" for

himself or to do something of which his descendants are proud. The
interest that people take in the "family history" is usually associated with vanity of some kind if the past has been glorious or even if
it has not, or else with ownership, whether of a name or of some
form of inherited property. For myself it's a question of giving some
thought to the millions of people whose numbers double and re-
double from generation to generation (two parents, four grand-
parents, eight great-grandparents, sixteen great-great-grand-
parents, thirty-two great-great-great-grandparents); I am interested in the anonymous horde of folk who enter into each and every
one of our lives, the human molecules of whom we have been made
since the first appearance on earth of the creature known as man.

Obviously there is no hope of recovering all their names, of
identifying all those individuals for more than a few centuries back,
a very short time indeed. They are lost forever, except within
ourselves. Still, we can attempt to delve as deeply as possible into
this world, or rather these worlds: we can attempt, as the saying
goes, to "dig down" into the past.

I embarked on this adventure at the age of sixty or so. When we
are allowed the time, there always comes a moment when we want
to sum up our accounts, a moment when we all ask what it is we
owe to various ancestors known or unkown, to various incidents or
accidents long since forgotten, and possibly even (what comes to
the same thing) to other lives. Precise answers to these questions are
obviously not within our grasp. When I look carefully at my close
ancestors. I believe I can identify certain common denominators in
our lives, but then there are common denominators in all lives. I
belong not so much to a family or families as to the human mix, the
dough of which we are all made. In this ever-changing world it is
almost impossible to identify what comes from one's ancestors,
what from one's education, what from the atmosphere of the times,
and what from sources less well understood. The most I could possibly say would be that I might have inherited from my father's
family a certain vigor, a certain spirit and durability.

G Is there no vanity in your wish to revive a million of your
ancestors?

Y What sort of vanity would it be? We've already discussed and
dismissed the possibility of genealogical vanity, a mania for which
there is very little justification. On the contrary, I see this attempt

to recover the millions of individuals of which we are all made as a source of deep humility.

G   Once again it is surprising that you didn't talk about yourself in this book.

Y   This French obsession with the "cult of personality" (one's own) surrounding anyone who writes or speaks is something that has always stupefied me. Dare I suggest that I find it frightfully petty bourgeois? I, me, my, I, me, my. Either the whole is in every individual thing or there is nothing that is worth talking about. As for myself, whenever I find myself at a "society" affair, I move as discreetly as I can away from the woman who tells me that "her" favorite dessert is marrons glacés or the gentleman, usually senile, who shows signs of wanting to regale me with stories of "his" romantic adventures. Readers who look for personal confessions in a writer's work are readers who don't know how to read.

G   It seems, too, that this book about the family is a book *against* the family in general.

Y   Yes, I am opposed to the idea of the family as a closed milieu. No family is. Even a dynasty like the House of France, which for royalists is the very symbol of France, is suffused through and through with foreign blood: Louis XIV was half-Spanish and one-quarter Italian. Louis XVI was half-German and one-quarter Polish. George Sand had royal as well as common ancestors. There is something of the prince in the humblest peasant (or at any rate there was, in the days when there still were peasants), and there are many commoners in every prince.

   Nevertheless, family documents constitute an excellent field of study, if only because, unlike more familiar historical documents, they haven't been twisted this way and that by scholars of opposing schools and points of view. One observation that I was able to make on the basis of studying such materials was of the relative stability, at least after the first five or six centuries of the Christian era, of life in a particular locale. Counties and provinces may have changed masters, but generally speaking the population remained settled. My paternal ancestors, save for a few forays into more northern reaches of Flanders, closer to Bruges and Antwerp, have lived "since time immemorial" between Cassel and Bailleul, Ypres and Béthune. In times of plague or war, people sought refuge within twenty leagues of where they were born. Persecuted Protestants fled to England or Holland. Nobles fleeing the Revolution moved to Germany for a few years. These places of asylum were still quite close to home, however. In our day this regional stability is increasingly breaking down. There are no more places of refuge.

G   What do you mean by the word "networks" (*réseaux*)?

Y   I explained what I meant at some length in *Souvenirs pieux:* a network is a group of families, related to or allied with one another, that eventually comes, as a net might, to blanket a whole region or territory.

G   Some of your characters, your grandfather in particular, have to pass through rites of initiation of one kind or another. What was your intention in describing these, and what is the importance of such rites of passage in a person's life?

Y   We are all of us constantly undergoing initiation. Every accident, every incident, every experience of joy or suffering is an initiation. Reading a good book or seeing an impressive landscape can also be initiations. Few people, however, are attentive or thoughtful enough to notice. Except, I suppose, people who are, or are presumed to be, "very simple," who notice in ways of their own.

G   How do you mean for us to understand the phrase, "the luck not to exist"?

Y   I received several indignant letters about that phrase, written, I suppose, by people who attach great value to life. What these people forget is that the word "luck" is an ambivalent one, for luck can be both good and bad. Personally, when all is said and done, I would be tempted to hazard the judgment that, for an individual, life does not necessarily represent a stroke of "good luck." It is of course a privilege, in the sense that life teaches us something. But I remember being told once by a clever friend that "to be born is to be caught up in the wheels of a machine from which there is no escape until you're worn out and broken down." To say nothing of seeing people around us worn out and broken down, which is even worse. I don't deny that there are moments of happiness, but there is, I think, something fundamentally insensitive and egoistic about those who assert, in vague and general terms, "life is beautiful."

G In that case, why say that "life's true face is a brazier"? The sentiment is rather surprising.

Y I'm surprised that it surprises you. Life has many things in common
with a brazier: heat (that heat that distinquishes the living from the
dead), instability, the mixture of dazzling light and dark smoke, and
the fact that like fire it feeds on destruction: life is devastating.
I've often said that every person is a volcano, which is another way
of saying practically the same thing. In another sense, how can one
fail to think of the sublime Buddhist meditation: "The world is a
fire, O my brothers! The fire of ignorance, the fire of hatred, the
fire of envy, the fire of rancor." At present we see many of these
flames leaping all around us. I do not deny the comforting presence
of the fire of love, but it often happens that that fire dies more
rapidly than the rest, or that it, too, becomes a fire that devastates.

G What is the precise meaning of the general title for the series of
books that you've begun with *Souvenirs pieux* and *Archives du Nord*—
—*Le labyrinthe du monde?*

Y Again, the meaning seems self-evident to me. You can't read the
morning paper or listen to the radio at night without being plunged
into a labyrinth of events and personalities, and at the heart of
every labyrinth one finds, whether sinister of aspect of deceptively
benign, a Minotaur. The Minotaur is one of the oldest symbols of
what we nowadays call the subconscious. Representations of
labyrinths have been sculptured, painted, engraved on walls and
urns or on the ground outside villages in nearly all parts of Europe
from Crete to Finland, and labyrinths figure in the most ancient
tales of all the peoples of the earth. I am therefore not claiming any
originality.

   Indeed, in this case I borrowed the title from a very great but
little-known work, *The Labyrinth of the World* by the great seventeenth-century Czech writer Comenius. My father translated it in
1904 or 1905, not from the Czech, a language he did not know, but
with the aid of an English translation. The idea was suggested to
him, I think, by a Protestant friend of his wife, a woman who, after
my mother's death, became my father's friend and adviser for a few
years and who will occupy an important place in *Quoi? l'Eternité*.
Comenius's book is a very beautiful one, differing by its bitterly
satirical tone from its near contemporary, John Bunyan's celebrated

Pilgrim's Progress, to which it is related by genre. I've always been astonished that lovers of "world literature" have not discovered this book, which is to writing approximately what Bosch and Brueghel are to painting. The concluding portion of the work is a purely mystical, or rather pietistic, section entitled "The Paradise of the Heart," which Michel also translated but with rather less enthusiasm than he brought to the earlier part of the book. He had little faith in a paradise composed of small groups of the devout.

And yet there is, beyond any doubt, a paradise of the heart, a happiness given to a mind, a soul, or even a body more or less freed from the bonds of futility, and this ineffable happiness somehow inexplicably survives in certain individuals alongside despair over the world's suffering, it, too, ineffable. But subjects such as these are not easy to discuss in the course of an interview.

G   And how are we to understand the title of the third volume, *Quoi? l'Eternité?*

Y   No one understands eternity. One simply recognizes its existence. Rimbaud's lines express amazed astonishment at this supreme "illumination."

G   But I assume that in *Quoi? l'Eternité* you are going to describe your childhood. Everything comes from there.

Y   Everything comes from much farther back than that, I think. All humanity and all of life course through our veins, and if their ceaseless flow happens to have chosen the path of a particular family and society, the one in which one happens to have grown up, that is just one accident among many that shape one's life. Unless he happened to be neurotically narcissistic, why would a person still young dwell on his own childhood? Later on there comes a time, as I said earlier, when we want to add up the accounts, to retrace certain paths in order to understand a little better where we are now and how we got there.

G   In the meantime, though, surely you've made use of your childhood in creating some of your characters.

Y   For certain details. In imagining some of the incidental circumstances of Zeno's or Alexis's childhood, I sometimes made use of my own memories. For instance, the anticipated arrivals and visits of various people, friends of the family and other children, who, in *Alexis,* come to stay in the castle, are experiences that any child living in the country will have had. But Alexis's childhood was essentially a melancholy one; mine was not. The "eggshell game" that Zeno plays as a child in the dunes and recalls later when he is a fugitive in peril in the same vicinity, was a game that I, too, played as a child.

G   Didn't you put something of Mont-Noir into *Coup de Grâce*?

Y   No. The castle in *Coup de Grâce* is a princely one; Mont-Noir was nothing of the sort. What's more, the fictional castle is located in Kurland, with its wide open spaces. In imagining Sophie's castle I thought of castles belonging to friends of mine in northern and central Europe. The same is true of Alexis's castle.

G   Which is located in the vicinity of Montagne-Blanche (White Mountain). How can one help thinking of Mont-Noir (Black Mountain)?

Y   It never occurred to me. There is a region in old Bohemia known as White Mountain, and it was that that I had in mind.

G   When did you first think of using your father as a character?

Y   Again, I think back to the ambitious novel that I planned when I was twenty, in which all the generations from Zeno to Michel would have appeared one after the other. but I soon dropped that vast and rather shapeless project.

G   At that time Michel was still alive. Did you already look upon him as a character?

Y   I would say rather that I looked upon him as a human being (*un être*). The Romans believed that the persona was something quite distinct from the individual or the human being (*l'être*), a kind of representative figure, something like a blueprint. Sitting opposite me right now is a character (*personnage*) by the name of Matthieu. I also know a little—very little—about this fellow Matthieu as an individual. But who are you? I recognize you as a human being without knowing you. Even today I don't know Michel in all his recesses. At age twenty my experience of life certainly did not allow me to know him fully.

G   It seems to me, though, that your approach was precisely the oppo-
    site. It was you who introduced yourself into the character.

Y   Oh, no, a thousand times no. I am not Michel any more than I am
    Zeno or Hadrian. I tried to recreate him—as any novelist would—
    out of my own substance, but that substance is undifferentiated.
    One nourishes one's created characters with one's own substance:
    it's rather like the process of gestation. To give the character life,
    or to give him back life, it is of course necessary to fortify him by
    contributing something of one's own humanity, but it doesn't
    follow from that that the character is I, the writer, or that I am the
    character. The two entities remain distinct. I love Zeno a a brother,
    but Zeno and I are not the same. I feel very close to Michel, but I
    can't judge how much of him there is in me. Most likely quite a bit,
    but in any case mixed in with a great deal that does not come from
    him. My judgment is further hindered by the fact that Michel and I
    lived in different circumstances and among different people. What
    I know about him is what he told me, and I tell his story as he told it
    to me.

G   Nevertheless, it seems to me that Michel now tends to take his place
    alongside your other two key characters, Hadrian and Zeno.

Y   Any character with whom the writer has spent a great deal of time
    quickly becomes a key character. He opens certain doors. I love
    Michel, and I write about him, but for years prior to his death I had
    other, unrelated preoccupations, and for years after his death he
    was not constantly on my mind. One doesn't go through life at
    one's father's side; in fact, it's more nearly the opposite. As a child I
    felt that Michel was an essential part of my life and of the world I
    lived in, which is normal: parents are a given, that's all there is to it.
    After his death, I confess that I thought of him only occasionally,
    though my affection for him grew rather than diminished with
    time. I put some aspects of his character into my books, combined
    with traits that were not his at all. In *The Abyss,* for example, I
    thought of him in connection with Henry Maximilian, the literate
    soldier of fortune. I gave Henry Maximilian something of my
    father's nonchalance, his carelessness of the future, his horror of
    words, and a rather rough-and-ready common sense that went hand
    in hand with follies of the imagination. But Henry Maximilian is
    not handsome; his manners remain those of a rustic, and he doesn't
    know how to make himself agreeable to women. None of these

statements describes Michel. The more I thought about *Souvenirs pieux* and *Archives du Nord,* the more the authentic character of Michel took shape in my mind.

G   And now you too are going to become a character. You're going to have to use the first person singular that you've hitherto avoided so assiduously.

Y   Frankly, I don't understand your insistence on the "I," when this "I" refers to a child born in 1903 who has gradually become the human being that I am or try to be. Hadrian says "I," and I think I succeeded in making him appear to be lucid. Zeno, Eric, Massimo, and Clement Roux all say "I" in monologue and conversation, and the third-person narration (to which you attach such importance) hides another "I," an "I" belonging to each of these characters. But a novelist knows his characters from without as well as within, he knows their ins and outs, he sees, or may even have experienced in advance, the fate that lies in store for them. His own "I" is far more likely to fall into traps or follow a false trail. A passenger on a moving train can't see where he's going, can't lean out the car window to watch the train move through space. Hadrian and Zeno, moreover, are aware of the movement insofar as it affects them. Zeno, plunged into the abyss of his past life, "disappears like ash in the wind," and Hadrian, near the beginning of the memoirs that I had him write, has these words to say, to which I gladly subscribe my own name, preferring to quote myself rather than repeat the same thing in different words:

> When I consider my life, I am appalled to find it a shapeless mass. A hero's existence, such as is described to us, is simple; it goes straight to the mark, like an arrow. Most men like to reduce their lives to a formula, whether in boast or lament, but almost always in recrimination; their memories obligingly construct for them a clear and comprehensible past. My life has contours less firm. . . .
>
> The landscape of my days appears to be composed, like mountainous regions, of varied materials heaped up pell-mell. There I see my nature, itself composite, made up of equal parts of instinct and training. Here and there protrude the granite peaks of the inevitable, but all about us is rubble from the landslips of chance. I strive to retrace my life to find in it some plan, follow-

ing a vein of lead, or the course of some subterranean stream, but such devices are only tricks of perspective in the memory. From time to time, in an encounter or an omen, or in a particular series of happenings, I think that I recognize the working of fate, but too many paths lead nowhere at all, and too many sums add up to nothing. To be sure, I perceive in the diversity and disorder the presence of a person; but his form seems nearly always to be shaped by the pressure of circumstances; his features are blurred, like a face reflected in water. I am not of those who say that their actions bear no resemblance to them. Indeed, actions must do so, since they alone give my measure, and are the sole means of engraving me upon the memory of men, or even upon my own memory (and since perhaps the very possibility of continuing to express and modify oneself by action may constitute the real difference between the state of the living and of the dead). But there is between me and these acts which compose me an indefinable hiatus, and the proof of this separation is that I feel constantly the necessity of weighing and explaining what I do, and of giving account of it to myself. In such an evaluation certain works of short duration are surely negligible; yet occupations which have extended over a whole lifetime signify just as little. For example, it seems to me as I write this hardly important to have been emperor.

By the same token, perhaps, it seems to me as I utter these words hardly important to have been a writer.

G How do you intend to describe your childhood in *Quoi? l'Eternité*?
Y I plan to use the simplest and best method, concentration, which empties the mind and leaves it free of everything but the object or memory of interest. Everything that was is preserved in our nervous tissue and can be brought back to the surface if only we allow it. I have some memories of childhood that are important to me because they are beautiful and seem to shed light on certain aspects of childhood neglected by educational psychology and still more neglected by what people here call "drugstore psychology." But *Quoi? l'Eternité* will not be merely an essay on childhood. It is also the story of the last twenty-five years (which is to say the last third) of Michel's life: a Michel who was of course interested in his

daughter and who loved her, but who also loved other women, some of them admirable, some mediocre, some dangerous, and who was also interested in quite a few subjects other than his child and mistresses. What is more, the book, which begins in 1903 and will most likely end in 1929, is also the story of a Europe drifting toward war, finally experiencing it, and then once again slipping, at an ever-accelerating rate, into yet another war. One of my childhood memories is of the 1914 alarm. Amid all this a child's growing awareness of the world naturally occupies an important place in the book; but this has to be kept in proper perspective.

Who will be the protagonist of *Quoi? l'Eternité?* I don't know yet: books must be allowed to fashion themselves slowly.

G   Your difficulty with talking about yourself is unusual. You are practically the only writer who experiences such difficulty. Writers are rarely reluctant to tell their own stories.

Y   Many don't tell their stories so much as they repeat them.

G   What do you think about the way in which Jean-Jacques Rousseau talked about himself, for example?

Y   The answer depends on which part of the *Confessions* you have in mind. The account of his childhood and adolescence is overwhelming: we love the Jean-Jacques we meet there, as we might not have done had we known him at the time. What is most unusual is that he created a genre, a genre that, it is true, is today thoroughly overworked and somewhat in disrepute: total sincerity, or at any rate sincerity that takes itself to be total. Rousseau wanted to say it all—moving things, exquisite things, and things that to us seem ignoble. For us it is particularly moving that the child of Geneva, the vagabond of Turin, and the adolescent of les Charmettes gets it all off his chest, so to speak, in protest against the desiccated, polished, gilded society of his day, which caused him so much suffering. What would have been a mere picaresque adventure in the hands of another writer became human truth in the hands of Rousseau. But this miracle does not last. Rousseau in Paris, Rousseau moving in with Thérèse, Rousseau bickering with Diderot—here Rousseau was unable to penetrate as deeply into himself. The place to look for the deeper truth about Rousseau as a lover is not in the few rather insipid pages in the *Confessions* where he describes his affair with Mme d'Houdetot but in the second part of *La Nouvelle Héloïse*. This is one case among many in which the novel takes us further than the biography.

G   Are there writers whose work has been useful to you as a guide, if not as a model, in your current work?

Y   I've never asked myself that question, but I'm tempted to respond, as I've said elsewhere, that for me Tolstoy remains the supreme master. Nevertheless, *Childhood and Youth* does not seem to me one of his best books; perhaps he wrote it when he was still too young. One senses a desire somehow to conform to certain conventions, which later became foreign to him; perhaps the young Tolstoy had not yet cast convention aside. As always, though, he is without equal when it comes to eliciting a pure feeling, pure memory, which is not so much that of an individual as that of a human being (if you will allow me to persist in this distinction). To give one example, there is the memory of the bathtub's smooth wood, the child's first contact with the matter of which things are made. Or again, to mention a subject that is very important to me, the first intimation of a certain moral or spiritual inclination, of a certain law. I am referring to the moment when a child who is enjoying himself dancing suddenly becomes disgusted when the dance explodes in what seems to him a frenzy of wild vulgarity. This book, along with parts of *David Copperfield,* which like the Tolstoy is a somewhat fictionalized account of the author's youth and which is nowadays read too little and too superficially, is one of the rare autobiographies of childhood in which one feels a man being born.

A Craftsman's Calling

MATTHIEU GALEY:
Are you sure that your readers understand what you're up to?
MARGUERITE YOURCENAR:
I'm sure of the contrary. Some readers look for themselves in whatever they read, and find just what they're looking for. Whatever they touch changes not into gold as it did for Midas but into their own substance. Others begin with a preconceived notion of the writer, which is often worse. A critic who shall remain nameless, a man not devoid of poetic intelligence but utterly devoid of judgment, somehow came up with the idea that I had drawn my own portrait in Electre of *La chute des masques* and in Martha of *The Abyss*. But Electre and Martha are monsters: Electre owing to embittered hatred that mistakes itself for love of justice; and Martha, apparently a strong woman, because she is ruined by almost pathological cowardice—incapable of taking care of her cousin, ill with the plague, incapable of saving her half brother Zeno when he is condemned to the stake, she is a woman who renounces her parents because they end badly and who renounces her beliefs because she is afraid of running any risks. This same critic was of the opinion that the chapter of *The Abyss* entitled "A Noble Abode" was a glorification of Renaissance architecture when in fact it was a scathing satire: built for reasons of prestige, those luxurious dwellings with their myth-encrusted ceilings gave shelter to human beings utterly devoid of decency and courage. Such interpretations are distressing to read and sometimes odious. On the other hand, there was a Catholic priest who wrote me that he would like to die the death of the Prior of the Cordeliers. Many anonymous letter-writers assure me that *Memoirs of Hadrian* helped them to live. I think, by the way, that the number of people who do understand is steadily growing. Perhaps a writer is not really known until the *Complete Works* are published.

G   Don't you find this a discouraging state of affairs?

Y   It would be practically hopeless if comprehension were what one
    was looking for. But the writer's master is chiefly a certain need of
    expression, which is a very mysterious thing. Why one feels this
    need I do not know, but there are situations and thoughts that insist
    on being written down or told, for inexplicable reasons.

G   Is writing an effort for you? Does it cause you pain?

Y   No, it's a job but it's also practically a game, and a pleasure; for the
    important thing is not the writing but the vision. I've always
    written my books in my mind before writing them down; I've
    forgotten some ideas for ten years' time before finally giving them
    shape as words on paper. The scene between Zeno and the canon,
    for example, was one that I imagined, and I might almost say
    composed in my head, while listening to music, Bach, I think, at a
    friend's house one afternoon in 1954. As I was leaving, I said to
    myself, I don't have the time or the opportunity to write this down
    at the moment, and I'm sure I won't have time for the next few
    months and perhaps not for years. Either it will come back to me or
    it won't, we'll see. Years later, it did come back.

    In 1957—I remember the exact date because it's associated in my
    mind with a trip—I went to Canada to give some lectures. I wasn't
    in very good health at the time, and I had to take a train from an
    out-of-the-way railroad station somewhere in the United States.
    The train was to leave at three in the morning, and I had taken a
    small room in some sort of inn. I remember that it was cold and that
    I lay down on the bed without pulling down the covers. During the
    next three hours I composed in my mind a fairly long story, "La
    mort conduit l'attelage," which I have since renamed "Comme
    l'eau qui coule" and am just now finishing. That was in 1957, and I
    didn't touch the piece again until last year. I remembered the story
    as if it were told by someone else, as if a river had begun to flow
    again after remaining frozen for more than twenty years.

G   Does that happen often?

Y   Fairly often when I find myself in circumstances a bit out of the
    ordinary. It may have something to do with getting away from
    one's habits, escaping the routine. I should add, though, that habits
    are also useful in literary creation, because they contain an element
    of ritual. Getting up in the morning, going down to light a fire in

the kitchen, feeding the birds, looking at the sun from the porch—
all these are rituals, which eventually become quite impersonal.

G   There are also writers who get up every morning and sit in front of
their desks at a specified hour in the hope that inspiration will strike.
Is this the case with you?

Y   When I sit down at my desk, I know exactly what I am going to do,
since I've already written it all out in my mind. Obviously the act
of writing reveals some things that stand out and others that ring
hollow, points up errors, and leads to fresh discoveries; but the
facts, the ideas, are already in place. For a critical essay my approach is very different. It is possible to spend six months just
gathering materials. That was the case with both my preface to *La
couronne et la lyre* and my study of Thomas Mann, which required
endless checking, reading and rereading of texts. One is constantly
asking, Am I wrong? Why? How? The nature of the work is
different, since it involves this constant checking. But when it
comes to fictional invention, the bulk of the work is done when one
sits down to write.

G   But still, you don't write from dictation.

Y   The writer's calling is an art or, rather, a craft, and the method
depends somewhat on the circumstances. Sometimes I take a pad of
paper and scribble my text in a hand that unfortunately becomes
unreadable after four or five days, which in a sense fades away like
flowers. But on other occasions I'll go directly to my typewriter
and type out a first draft. In either case I'll take several stabs at
every sentence and write them all down. Later on, I erase those I
don't like and keep those I do. I also work with scissors and paste,
but not always. And if you're fond of writers' idiosyncrasies, here's
one: on the third or fourth draft, pencil in hand, I reread my text,
by this point practically a fair copy, and eliminate whatever can
be eliminated, whatever seems useless. Each deletion is a triumph.
At the bottom of every page I write, "crossed out seven words,"
"crossed out ten words," as the case may be. It gives me great
pleasure to get rid of what is futile.

G   At what point do you decide that a draft is final?

Y   When I feel that I've said all I could say, and said it as well as I possibly could. At that moment I feel that my job is done, that the

work is finished. It's like making bread: there comes a point when you feel that it's time to stop kneading. At that point you experience a feeling of amazement—which I feel upon finishing any kind of work, not only books—a feeling of satisfaction and astonishment that the job is done, that you've made it through, come to the end. I suppose an athlete has the same feeling when he scores a point. He wasn't sure that he would.

G Doesn't your working method depend on the book itself, its subject or the form you've chosen?

Y Indeed, it is different in every case, in that there's a different puzzle to be solved each time. Painters will tell you the same thing: every portrait poses new problems. Even Rembrandt must have hesitated when he had to paint a new model. On the canvas the model is represented both as individual and as human being, as a seventeenth-century bourgeois down to the very warts and at the same time as a representative of humankind. Still, this didn't prevent Rembrandt from painting a Rembrandt in each instance, because his style was his own.

G That's also true of you.

Y What happens is that a form comes into existence without your being aware of it. I realized this when I reread my very first books: I wrote very badly. There were moments of unnecessary vagueness. Quite recently I made a few changes in my story "Anna soror"—it wasn't a matter of rewriting but simply of tightening up all the bolts, so to speak—and that experience brought home to me what was lacking in the original: the botched passages were too vague or too stiff. Tightening and loosening are jobs for a mechanic. But I was aided by the fact that, with *Alexis,* I submitted myself to the discipline of the French *récit.*

G Yet your diction has remained unchanged.

Y No, because once again that depends on the subject. Speech, whether oral or written, is like flowing water. The diction required to express the thought of an almost illiterate laborer is quite different from that required to express the thought of Hadrian. Zeno required yet another vocabulary. For with him everything was different: the country, the substance of the man, the temperament, the talents, the possibilities of the language.

G The author remains.

Y   The author depends on his subject, his characters. This is one of the things that has always made me very suspicious of scholars. A scholar will say, "Such and such a poem cannot be by Theognis or Theocritus" after comparing it with other texts by the same author. But if the subject happens to be different, or if the author happens to have been ten years older when he wrote the second text, the criteria used don't prove very much. In a person's writing, in a style, there exists a sort of undergirding that is properly part of the author's own nature. But I'm not even sure of that: the final form of the work depends on the subject and the moment.

G   Your writing exhibits a characteristic solidity in every sentence.

Y   I try to eliminate what isn't essential, and I try not to give in, as I did in my youth, to the temptation to add ornament. Back then I thought it was necessary to round off each sentence. Now I look instead for the sharpest possible sentence, the simplest images, and I don't try to be original at all costs. In fact, I don't try anything at all; my writing is the way it is.

G   People often say that you write in marble or in bronze.

Y   I don't have that kind of polish, except perhaps in *Hadrian,* where the polish comes from Hadrian's era and from the lapse of time. In *The Abyss* it seemed to me, on the contrary, that I worked in granite, and in *Archives de Nord* I felt as though I was kneading a very thick dough. Yet that density is not a defect, in my view, but a characteristic of the society I was writing about. I know about dough, mind you: remember that I make my own bread.

G   Bread is made according to recipes.

Y   One never rereads a recipe. Only a bad cook turns every five minutes to the cookbook. You have to vary things according to your mood, you have to adapt the recipe to the materials at hand. Bread is never made twice in the same way. And sometimes things go wrong. Winters here are very cold. It's hard to get the dough to rise without heating the kitchen as hot as an oven. You can never be sure that it will work. There are stages in bread-making quite similar to the stages of writing. You begin with something shapeless, which sticks to your fingers, a kind of paste. Gradually that paste becomes more and more firm. Then there comes a point when it turns rubbery. Finally, you sense that the yeast has begun to do its work: the dough is alive. Then all you have to do is let it rest. But in the case of a book the work may take ten years.

G   During those ten years you live with your characters. Are they with you constantly?

Y   They are with me, and so are the characters from life, past or present, whom I like or who interest me. Though I don't know you very well, you too will be with me after you leave. I don't think I ever relinquish a person I have known, and surely not my fictional characters. I see them, I hear them, with a clarity that I would call hallucinatory if hallucination didn't mean something else: the capture of a person's mind against his will, possibly coerced and sometimes accompanied by a feeling of fear. No doubt it won't help matters much nowadays if I explain what I mean by saying that the presence of my characters is for me the equivalent of what the presence of angels or familiar saints is (or might be) for a Christian, or the equivalent of what the presence of bodhisattvas is for Buddhists—important, familiar figures that we perceive and to some extent create out of our own lives, though at the same time their origins lie partly outside us. A character whom we create can never die, any more than a friend can die, if you understand what I mean.

When one spends hour upon hour with an imaginary character or a character who lived in the past, one's conception of that character ceases to be a product of the intelligence alone; emotion and affection also come into play. Little by little you withdraw from the world and silence your own thoughts. You listen to a voice and ask, What does this person have to tell me, to teach me? And once you have heard that voice well, it will never leave you. The character's presence is almost physical: in a word it's a "visitation." What is rather strange is that sometimes the first visitation occurs at a time when we know very little about a character who will later take on a tremendous importance. The character imposes himself upon us, sometimes by way of the surroundings, as though we were already prepared, unwittingly perhaps, to receive him. This was how it happened one Sunday in the Franciscan church at Salzburg, when I "saw" the Prior of the Cordeliers, who until then had been a very minor character in a work already in progress (I had imagined him merely offering Zeno a ride to Bruges in his hired carriage); yet he eventually became one of the book's protagonists. Other characters continue to live their lives even after the book has come to an end.

Another book could even be written about them.[1] That's why, at the end of *Rendre à César*, I included a page headed "Vital Statistics," which recorded, for each character still alive at the end of the play, the place and date of death; the reader is free to fill in the interval as he chooses. In some cases, particularly in the past, I took control of my characters too soon, before they had had time to tell their stories in full, and ruined what I was writing; but eventually I would set back to work. I wrote one or two complete versions of *Hadrian*—beginning to end—only to discard them. The reasons for my failure are not difficult to understand: I hadn't read enough about him; I hadn't seen enough of the landscape in which his life unfolded; and I hadn't thought enough about certain subjects to be able to make Hadrian talk about them. But one day the character of Hadrian came back to me, and I must say that I went back to work with indescribable joy.

G So that's why you've rewritten so many of your books.

Y I rewrote only those books that seemed to me botched in one way or another. Neither *Alexis* nor *Coup de Grâce* nor *Fires* nor any of the plays were rewritten.[2] The stories in *Nouvelles orientales* were partly rewritten because I found the style of the first version too ornate. *A Coin in Nine Hands* was rewritten from beginning to end, because in 1933 I had attacked a problem that proved too complex for me, stylistically and psychologically: my first attempt to draw present-day characters from life failed because I went about it too hastily; I was still too close to the incidents described. As soon as I had completed the final versions of *Memoirs of Hadrian* and *The Abyss,* I felt that not a word could be changed or added to either work, now that they were done. It's the same as a cook recognizing that the moment has come to take the vegetables off the stove.

G But, to continue your metaphor, when it came time to serve some of the dishes, did you find that they had in fact been cooked to perfection?

---

1. It seems to me that I told this story a while back. In a lengthy conversation, some repetition is inevitable.

2. Except for a short, early vesion of *Qui n'a pas son Minotaure?* from around 1934.

Y   I made mistakes. A young writer often makes mistakes about the quality of his or her work. I published mere drafts, nothing more than that. I approve of Rouault's attempts to buy back paintings that he considered failures so that he could burn them. If a hasty draft was by some misfortune published too soon, I am at least capable, as long as my author's rights have not lapsed, of preventing that worthless work from being reprinted; one day, perhaps, I may even rewrite the piece, since the characters continue to exist and for the moment at least so do I.

G   In other words, it is the characters who come begging for your attention.

Y   Something like that. In one sense they are more real than I am, for I change, move on, transform myself, whereas our characters soon acquire some of the characteristics of a nonductile material: they assume a particular shape and won't allow us to change it beyond a certain point.

G   Don't they form a kind of screen between you and reality?

Y   On the contrary, they each provide one more avenue by which I can penetrate reality. Through them I've lived many parallel lives. The same is true of my friends of flesh and blood. I myself have never been a great collector of painting, but my friend Everett Austen has. I myself have never worked from morning till night to provide for my aging parents, but my friend Erica Völlger, a Swiss seamstress who found herself stranded in a Harlem apartment, did. I myself have never been (or even dreamed of being) a young woman admired by all for her beauty and elegance, but my friend L.K. has. Our experiences mingle with and authenticate one another. Any sympathy, any comprehension extended to others, past or present, real or imaginary, enhances our chance of making contact with reality, regardless of whether those other beings accompany us through life or stand in our path.

In moments of fatigue I've occasionally had the sensation of holding Zeno by the hand. I think it was when I met you initially, in the offices of *L'Express,* for the ritual "exclusive interview," that I first expressed a thought which since that time I've frequently had occasion to repeat: "No matter what happens, when I die I'm sure of having a physician and a priest at my side, Zeno and the Prior of the Cordeliers."

G   And where will Hadrian be?

Y   Present as always, or at any rate nearby, but for a mere personal
matter one can't disturb the man who spent twenty years of his life
trying to "stabilize the earth." Everything I tried to say about
Hadrian seems somehow to have worked an effect on me. His
lucidity fortifies what little lucidity I possess. In times of crisis I
think of the crises that he went through and overcame. His *disciplina
augusta* and *virtus augusta* sustain me; his last motto, from the time of
his illness, suits me even better: *Patientia*. With all his passions, curi-
osities, and pleasures, his gloomy marriage, his collections, his
gardens, Hadrian remained to the end the great administrator that
he was. Similarly, I wanted to show Zeno, for all his absorption in
metaphysical and alchemical speculation, practicing as a physician,
a poor man's physician, to the very end of his life. Both men, for all
their differences, shared "the desire to be useful." When Zeno tries
to escape to England, his only hope of salvation, he becomes discouraged by the thought that there, too, life will have its compromises and its lies. He spends the night by the seaside and at dawn
takes a swim in the ocean. His thoughts turn to the sound of the
waves, which have gone on since the beginning of time, and he
resigns himself to the transition that is death, which still will not
propel him outside the universe. Contemplation brings peace. But
all he has left is a morsel of bread and a small bottle of water. He
realizes that he will remain to the very end dependent on other
men, on the farmer's well and the baker's bread: he must serve
them and be served by them. For me, to serve and to be served are
identical: each man is in the world, and shares it with the rest of
humankind.

Solitude,
to Be Useful

MATTHIEU GALEY:

The writer, even if he has his characters for constant companions, is by nature a lonely figure, at least in theory. Are you?

MARGUERITE YOURCENAR:

We are all alone: alone at birth (how lonely the newborn infant must feel!); alone in the face of death; alone in illness, even when we are well cared for; and alone in our work, because even the forced laborer and the assembly line worker are on their own—we all work by ourselves. But writers are not, as I see them, more alone than other people. Take my little house, for instance: people come and go almost constantly, with something like the regularity of breathing. Very seldom have I felt alone in my life, and even then, never entirely alone. I'm alone when I work, if to be surrounded by ideas and characters born of one's own mind is to be alone. I am alone very early in the morning, when I observe the sunrise from my window or the porch. And I am alone at night when I shut the door of my house after gazing out at the stars. Which is tantamount to saying that I'm not really alone.

But to reiterate, in the ordinary course of life we depend on other people and they depend on us. The people whom I employ (without whom I would have a hard time keeping up a fairly isolated house like this one, since I lack the time and the strength to do all the work that needs to be done in the house and garden) are friends of mine. If they weren't friends, I wouldn't hire them. I'm not a person who thinks you can call it even with someone just because you've paid him for his labor (or received payment for your labor), or just because you've paid a few cents for a newspaper or a few dollars for your dinner. (Incidentally, this is the basic idea of *A Coin in Nine Hands:* a coin passes from hand to hand, but each person who comes into possession of it remains isolated, alone.) That's why I like living in very small towns or villages. When the grocer comes to make a delivery, he'll stay and have a glass of wine or cider with me, when he has the time. If a relative of my secretary falls ill, I worry about the sick person, whom I've never met, just as much as if he or she were a relative of my own. I have as much respect and esteem for my cleaning woman as I might have for a sister. In summertime children from the kindergarten come every now and then to play in the yard. The gardener who tends the property across the way is a friend who comes over when it's cold to visit with me and to drink a cup of coffee or tea. Of course I also have friends outside the village, friendships based on shared tastes (in music, painting, or books) or shared opinions or sentiments. But friendship, whatever other grounds it may have, is to my mind primarily a product of spontaneous sympathy for another person; less often it grows out of sympathy that develops more slowly. But in any case friendship derives from sympathy coupled with the habit of helping each other out. A person who is open to other people is never really what you would call alone. Class (a detestable word which I would like to see stricken from the language, along with caste) does not count. Culture at bottom counts for very little: please understand that I don't say this to denigrate culture. Nor do I deny the existence of the phenomenon referred to as "class"; but human beings are constantly transcending it.

Not that indifference, suspicion, and hostility don't exist here, for if they didn't this island would truly be "the heart's paradise," which it cannot pretend to be. But one encounters these things somewhat less often here than in New York or Paris. To mention just one example: as you know, I recently lost a very close friend, who, during the final years of her life, "went out" very little. It was understood, however, that she and I would take Christmas dinner at the home of friends who live on the island. Now these friends are quite wealthy though not super-rich (I'm obliged to mention these details to make the point of the story clear), and they own a fine stretch of woodland along the coast, a refuge for birds and animals which they feed when it snows or the temperature drops below freezing. To round out the description of this couple, let me add that they are Irish Catholics. Two years ago (for what turned out to be my late friend's last Christmas) it was agreed that the four of us would have dinner together and that no other guests would be invited, in order to avoid tiring our ailing companion. On Christmas morning I picked up the telephone and heard the sound of Mrs. G's voice. "In the village this morning," she said, "I ran into the man who sweeps the streets. It's no secret that his wife has just left him and their fourteen-year-old son. I invited both of them. I hope you won't mind and hope that Grace won't find them too tiring." Of course we didn't mind, and that night all six of us shared a fine Christmas dinner in front of the fireplace, enjoying a warm feeling of friendship. I'm almost embarrassed to call attention to the occasion, which should really require no comment.

G   In modern societies, however, there are a great many lonely people.
Y   There are many reasons for this, having to do with the breakdown of traditional social groups and with the social or class barriers that people incorrectly assume divide us from one another. There are also too many unexamined social customs, and the nefarious influence of bureaucracy also plays a role. Many nurses tell me that they feel much more isolated in large hospitals than in medium-sized ones. Such involuntary solitude is a great crime. I think, as is involuntary promiscuity, which is the other side of the coin; some teachers, for example, try to make sure that their students are never left alone for a single moment. It's up to each of us to reach out to others without coercing them in any way. Perhaps one must love solitude in order not to be alone. Why do birds return in the springtime? Because "their trees," abandoned in the fall, have survived what might be called, misleadingly perhaps, the loneliness of winter and are there waiting for them.[1]

G   What about loneliness due to the absence or loss of another human being?

1. I am aware of the fact that a legend has grown up around my presumed solitude, partly because of the name of this island but partly, too, because throughout my life, even when I was young, wherever relations with other human beings who really mattered were concerned, whether lasting or brief, intermittent or continuous, I've always tried to keep them in the shadows that conform so well to the important things in life. As a result, when people began to take an interest in me, a legend developed, or several legends. I've seen excited visitors arrive here thinking that Mount Desert Island was a sort of Capri. Others have cast inquisitive glances at the bottles in my kitchen, thinking they detect an odor of alchemy or magic. And I could tell you many other stories of the same sort. But such myth makers have their value: they teach the poet-historians to be wary of historical gossip.

193

Y   Each loss is a catastrophe not simply emotionally but metaphysically as well: how are we to *comprehend* the words "loss" and "absence"? Obviously the feeling of loss is something for which one
    can never console oneself, though the vital forces frequently, and
    almost miraculously, guarantee recovery. When one of my dogs
    dies I never get over it; I get another, which I love instead of, and
    to some degree because of, the others that have gone before.

G   But what if it's a human being who dies?
Y   It's not so very different. Every life is punctuated by deaths and
    departures, and each one causes great suffering that it is better to
    endure rather than forgo the pleasure of having known the person
    who has passed away. Somehow our world rebuilds itself after
    every death, and in any case we know that none of us will last forever. So you might say that life and death lead us by the hand,
    firmly but tenderly.

G   Another possibility is that a person will close himself off from
    others, for example by devoting himself exclusively to his work.
Y   Which would be tantamount to making a prison of one's self. I
    don't think that the work done in such circumstances would be very
    good. I don't believe writers who say, "I devote all my time to my
    work." They probably spend a good part of the time chatting,
    smoking, relaxing in someone's living room or in a café. The mind's
    powers to concentrate on work are so strong, and therefore so
    exhausting, that I can't imagine anyone sustaining such concentration twenty-four hours a day or even twelve hours a day. In any
    case, to work with such intensity would be to cut oneself off from
    necessary reserves, from needed nourishment, just as never to look
    at the sun or the trees would be to cut oneself off from nature. In
    addition to the natural environment there is also a human environment which is just as essential to us, even if some people don't
    place much value on it.

G   So you never work around the clock?
Y   No, but the thought of my work is with me always, though it
    doesn't prevent me from doing other things— practical, material
    things—which don't interrupt my thinking about the work in the
    slightest. In Tibetan religious disciplines novices used to withdraw

into their cells for long periods, up to a year, to learn how to create, piece by piece in their minds, the image of a protective deity. When finally they emerged, they would work hard not to lose sight of that deity, in spite of all worldly distractions. Later, orders would come commanding the novices to return to their cells and, through the same piecemeal process only now in reverse, to rid themselves of their protectors, thereby regaining the absolute, which has no shape. Therein lies a lesson for all of us. And for the novelist in particular. I told you earlier that I composed the scene of Hadrian's death, which came at Baiæ in the year 138, right here in this room on a cold winter night in 1950. What I forgot to mention was that, at the time, a half-dozen workers were painting and doing repairs in the next room, and every now and then I stopped my writing to chat with them.

G   In the famous "Marcel Proust Questionnaire," which I understand you don't care for, perhaps because it was Jean-Louis Vaudoyer, your first hostile critic, who compiled it, you say in answer to one of the questions that you would like to be useful. In what ways can a writer be useful?

Y   Every writer is either useful or harmful, one or the other. He is harmful if he writes rubbish, if he distorts or falsifies (even unconsciously) to achieve an effect or to cause a scandal, or if he subscribes without conviction to opinions in which he does not believe. He is useful if he clarifies the reader's thinking, rids him of timidity or prejudice, or makes him see and feel things that he would not otherwise have seen or felt. If my books are read, if they reach one person, a single one, and help that person in some way, if only for an instant, I consider myself useful. Furthermore, since I believe that all our impulses endure forever, just as all things continue to survive in one form or another, this usefulness can perpetuate itself indefinitely. A book may lie dormant for fifty years or for two thousand years in a forgotten corner of a library, only to reveal, upon being opened, the marvels or the abysses that it contains, or the line that seems to have been written for me alone. In this respect the writer is no different from any other human being: whatever we say or do can have far-reaching consequences. We must endeavor to leave behind us a world a little cleaner, a little more beautiful than it was, even if that world extends no farther than our backyard or kitchen. If the passage in *Souvenirs pieux* on the massacre of the elephants has discouraged one wealthy hunter from going to Africa to kill an elephant or one woman from going out and buying an ivory trinket, then my writing that book will have been justified.

Writers and Sages

MATTHIEU GALEY:

Which authors do you read, or rather, reread?

MARGUERITE YOURCENAR:

I very much like to read and also to reread, much as music lovers like to play the same piece again and again or listen to the same record over and over. Of writers from the generation preceding my own, I've reread a great deal of Hardy, Conrad, Ibsen, Tolstoy . . . some Chekhov, some Thomas Mann. . . . And the book that has been reread, if not most often then at least with the most beneficial effects, is Gandhi's *Autobiography*.

G   Again, not a single French writer on the list.

Y   Now that you mention it—I hadn't thought about it. I reread Balzac of course, and Saint-Simon and Montaigne, but they're much earlier. Of the great writers living at the turn of the century, I think that the one I would single out above all others is Marcel Proust. What I like in his work is the vast thematic architecture, the exquisite perception of the passage of time and of the way it alters individual personalities, and a sensibility unlike that of any other writer. I've reread Proust seven or eight times.

G   Yet your own work has little in common with Proust's. What attracts you about him?

Y   As I said, his genius. It makes very little difference to me that his methods and his choices are different from my own: on the contrary, I see the situation as an opportunity to learn and benefit from what is alien to me. And in any case, what does it mean to say that something is alien to us?

G   I should have thought, rather, that you would reread the classic authors of the seventeenth and eighteenth centuries. Proust is the egotist par excellence.

Y His egotism doesn't bother me. My own would. What might possibly bother me about Proust is rather his tendency to combine
admirable realism (no one has ever captured the sound of different
voices better than Proust; this was a gift that Balzac lacked, or
disdained to use) with a kind of misrepresentation. I have some
difficulty accepting "budding young ladies" who are not very
young-lady-like; wildly improbable scenes (which Proust I daresay
considered pivotal) such as those in which the hero turns into a
voyeur (Marcel outside the Vinteuil home, Marcel spying on
Charlus); and conversations in which the author reproachfully
imputes to others views that were probably his own, such as
Charlus's reflections on the absurdity of the war in 1917, of which
Marcel is supposed to disapprove though Proust's own thoughts on
the subject could scarcely have been very different. But a great
writer has to be accepted entire. It is impossible to imagine
Remembrance of Things Past other than as it is.

G And what do you think of that other egotist, Gide?

Y Young writers of my generation were indebted to him for his
rediscovery of that quintessentially French literary form, the *récit,*
which had fallen into disuse; Gide made us understand that it was
still possible to work with this form and that it might be useful. Nor
should it be forgotten that for the generation just reaching adolescence at the end of World War I, *Les nourritures terrestres* was a
lesson in fervor and gusto. In the meantime the style has dated and
the point of view seems at times slightly false when compared with
what came after, but it's only natural that this should be so. You
have to read Gabriel Germain's description, in *Le regard intérieur,* of
Father Teilhard de Chardin quoting a passage from *Nourritures
terrestres,* with greater intensity perhaps than Gide intended, to
understand what that brief work could have meant to ardent and
attentive minds back in 1910. But it seems to me that Gide's thinking
quickly chilled, turned prosaic, and perhaps hardened in its mold.
He dreamed of a Goethean old age, but his last books trouble me
because the upheavals of the times had such small impact on them.
His *Thésée,* whose nonchalant humanist hero has all the answers,
seemed to him an authentic testament. To me it seems quite the
opposite, terribly behind the times, after the concentration camps,
after Coventry and Dresden, and after Hiroshima.

G   Is there a contemporary French writer whose work moves you?

Y   There are several I admire, for different reasons. One doesn't admire Proust for the same reasons as Simone Weil or Montherlant. But are Weil and Montherlant, and others I might name, really still contemporaries? Well, of course I did know Montherlant somewhat, and Simone Weil was someone I might have known. In any case, both stand outside time, each in a different way. I frequently reread Montherlant's diaries, which are almost always very fine when he is contemptuous and painful to read when he tries to defend or explain himself. But novels such as *Les célibataires* and *Le chaos et la nuit* I think are genuine masterpieces. I hesitate to say as much about *La rose de sable,* though it does contain some admirable pages, at the very least the scene showing the two men caught in the native quarter during an uprising. I'm also hesitant about *Les garçons,* despite the unforgettable portrait of the mother of the main character; what bothers me are the pointless transpositions and, even more, the cuts to which the author himself calls attention by marking them in the margins. Either what he wrote was beautiful and valuable, in which case he should have left it in and braved whatever criticism he feared for political imprudence or sexual immodesty, or else the passages were of no value, in which case why signal their absence? Nothing is more moving than a text mutilated by time, whose missing pages leave one free to dream, but such effects cannot be produced at will.

G   Apart from Montherlant, any other living writers?

Y   I admire the work of Roger Caillois. I also admire some of Ionesco's plays and some of E.M. Cioran's aphorisms, but I don't have the time to follow my contemporaries step by step. Nevertheless, what strikes me about the bulk of the French poems and novels that come my way is the degree to which most remain narrowly subjective, confining themselves to private dreams or nightmares or often feeble reveries, while a few lose themselves in arid personal deserts. The image they give of the present era frequently seems to have been overtaken by reality.

G   You don't preach by example. Your classicism, your style, and the sources of your inspiration all suggest comparison with nineteenth- rather than twentieth-century writers.

Y Which ones do you have in mind? Stendhal and Balzac, or Renan and the Goncourts? They're all thoroughly different from one another. As for the word "classicism," I confess that I don't understand it in the slightest. If by classicism one means that an author does not write in a style that is sloppy or full of pointless acrobatics, say so. In fact, the word, which in my opinion is chiefly a textbook classification, seems to offer a first-class burial to any writer supposed to be of some value but whose work no one reads. I also have a hard time understanding how "the sources of my inspiration suggest comparison with nineteenth-century writers," who in any case are the opposite of classics. If you're talking about *Souvenirs pieux* and *Archives du Nord,* then obviously the nineteenth century is the subject of those books. But *Hadrian* quite literally could not have been written before 1945, and *The Abyss* had to wait twenty more years. That said, let me reiterate that I tremendously admire certain nineteenth-century writers, most of whom, as you have pointed out, were not French, although Hugo is certainly one of the greatest names on the list. Tolstoy, Ibsen, Dostoevsky, and Nietzsche[1] (each different from the others, as I hardly need point out) surprise us by their unbelievable resources of spirit and generosity. There is always more they have to tell us, one feels, then they have already done. And their power of protest places them in an eternal avant-garde.

G That isn't the case with you, precisely.

Y I disagree completely. As it happens, the issues that concern and upset me have as yet captured the interest of only a minority of my compatriots, but I believe that these issues will become increasingly important as time goes by. I am at times astonished by the conventionality and obsolete flavor of the ideologies that, in France, are still put forward as current, not to say brand new. Consider the issues. The population explosion, which is turning people into the inhabitants of a termite colony and paving the way to future wars; the destruction of the planet by air and water pollution; the extinction of whole species, which is tipping the vital equilibrium between humans and the environment; the confrontation of each of

1. Nietzsche has been misused, but that is no reason for denying his greatness.

us with himself and with God (however that word be interpreted); the disturbing new directions taken by scientific research—in France, none of these things, on which everything depends, have found their way into literature, and, while there are fortunately some people who are concerned, they are not men of letters.[2] The group that claims to be today's avant-garde will be tomorrow's rear guard.

G What solutions do you have for all these problems?

Y The first response to any question is to state the question. By attending to these problems we may not save the world, but at least we can avoid adding to its ills. "Save" is an unfortunate choice of words; let me say, rather, that we may not reform the world, but at least we can reform ourselves, and we are, after all, a small part of the world. Each of us has more power over the world than we imagine. No person can save himself unaided. Christianity has placed too much stress on individual salvation, and this was correct in the sense that every sould saved is a gain for all humankind. But it created the false impression of a kind of spiritual egotism, which in fact the saints never had. "As long as there is a single deaf old woman or blind beggar in the streets," says Father Chica in *Rendre à César,* "as long as there is a single ass whose open wounds ooze under its heavy burden, or a single hungry dog on the prowl, let me not slumber in God's tender mercy."

G Are you more pessimistic than you used to be?

Y Pessimism and optimism are two words that I reject. The point is to keep one's eyes open. The physician who tests a patient's blood and stools and checks his temperature and blood pressure is neither optimistic nor pessimistic: he does his best based on the facts. But if you want to use the wretched word, I am pessimistic when I notice how little the mass of humanity has changed over thousands of years. The greatest reformers have all come up against the virtual impossibility of changing man, but when they die the lessons they've learned are generally forgotten.

2. Roger Caillois and a few others, whose names escape me at the moment—but how could I forget Etiemble?—are, I think, admirable exceptions.

G Even Christ's lesson?

Y Christ knew that only a small portion of the seed is sown in fertile ground.

G So there is no solution?

Y I see only incomplete solutions, which are all the more moving for being incomplete. Saint Francis, Saint Bernard, Meister Eckhart all offer incomplete solutions. Mother Teresa saving the dying on the streets of Calcutta, Dorothy Day and her associates taking in tramps from the streets of New York, Gandhi visiting the untouchables—all offer incomplete solutions. The most insignificant defender of civil or human rights contributes his share. Other names come to mind: Ralph Nader in the United States has begun a battle against the big food monopolies that sell products treated with harmful chemicals; Rachel Carson was the object of ridicule for having been one of the first to point out the danger of ecological disaster; Margaret Sanger has become an object of hatred for her championing of contraception; in France, Madame Gilardoni, who honors me by counting me among her friends, has been fighting against the cruelty inflicted on animals in slaughterhouses. It would not be correct to say that the efforts of all these people have been useless. But reformers come and go, the initial ardor dissipates, and until a new leader comes along error and evil continue to proliferate in the face of inertia.

G Reformers generally leave their writings behind them.

Y But someone has to read them. Remember, too, that many obscure saints and simple heroes didn't write at all. The same can be said of some more illustrious figures. We know the teachings of Jesus and Buddha only through the writings of their disciples. Leave the case of Jesus aside, so as not to ruffle too many sensitive feathers. Take Buddha instead. Buddha always denied the importance of the gods and, as a "delivered man," felt superior to them. Ultimately his disciples made him into a god. Think of Socrates, who, according to legend, when he looked at Plato's early writing muttered, "What things that young man has me saying!" Yet something remains. Certain elements of Mahayana Buddhism are admirable, and I am one of those adolescents who have never forgotten their first encounter with Plato.

G Do you think that the lesson of Francis of Assisi can still be understood?

Y More than ever, and many young people do understand it. Francis is the teacher of us all—the Francis of the Canticle of the Creatures, the greatest protester of all, who threw his clothing in the face of his father, the wealthy fabric merchant, and who loved poverty for its own sake as some of us are again learning to love it. Remember that Francis rolled naked on a bed of thorns to vanquish his carnal feelings, which is something most of us would never agree to. But I understand him: he wanted to be free even with respect to his own flesh.

G Whom do you see of equal stature?

Y I've already mentioned quite a few great names. The perpetual influx of individuals worthy of admiration and love, the almost instinctive urge of certain human beings to achieve transcendence, is consoling and reassuring; it's our share of optimism, if you will. But a few rays of light aren't enough to dispel the darkness of night, and a few waves cannot move the ocean. Let me put it this way: Whenever one looks at a flower or a beautiful loaf of bread, one is optimistic, and whenever one thinks about those who denature bread and kill flowers, one is pessimistic.

G In politics, it is common to think of the leftist as optimistic because he believes in progress, in contrast to the rightist, who takes the view that his fellow man is not perfectible.

Y The man of the left, in keeping with his credo, evinces faith not in a certain progress but in the *certainty* of progress, which is a more serious matter and calls to mind the early Christians, who believed in the imminent coming of the Lord, in Parousia. In this day and age, which has seen the disasters that accompany technological progress, to have such faith would be to believe in a fool's paradise. Tell me how the leftist who clings to his optimism at all costs is different from the right-wing capitalist, who also dreams of progress, or at any rate did until recently? Every time I go to a supermarket, which, by the way, is something I do rarely, I think I'm in Russia. What food is available is determined by higher authority, and it's the same wherever you go: here the monopolies decide, in Russia the state agencies do. In a sense the United States is as totali-

tarian as the Soviet Union, and in both countries, indeed everywhere, progress (that is, immediate increase in people's well-
being), or even just preservation of the status quo, depends on an
increasingly complex and fragile organizational structure. Like the
rather smug bourgeois humanism prevalent at the turn of the
century, the dream of constant progress is out-of-date. People need
to relearn how to love the human condition as it is, to accept its
limitations and its dangers, to take a hard look at things as they are,
and to renounce the dogmas of party, country, class, and religion—
all of them uncompromising and hence doomed. Whenever I knead
dough, I think of the people who grew the wheat, of the middlemen
who artificially drove up the price, of the technocrats who ruined
the quality—which is not to say that technology is necessarily evil
but simply that it has placed itself in the service of greed, which is
evil, and that much of technology is possible only at the price of
considerable concentration of resources, which is always full of
potential dangers. I think of people who have no bread and of
others who have too much; I think of the land and of the sun that
makes the plants grow. I consider myself to be both an idealist and a
materialist. The would-be idealist fails to see the bread or its cost,
and the materialist, paradoxically enough, neglects the significance
of that vast, divine substance that we call "matter."

G   To follow your advice, it would be necessary to change the think-
    ing of most people.
Y   Even if that is impossible, it is necessary to try. In the *Bhagavad-Gita*
    there is a passage where Krishna says to Arjuna, "Fight as if the
    battle were useful for something; work as if the work were useful
    for something." Closer to home, there is the motto of William of
    Orange, which you probably know: "Enterprise does not require
    hope."

On Being Saints
When God Is Dead

MATTHIEU GALEY:
To take what you say literally would be to ask men to be saints.
MARGUERITE YOURCENAR:
I will answer you by citing one of the most beautiful sentences in all
of French literature. Hold on to your hat; it's from Léon Bloy:
"The only calamity is that we are not saints." The word "saint"
frightens people, but they're wrong to be frightened. Let me, if I
may, remind you of the story of the three schoolchildren in four-
teenth-century Flanders who went to see Ruysbroeck the Admirable and said to him, "We would like to be saints, but we don't
know how to go about it." Ruysbroeck, who was not especially elo-
quent, reflected a while and no doubt scratched his head before answering, "You are saints as much as you want to be." (*Vos estis tam
sancti sicut vultis.*) It is in our power to be more saintly, which is to
say, better than we now are, just as it is to some extent in our
power to make ourselves more beautiful or intelligent.

G   Have you achieved this form of sainthood?
Y   I wish I had, because I believe that perfecting oneself is life's prin-
cipal purpose. But my attention flags; willfulness or sloth gets the
better of me; or I succumb to the stupidity that afflicts all of us at
times. I am not at every moment what I ought to be. I do my best,
when very often I might do better than my best.

G   What you're describing is an asceticism that is not without certain
dangers. For it may confer power that is subject to possible abuse.
Y   Indeed it may, and that's why both Buddhist and Christian wisdom
warn against this power, which is frequently an early, if secondary
and quite negligible, product of ascetic practices. Therein lies the
whole, vast difference between religion in the broadest possible
sense of the word and magic. Magic wants to *coerce;* true religion

counts on fervor and love. Ancient alchemists issued similar warnings against the abuse of power, though alchemy frequently verged on magic. You surely remember the three stages of the alchemical process: the black, which is renunciation and destruction; the white, which is utility and service; and the red, which is the appearance of supreme powers in the operator. "Beware of allowing the red to appear too quickly," the alchemists constantly reiterate. I tried to make a similar point in another context, in depicting the stage in Hadrian's life when, being happy, powerful, useful, and beloved, he allowed himself in peak moments to become almost intoxicated with his success, while in less heady moments involving himself in facile, indeed futile, pursuits. The death of Antinous intervenes at a time when the man for whom he is making his sacrifice has fallen markedly beneath himself. That's why I have Hadrian say, after the fact, "Had I been wise, I would have been happy up to the moment of my death." For it's wisdom that preserves us from the abuse of power.

G   But aren't there also temptations in the realm of knowledge?

Y   There are, and these consist essentially in the abuse of knowledge, in the use of knowledge as a sorcerer's apprentice might use it. Materially and morally, this is the way of so-called modern man. There is also the temptation of credulity, which most ideologies require of their adepts. And there is the temptation of fanaticism and the horrors it entails, which are propagated through history. It cannot be denied that fanaticism has been particularly prevalent among Muslims and Christians, each religion being convinced that it alone possessed the truth about the one God; and, when circumstances allowed, fanaticism has also flourished among Jews, another "people of the Book." And it thrives nowadays in secular sects of every variety. It is always dangerous to claim exclusive possession of a truth or a God or an absence of God.

Finally, there is the temptation of fraud and deceit. I confess that I don't like the Gospel episode in which Jesus curses the fig tree and then later, upon returning to the same spot, points out to his disciples that the tree has lost its leaves. In this passage it strikes me that Jesus is behaving like a fakir, who by waving his magic wand makes flowers bloom or wilt. I hope that the story is apocryphal.

G   Do you regard love as yet another form of domination?

Y   Yes, unfortunately, in most cases; if it were otherwise, jealousy would not be so widespread an instinct. Some people think they can possess another through domination. This obviously is not true love, of which it has been said, "Love is patient; it is good. It does not boast; it does not swell with pride; it does not seek its own profit; it does not take offense; it pays no heed to slander." The unfortunate thing is that, out of concern for propriety or modesty, we bestow the name of love on something that stands in its place and even claims some of its privileges but that is not love, not in essence at any rate.

G   To get back to miracles, Jesus also walked on water.

Y   And a wonderful story it is: it's pleasant to think of that grand figure striding across the waves to the endangered bark. It's a miracle of charity, since Jesus' purpose is to save Peter and his companions. But when bystanders ask him to perform a miracle, Jesus refuses, just as Buddha makes fun of the monk who boasts of having learned how to walk on water after ten long years of trying, when it would have been so much simpler to have used the ferry.

      These wonderful stories remind me of another: you know how much I like simple stories that are also fables. Do you remember Tolstoy's tale about the Orthodox bishop who goes to inspect convents along the Arctic coast near Archangel? He disembarks at a poor convent whose monks are so ignorant that they don't even know their Our Father. The bishop patiently spends several days teaching it to them and then returns to his ship and again sets sail. A few leagues out to sea, what does he see? Three monks running across the waves toward his vessel. The bishop, somewhat green around the gills, leans over the ship's rails and says, "Why did you come?" "Excuse us," the monks reply, "but we've already forgotten the prayer you taught us." The bishop answers, "You already know enough as you are, brothers. Go back to your monastery." It's a beautiful story, despite its somewhat anti-intellectual overtones. It reminds us of the natural and supernatural gifts of simple people.

G   The monks were believers, though, whereas God seems increasingly absent from today's world. How can one be a saint when God is dead?

Y   The question is, what God are we talking about? In France, and
    elsewhere for that matter, popular religious education (as well as
    secular education, insofar as the public schools are merely the
    negation of the church schools and defined in relation to them) has
    promulgated a crude, anthropomorphic concept of God. People
    find themselves faced with insuperable contradictions. No one has
    ever taught them to rise above the image of God as Santa Claus or
    the bogyman, neither of which is adequate. Forced to make do with
    such naïve stereotypes, or to subscribe to more abstract dogmas
    derived from the same underlying concepts, such as divine justice
    and goodness, people naturally draw the conclusion that God is dead.

    The problem did not arise for a Spinoza or a Meister Eckhart; for
    them God was somehow the supreme substance. Nor, I think, did it
    arise for Saint Augustine. By God I mean what is deepest in us yet
    at the same time as far as possible from our weaknesses and errors. I
    haven't the slightest feeling that the eternal Being is dead, by what-
    ever name one chooses to call the unnamable, whether it be Eck-
    hart's *sol,* by which he no doubt meant our terra firma, or the Void
    of Zen, which doubtless refers to that which is absolute and pure.
    What dies is not God but the always limited forms that humans give
    to Him.

G   The ancients too must have had to grapple with the problem of
    anthropomorphism in the conception of God.
Y   In their own way, yes, and ancient religion certainly suffered from
    the penchant of poets and satirists for describing the amorous
    adventures of the gods, whose behavior is scarcely distinguished
    from that of mortal contemporaries; the writers simply lost sight of
    the fact that the multifarious couplings of the gods had once had a
    cosmic and sacred character.

    Moralists began very early to complain of the fact that such
    accounts might well impute an act of savage vengeance to Apollo
    or an act of theft to Hermes. Let us not forget, though, that the
    ancient gods were thought of in the first place as antagonistic forces
    that ruled the world, as devoid of intentions for good or ill as the
    wind, the rocks, and the waves.

    Little by little, as philosophers gradually brought polytheism
    under the symbolic sovereignty of Zeus, protests began to be heard
    against a ruler of the universe who did not invariably take the side
    of justice. Prometheus had many imitators. On the whole, though,

the problem was not posed in the same terms as it is today. The thinkers of antiquity knew that their gods were mortal, because they knew that their universe was mortal. Ancient and oriental civilizations were more sensitive than we are to the cycles of things; to the succession of generations, both divine and human; and to change within stasis. Western man is virtually alone in wanting to make his God into a fortress and personal immortality into a bulwark against time.

G   But how could anyone believe in gods known to be mortal?

Y   How can we believe in the presence of a person who one day must die? We accept the disappearance of a creature's form and individuality. In the meantime that creature is present and beloved.

   When I attempted to say a few words about Greek religion in the preface to *La couronne et la lyre,* I noticed that the literary and philosophical texts that dealt with the gods originated exclusively in the cultivated classes and were read only by those same classes. Popular piety most likely remained what it had always been down to the end of the antiquity. The devout continued to pray to their gods, to such a degree that those gods survived and found a place in the orthodoxy of the Christian Middle Ages.

G   But then how did the change from one religion to another take place, specifically in the popular imagination?

Y   To begin with, much of the old world survived in the new. People worshippéd the Panagia, the All Holy, as they had worshipped Demeter, in the same locations. Hagia Sophia is the temple of divine wisdom, just as the Parthenon had been.

   Furthermore, in any troubled period (like our own, for example), traditional religions, grown rigid with age, cease to be adequate: Isis, Serapis, Mitra, and the apotheosized emperors themselves became saviors from whom people expected aid. In England even today one can still spend a dreamy hour in Mitraic sanctuaries, and there are icons of Isis in northern France among the small antique bronzes of Bavai. After Christ came, all of this hung in the balance. Eventually, the world discovered that it had become Christian, because Christianity had in the meantime become official, all powerful, and the persecutor of cults outside its purview. Christianity had, I dare say, become fashionable, but it prevailed also because some people believed sincerely and humbly in Jesus. It

seems that no poet except Palladas, a modest grammarian who lived
in Alexandria in the fourth century, was greatly moved by what
seems to us such a profound change.

G   Didn't they see the danger that Christianity represented for their
    society?

Y   No, because their society had itself begun to disintegrate. What is
    more, among the Byzantine *literati,* pagan tradition coexisted for
    centuries with faith in Christian dogma and became what it had no
    doubt been since long before the official advent of Christianity,
    namely, literature. In some cases, though, it is possible to detect a
    difference. In order to persuade the woman he loves to give in to his
    wishes, one poet who is labeled Christian, Paul the Silentiary, a
    contemporary of Justinian, tells her that it wouldn't matter to him
    if they were caught in the act by a stranger, a neighbor, his wife, or
    a priest. That is throwing down the gauntlet in a manner unknown
    to the ancients, which is Christian or post-Christian.

G   What comparable dangers threaten our own civilization?

Y   The dangers that threaten us are immediate and physical and so
    overwhelming that they all but dwarf the significance of the
    various ideological conflicts that divide us. If man survives, and it is
    by no means certain that he will, one might then dream of a postin-
    dustrial society, which is to say, a society that would use no more
    than the indispensable minimum of technology, a society that would
    be both postcapitalist and postcommunist. One can always dream.
    But the almost seismic upheavals now shaking the entire globe are
    not very propitious signs for the coming of a golden age. How can
    we guess what will happen over the course of the next generation?

G   You have no premonition at all?

Y   No one can see the future, because everyone is blinded by the pres-
    ent. People imagine that life will continue as it is or, what is almost
    equally simplistic, change into its opposite, when the truth is that
    events follow a twisted path whose outline cannot yet be glimpsed.
    Lucien Febvre pointed out that nobody could have imagined the
    change that occurred in less than forty years' time in the nature of
    the French people: in the era of François I they were lighthearted,
    adventurous, religious but not excessively devout, confident of
    life's goodness and value, and, if lewd and ribald, joyfully so; by the

time of Henri III they had become enflamed by the religious wars, refined, agitated, and as excessive in devotion as in debauch. Similarly, one might contrast the Europe of Prince de Ligne with that of Louis-Philippe, or Nero's Rome with that of Marcus Aurelius. The point is not merely that the change was total but that it took a direction that not even the most judicious observers could have imagined. The slogans we all read on the walls of Paris in 1968 have already lost their meaning, in just ten years' time. The motorists who used to vent their hostility on the highways by driving nowhere at top speed only a short while ago never even suspected that the gas crisis would threaten their "standard of living" and shift the world's economic balance. Only a few scientists are even now concerned with the problems of acid rain and depletion of the ozone layer. The real drama escapes the actors' grasp.

G   Perhaps the problem is simply one of education.
Y   Yes, but it's still enormously complex. What I'm going to say next will be based on my observation of the educational system in the United States, but what I've seen of education in other countries leads me to believe that things are no better anywhere else. The United States government is only now beginning to concern itself with the problem of illiteracy, which for years has been disguised by the spending of millions of dollars on "education for everyone." There is no denying that children do learn a certain amount at school. But what they learn doesn't really *stick,* because of their total lack of psychological preparation. The American child, driven to school by bus and stupefied by television, is losing contact with reality. There is an enormous gap between the sheer weight of the textbooks that he carries home from school and his capacity to interpret what is in them. I know a young boy of seven who has a superb atlas, but when you ask him, "Do you know what a river is? Have you ever seen one?" he answers no, even though he has made several trips from here to Florida. "But you cross the Penobscot River Bridge every day," I point out. "Oh, yes, I do cross the bridge." He hasn't established any relation between the bridge and the river. Most scouts are incapable of finding their way without a compass, though this is a feat that any country person could have performed a few years ago.

G   That's a rather special case.

Y   On the contrary, it's quite typical. The same thing can be said of
arithmetic. How many teenagers would rather be paid less for the
work they do in the yard than have to perform a calculation involving fractions. "Let's just say I worked for two hours," they'll tell
me. This happens especially when the computation involves time.
They can't deal with the fact that there are sixty minutes in an
hour, which can be divided into intervals of fifteen, twenty, or thirty
minutes, whereas the fractions of a dollar are decimals. The same is
true of geography. I can't tell you how many adolescents and even
adults I've seen get excited about the Korean War or the war in
Vietnam who wouldn't have been able to locate either country on a
map, not even approximately. A young woman of twenty-seven, a
lively, intelligent person, by the way, thinks that Guatemala is in
the South Seas and that Vienna is the capital of Switzerland. You
will say, What difference does it make? And no doubt you're right,
but when you stop to think that such people elect the people who
must make decisions affecting the entire country, you're seized by
fear. You also notice that the television images that they watch constantly, in apparent passivity, pass before their eyes without
teaching them a thing.

G   It's the principle of democracy that you're condemning.
Y   I am condemning the ignorance that currently reigns in both the
democratic and the totalitarian countries. This ignorance is so
powerful, and frequently so pervasive, that it almost seems deliberately intended by the system, not to say the regime. I've often
thought about how children could be educated. There should, I
think, be basic courses at a very simple level, which would teach
children that they are living in the midst of the universe on a planet
whose resources they will one day need to conserve, that they
depend on the air and the water and on all living creatures, and that
the slightest error or act of violence could possibly destroy everything. They would learn that men have killed one another in wars
that have never done anything but lead to other wars, and that
every country doctors its history to make itself look good. They
would learn enough about the past to feel a bond to the men and
women who have gone before them and to admire where admiration is due, but without setting up idols; nor should there be
idols for today or for any hypothetical tomorrow. Some effort
should be devoted to familiarizing the children with both books and

things. They should know the names of plants and should be taught about animals, but without recourse to the horrible vivisections that children and teenagers are now required to perform on the pretext of learning biology. They should learn how to give first aid to the injured. Sex education would include attendance at a birth, and education of the mind would include witnessing the gravely ill as well as the bodies of the dead. Teachers would also instill the simple ethical ideas without which life in society is impossible, something that elementary and middle schools in the United States no longer dare to attempt. In religion, no practice or dogma would be imposed, but something would be said about all of the world's great religions, and particularly about those prevalent locally, in order to kindle respect for religion in the child's mind and to eliminate certain hateful prejudices. Children should be taught to love work, provided it is useful; and they should learn to see through the claims of deceptive advertising, starting with ads for sweets aimed at the young buyer, since consumption of such adulterated confections is likely to cause tooth decay and diabetes in later life. There is surely some way to speak to children of the truly important things sooner than we do now.

G   Your proposal would require education for everyone worldwide.
Y   To you it seems utopian, and in current circumstances it is, but what is utopian is not necessarily impossible. What I am proposing would be, for the first time in history, a humane education. We might at least try heading in that direction rather than continue our headlong race to the abyss.

G   Your system would also mean eliminating every vestige of nationalism, to say nothing of all ethnic groups.
Y   So much the better if nationalism is eliminated! But ethnic groups exist, they are a part of the established order, and there is no reason for them to adopt an aggressive stance unless they are victimized as they so often are today. It is our systems that are destroying the traditional ethnic groups of Africa, for example, in the new states that have been modeled after the colonial regimes they were supposed to replace and that, like their predecessors, run roughshod over tribal and linguistic boundaries. In the United States people have had to fight, and are still fighting, for courses to be taught in Spanish in areas where large segments of the population are of

Mexican or Puerto Rican extraction. France has tried to stamp out Celtic in Brittany and Flemish in the Nord (I was never so keenly aware of this as when I was studying the history of my family). It is states that destroy ethnic groups.

G Are you therefore in favor of the regionalist movements that have grown up recently in France?

Y Certainly, unless they are artifically manipulated and turn out to be merely another form of chauvinism.

G Do you think of yourself as Flemish?

Y I didn't think about my Flemish origins until fairly late in life, when I was writing *Archives du Nord*. But yes, in looking into the lives of my ancestors I think I discovered in myself something of what I have called "the slow Flémish flame." But I am as much French as I am Flemish, and not simply because half of my father's family (not a very likable lot to judge by what little I know of them) was native to the region of Béthune and never spoke Flemish, and my mother's family, which was Belgian and Walloon, spoke only French. What is more important and more objective than these criteria of blood and language is that I am French by culture. All the rest is folklore. Yet French culture, like any culture great or small, will wither and die if refused its part in the world culture. I have several cultures, just as I have several homelands. I belong to all.

Racism

MATTHIEU GALEY:
Living in America has familiarized you with a phenomenon
peculiar to the United States, namely, racism not only toward
blacks but also toward Indians, upon whom was inflicted something
akin, almost, to the Nazis' "final solution."

MARGUERITE YOURCENAR:
What you say is only too true. Many years before I thought of
living in the United States, a friend showed me a U.S. nickel of a
type that I believe has since been withdrawn from circulation, for
it's a long time since I've seen one. One one side of this coin is an
Indian's handsome profile, on the other side a buffalo. "Notice,"
my friend said to me, "how they stamp their coins with the images
of the two races they exterminated."

We have come a long way since the days when wealthy if un-
civilized hunters shot buffalo from the doors of speeding transcon-
tinental trains; the national parks now provide refuge for a few
remaining herds. Nor are Indians today subjected to violence and
brutality as in the past. But their reservations are threatened by
large firms determined to dig mines or build nuclear power plants
on what remains of Indian land.

The only Indians I know at all well are those of Maine, among
the poorest in America. The sight of their "reservations" pains the
heart. Alcoholism due to poverty is widespread. Ignorance too is
perpetuated by the reservation schools, which are ill suited to the
Indians' needs and turn out second-class citizens. As a result, Indian
workers can command only very low wages, and this in turn keeps
them isolated from the rest of the population and in a situation of
real inferiority. It would be unfair, however, not to mention the
social services that are available to Indians, as well as the individuals who labor on their behalf. A clever attorney, who happens to
be white, was able to prove in court that almost all of the state of
Maine belongs to the Indians, based on ancient treaties between the

Indians and the colonists. Some good may come of this recent court decision. In fact, the entire continent is an Indian continent, and it is striking to see the degree to which certain types of behavior associated with Indians have gradually begun to manifest themselves among whites, despite the absence of direct influence and the relative infrequency of intermarriage.

G   What do you have in mind?

Y   A growing interest in trials of endurance, in some cases carried to the point of savage stoicism. A social organization based on the clan, as is also common among Scottish and Irish immigrants. A tendency to emphasize communal life over private life, as the Indians used to do in their huge village "dormitories." A feeling for and knowledge of nature, which I find in many people on this island, especially older people. With a single glance they can identify a plant, an animal, or a bird that most people wouldn't even notice. People commonly say that these folks have Indian blood. To speculate a little, perhaps it's worth noting that the use of hallucinogenic drugs was an old Indian custom. But it may be that equivalents of these things exist in all countries, that so-called primitive forms of life coexist, as they do here, with the most advanced technology.

G   Have any Indian religious customs survived?

Y   What I just said applies to religion as well. Halloween, the witches' feast, is actually the traditional festival of the dead, which is celebrated almost everywhere after the harvest has laid bare the earth, in which the spirits of the dead are thought to reside. The custom of children coming to beg candy and sometimes issuing threats if they aren't given any is common to the folklore of many nations. Still, the wearing of ghost costumes and death's-head masks is somewhat unusual and irresistibly calls to mind the Mexican festival of the dead a continent away.

G   What about racism against blacks? Does that exist here?

Y   It does, although there are few blacks in the region. Fewer than there used to be, most likely. Occasionally one sees an unobtrusive black tourist walking about, sometimes holding hands with a white woman, but such things no longer bother anybody. Still, it is dif-

216

ficult to find overnight lodging for a black traveler. No one will tell you bluntly no; they simply say that they have other guests or are expecting family. And anyone who puts up a Negro friend in his own house is looked at suspiciously.

G   You say "Negro" without embarrassment. In this country many whites refer to "colored people" or use other circumlocutions.

Y   To my mind, subterfuges and minced words only exacerbate the problem. It's much better to say "a Negress" without letting prejudice sully the word in any way.

G   Do you have many black friends?

Y   Few, unfortunately, because there is little opportunity to meet blacks here. I do meet them when I travel in the South. But when it comes to answering a letter or offering my hospitality, I naturally make no distinction between black and white. Or rather, it may be that I feel some additional sympathy for the black, something about which one has to be wary, because it's really racism in reverse. Liking a person simply because he happens to be black shows that the racial problem has not been entirely eliminated.

G   You haven't always been very tender toward Jews, though.

Y   I have many Jewish friends.

G   I was thinking of your books.

Y   Do you mean Eric, in *Coup de Grâce*? Racism was part of his education and his social group. But he is no more "tender," as you put it, toward Volkmar, the Baltic baron, than he is toward Grigori Loew, the Jew. On that subject, incidentally, nothing in Schlöndorff's film shocked me more than the cutting of the scene in which Eric, after a rearguard action, finds himself standing over the body of Grigori Loew. Without repudiating his anti-Semitism, which would have been out of character psychologically, he is affected by the thought that this man, his enemy, was perhaps the only person in the region with whom he might have enjoyed engaging in intellectual conversation. He decides, moreover, that this adversary was granted "the somewhat debased privilege of a noble death." Coming immediately after the passage in which Eric scornfully describes the extremely successful career of Baron Volkmar, this page was one of those that set the tone of the book.

217

G   And Hadrian?

Y   Hadrian, too, had many Jewish friends: Hellenized, liberal Jews. He
    had to confront the fanaticism of old Akiba, and I must confess that
    I myself find Akiba scarcely more sympathetic than Khomeini ("he
    may have been a hero, but he was no sage"). Jewish fanaticism is no
    more respectable than any other. Admittedly, Hadrian made a
    mistake; his blind spot was the same as that of the English or the
    Americans, who thought that by Anglicizing or Americanizing
    groups that remained apart from the mainstream of the times, they
    were doing them a favor. He could not understand that zealots
    would prefer to remain amidst the ruins of Jerusalem, destroyed
    earlier by Titus, rather than share in the profits and amenities of a
    new, Roman-style city. The inability of both sides to understand
    each other eventually brought on the war in Palestine and short-
    ened the emperor's life by a few years.

G   He made no effort to understand their religion.

Y   That's normal: How many top white officials made an effort to
    understand Hinduism in India or native cults in Africa? But let's not
    jump to conlcusions: Hadrian, fascinated as he was by all religions,
    no doubt discussed Judaism with his Jewish friends, just as, in
    another context, we know that he informed himself about "a young
    prophet named Jesus." Bear in mind, too, that it was in the nature
    of the Greco-Roman spirit to accept alien gods as other forms of its
    own deities, so that the intransigence of the Jews must have seemed
    very shocking.
        As for your charge of anti-Semitism in *The Abyss,* it is based on a
    misreading of the book. Florian, the young Flemish painter and
    vagabond, who is a fool yet not lacking in courage, finds the
    strength in the midst of torture to be outraged at the charge that he
    had subscribed to the doctrines of one Jacob Van Almagian, "a Jew
    to boot." All the popular prejudices that he carried with him to the
    stake are vented in this outburst. It is hardly necessary to point out
    that it is Florian who is speaking and not the author, for otherwise
    the author would be a poor novelist indeed. In the same book,
    Zeno, who initially describes as "hazy" the Cabalistic teachings of
    his old master, Don Blas de Vela, finds himself thinking of his
    former teacher more and more as he grows old, and ultimately
    discovers the wisdom in what he had first taken to be folly. At the
    age of twenty, determined to be accepted into the schools of Mont-

pellier, Zeno fails to come to the aid of the old Marrano after the latter is driven out by the monks, even though Brother Juan, Zeno's best friend, does try to help. Later on, however, Zeno compromises himself while attempting to stand up for the Jewish physician Joseph Ha-Cohen in Genoa, and right up to the end of his life his thoughts revert several times with affection to Don Blas de Vela. So much for the anti-Semitism of *The Abyss*. What other counts are there in your indictment?

In *Souvenirs pieux* the most attractive person Michel meets in Brussels is a Jewish antique dealer.

In *Archives du Nord,* in the quite authentic episode involving the purchase of the Baron of Galay's castle in Hungary by a Viennese Jewish merchant, I tried to balance the ruined Hungarian's elegant nonchalance against the indescribable human warmth of the Jew, who did not wish to take undue advantage of the situation and who, as the heir of a millennial tradition, felt pity perhaps tinged with contempt for the aristocrat forced to sell up his ancestors. So much for the anti-Semitism of *Souvenirs pieux* and *Archives du Nord*.

In fact, I've spent a good deal of time studying, with passionate interest, the Jewish religious tradition, and especially the Cabalistic and Hassidic components of that tradition. And I continually draw sustenance and encouragement from contemporary Jewish writing such as Martin Buber's and certain works of Elie Wiesel's.

G   Many members of the bourgeoisie were anti-Semitic, particularly at the time of the Dreyfus affair. What was your father's opinion of that case?

Y   To simplify matters, let me cite once more from *Souvenirs pieux:* "From love of justice, Michel was for Dreyfus." But the problem of anti-Semitism never arose for him. I never heard him speak disdainfully of a Jew when I was a child, and I'm quite sure that years went by before I understood the difference between a Jew and a Christian. Admittedly, there is a scene in *Archives du Nord* in which Michel calls the wife of the somewhat dubious physician whom he held responsible for Berthe's death a "filthy Jewess." This was an insult, I think it is fair to say, of a rather conventional sort, let slip by a man beside himself with grief. Yet, respectful as he always was of very ancient races, he was fond of remarking, whenever he heard of a Jew being treated in a somewhat high-handed manner, that "at least some of them can truly call themselves noble, since their genealogies date back for centuries!" In certain Jews he had known at one time or another, moreover, he had been struck by a kind of wisdom different from that prevalent (or not so prevalent) in the so-called Christian world (but it is difficult to pinpoint precisely what the shade of difference was).

For my own part, I am quite willing to repeat the disdainful epithet that free spirits in the Middle Ages applied to the "three religions of the Book," Judaism, Islam, and Christianity: "the three Impostures." Make no mistake about it: my gentleness, and perhaps some measure of pride, are due to my Catholic roots. I would not be all that I am if Catholic piety had not affected me as a child, and if, somewhat later, I had not loved the Greek Orthodox ceremonies and prayers as much as I did. In Islamic countries, and in places like Spain where Islam has left its mark, I have experienced the austere grandeur of that religion. And just a moment ago I mentioned my interest in Jewish mysticism. The imposture is not in the dogmas, rites, or legends, in which the human psyche can find much to admire and to nourish itself, but in the insolent assertion, all too often made by adherents of all three religions, that they alone are in direct communication with God.

And Feminism?

MARGUERITE YOURCENAR:
I am opposed to particularism, whether it is based on nationality,
religion, or species. So don't count on me to support sexual particularism either. I believe that a good woman is worth just as much as
a good man, and that an intelligent woman is worth just as much as
an intelligent man. That is a simple truth. If the issue is one of
fighting to insure that women with qualifications equal to men
receive the same pay, then I am involved in the struggle. If it is to
defend a woman's right to use contraceptives, then I am an active
supporter of several organizations that do just that. Even if the issue
is abortion, if the man or the woman involved was for some reason
unable to take appropriate steps in time, or ignorant of what those
steps might be, then I am for abortion, and I am a member of a
number of groups that aid women in trouble, though I should add
that abortion, in my view, is always a very serious matter. However, in a world that is already overpopulated and in which poverty
and ignorance are the lot of the majority, I believe that it is
preferable to end a life at its inception rather than allow it to
develop in shameful conditions. When it comes to education or
schooling, I am of course in favor of equality between the sexes;
that is self-evident. As for political rights, not only the right to vote
but the right to participate in government, I am strongly in favor of
equal rights for women, though I doubt that women, or men either,
will be able to do much to improve the current detestable political
situation unless there is a profound change in both sexes as well as
in the methods of political action.

I have, on the other hand, strong objections to feminism as it now
presents itself. It is usually aggressive, and aggression rarely
succeeds in bring about lasting change. Furthermore—and this will
doubtless strike you as paradoxical—feminism is conformist with
respect to the existing order, in that what women seem to want is
the freedom and well-being of the bureaucrat who goes to work

221

each morning briefcase in hand, or of the worker who each day punches in and out of his plant. The ideal that women wish to imitate, apparently, is that of bureaucratic, technocratic homo sapiens, and they fail to see the frustrations and dangers implicit in that ideal because, like men, they think (in this respect at any rate) in terms of immediate profit and individual "success." What is important for women, I think, is to take an as-active-as-possible role in useful causes of every description and to win respect by their competence. A century ago the English authorities showed themselves to be harsh and grudging toward Florence Nightingale and her work at the Scutari hospital, but they couldn't do without her. Every gain that women achieve in the areas of civil rights, urbanism, environmentalism, and in protecting the right of animals, children, and minorities, every victory over war and over the monstrous exploitation of science by the forces of greed and violence, is a triumph for women if not for feminism, and in any case feminism reaps the benefit. I even believe that women may be better equipped to play this role than men, because women are in day-to-day contact with the realities of life, of which many men remain comparatively ignorant.

I also find it distressing that women seem willing to play a double game. There are magazines, for example, that follow fashion (there are fashions in opinion just as there are in clothing) by publishing supposedly incendiary feminist articles, while at the same time serving up for the benefit of female readers idly flipping pages at the hairdresser's the same old photographs of pretty young girls, or rather, young girls who would be pretty if they weren't all too plainly the embodiment of some advertiser's ideal. Today's bizarre commercial psychology forces models to sulk and pout in ways that are supposedly seductive, exciting, and sensual, at times using seminude females in layouts bordering on the pornographic.

That feminists tolerate these woman-objects astonishes me. I'm also astonished that they still flock in droves to buy the latest fashions, as if fashion and elegance were the same thing, and that millions of them acquiesce, quite unwittingly to be sure, in the torture of the hundreds of animals martyred every year in tests of cosmetic products, to say nothing of the thousands of animals that suffer in traps or are clubbed to death on ice floes so that these same women can grace themselves with bloody furs. Whether those furs are bought with money earned by the women themselves in their "careers" or given as gifts by husbands or lovers has no bearing on the issue. In the United States one frequently sees advertisements that show a pretty girl smoking a cigarette with a slightly defiant air, and this image presumably induces readers of the magazine to go out and buy cigarettes, despite the warning in almost invisible fine print at the bottom of the page that smoking may cause cancer and endanger health. I think that on the day women succeed in out-lawing this kind of advertising, their cause will have taken a major step forward.

Last but not least, women who use the word "men" and men who use the word "women," generally to complain about supposed flaws in the opposite sex, inspire tremendous boredom in me, as people generally do when they mumble platitudes. There are specifically "feminine" virtues that feminists pretend to disdain, though that hardly means that the virtues in question were ever shared by all women: gentleness, kindness, subtlety, delicacy— virtues so important that a man who did not at least possess a modicum of them would be a brute and not a man. There are also so-called masculine virtues, though, again, this hardly means that all men possess them: courage, endurance, physical strength, self-control—and any woman who didn't share at least some of these qualities would be a slight or spineless creature indeed. It would be lovely if these complementary virtues could be combined for the good of all concerned. But to eliminate the social and psychological differences that do exist between the sexes, however fluid and variable they may be, strikes me as a deplorable thing, on a par with all the other forces that have lately been driving mankind in the direction of dull uniformity.

G   Didn't you ever suffer from being a woman?

Y   Not in the slightest, and I never wanted to be a man, nor would I have wanted to be a woman had I been born a man. Besides, what would I have gained from being a man, other than the privilege of taking a somewhat more direct part in a number of wars? To be sure, it is just this sort of advancement that the future seems to hold in store for women too.

G   In the Mediterranean countries, where you lived for many years, didn't you ever feel that you were "creating a scandal"?

Y   Never, except perhaps once when I went swimming in the nude

below the ruins of Selinunte and no doubt shocked several
contadini who happened to pass by. But in the Mediterranean countries, you must remember, I was a foreigner, and people tolerated
in foreigners what they would not tolerate in their own women.

I don't mean to imply, though, that Mediterranean women are as
mistreated as they are often said to be. Quite often I saw Greek men
in the villages berated by their wives because they had tarried too
long in some café, drinking a *metrio* or *poligliki* with three glasses of
water. I have the impression, moreover, that today's militant
feminists are extrapolating from current ideas and conditions when
they discuss the very low status of French women in the past. Mme
Du Deffand certainly never dreamed of entering the Académie
française. But she invited members of the Académie to her salon
and very likely entertained them on her own terms. It is hard to
think of women like Marguerite d'Angoulême, Marguerite de
Navarre, and Mme Roland[1] as having been mistreated. In *Souvenirs
pieux* and *Archives du Nord* I portrayed three nineteenth-century
women, tyrannical wives and mothers, and two of them I showed in
an odious light, while the third was more attractive, a woman who
even at a ripe old age still resembled a fine frigate in full sail. But it
is impossible to be sure that even Reine Bieswal de Briarde always
exerted a beneficial influence, since she forced her son, my
grandfather, to make a rather unhappy marriage for the sake of
money.

G   What do you think about rape?
Y   That it is a crime, one of the most repugnant of all crimes. If I be-
    lieved in the death penalty, I confess that rape is one crime to which
    I would be tempted to apply it. A rape can ruin a woman's life and
    psyche forever. In most rape cases only psychiatry can find ex-

1. Marguerite d'Angoulême, 1492–1549, sister of King Francis I of France,
poet, and patron of the arts.
Marguerite de Navarre, known as Queen Margot, 1553–1615, daughter
of King Henry II of France and wife of King Henry III of Navarre (later
Henry IV of France, who repudiated their marriage); writer, poet, and
patron of the arts.
Madame Manon Philipon Roland, 1754–1793, held a celebrated Parisian
salon before being guillotined during the Reign of Terror; memoirist.—
Trans.

tenuating circumstances. Occasionally, though, rapes are motivated by female sexual provocation, whether conscious or not.

G   That is the kind of argument put forward by the most "macho" of men.

Y   I've never heard anything of the sort except from the lips of women: mothers, sisters, or relatives of the victim forced to conclude, against their will, that the woman was imprudent. A woman who goes hitchhiking wearing fancy clothes and make-up and half-naked besides is quite naïve if she doesn't expect the worst. Last year, a twenty-seven-year-old tourist went hitchhiking through the national park here, on roads that she must have known would be quite deserted, and got herself raped and murdered by some imbecile brute; there is no way around the fact that such want of prudence comes dangerously close to stupidity, or else involves a good deal of provocation. That of course in no way diminishes the extraordinary sadness of such a horrible end.

G   Sad, yes, but also revolting. A man wouldn't have run the same risk.

Y   But he would have run others: the danger of war, of working in a mine, of doing dangerous jobs hitherto rarely open to women (I'm thinking just now of two quarry workers from this island who were buried alive in a rock slide). And above all the danger of having been brought up so vilely, so wretchedly, amidst such frustration and hatred and unsatisfied envy as to become the kind of man *capable* of wanting to commit a rape. Rape is the crime of a society that has been unable to resolve not so much the problem of the sexes as the problem of sexuality. Children must be taught very early in life a truth known to primitive civilizations, that coitus is a sacred act and that sexual satisfaction depends in large part on mutual tenderness and good will. (Incidentally, the rapist involved in the incident I mentioned earlier was a recidivist; it emerged that a warrant had been issued for his arrest on a charge of having bludgeoned his brother in a fit of rage.) Sensual pleasure cannot be had through violence or money or even insane love. Mutual understanding is indispensable.

G   But such comprehension requires equality between the sexes.

Y   Equality doesn't mean identity.

G   In your books, however, you've always hidden behind men in giving your view of the world.

Y   Hidden? The word offends me. In any event it isn't true of *Fires*, in which it is a woman who speaks almost the whole time. Nor is it true of *A Coin in Nine Hands,* in which male and female characters balance one another. Nor is it true of some of the "oriental tales" such as "Le lait de la mort" or "La veuve Aphrodissia." In *Memoirs of Hadrian* the object was to present a final vision of the ancient world as seen by one of its last great figures, and this had to be a person who had enjoyed supreme power, known war, traveled widely, and concerned himself as a high official with economic and political reform. History offered no woman who filled the bill; yet hidden away discreetly in the shadows Hadrian does have his female paradrome. The woman I have in mind is not one of his young mistresses but Plotina, his counselor and friend, a woman with whom he was associated in "amorous friendship," to quote verbatim from one of the ancient chronicles. In *Coup de Grâce* it is Eric who has the advantage of lucidity, if only because he is the narrator, but it is Sophie who, as he says, "takes the lead," with such generosity and spirit as to dumbfound even Eric. They too are paradromes; they understand each other to the bitter end, despite all their differences, and even in the moment of death. There are also women and young men in the life of Zeno, a character infinitely more intellectual than he is sensual, but who accepts what little life has to offer him of sensual gratification only to renounce it in the end. But he too has his discreet paradrome, the Lady of Froso, the only women who might have been his companion and shared his medical work; and Zeno can't be sure that they didn't have a son together. But it would have been impossible to convey the whole broad panorama of the sixteenth century through the Lady of Froso in her Swedish manor, just as it would have been impossible to convey the ancient world through Plotina.

G   If women's lives are as limited as you claim,[2] how do you account for the fact that there are novelists who are interested exclusively in women?

2. I must take the liberty of interrupting my interviewer to protest one more time. A traditional woman's existence was not necessarily limited in every sense: Phaedra and Andromache (and even—why not?—Felicité in *Un coeur simple*) essay the infinite.

Y   Precisely because they are women, perhaps, and interested only in themselves. If men were the same way, we would not have Virgil's Dido or Mme Bovary or Mme de Langeais or Anna Karenina. Still, when Tolstoy and Flaubert want to describe the great currents of the nineteenth century, they are forced to choose male characters: Prince André and Pierre Bezukhov for the Napoleonic period, or, to capture the social and political life of nineteenth-century France, either that rather tarnished mirror, Frédéric Moreau, or that more somber mirror, Vautrin.

G   Still, there have been exceptional women in history who might have inspired you.

Y   They did inspire me in some of my essays and, as we've just been discussing, as deuteragonists in some of my books. The life of a woman of action like Florence Nightingale might have tempted me; Strachey has told her story and very well too, whatever people may say. Antigone and Mary Magdalene are sublime chracters, however good or bad the poems I've written about them may be. Yet there is, in some very great men, a tendency toward complete impersonality, of which Hadrian speaks to us: "A man who reads, reflects, or plans belongs to his species rather than his sex; in his best moments he rises even above the human." Such impersonality is much more rare, at least up to now, in even the most eminent of women.

G   You are a counterexample.

Y   Even if that is true, one swallow does not a summer make.

A Writer in
Her Times

MATTHIEU GALEY:
Among the current major issues in which you take an interest,
ecology seems to be a primary concern.
MARGUERITE YOURCENAR:
Yes, and it has been for some time now. Indeed, I believe I was
aware of the issue before it began to claim the attention of the
media. In any case, ecological matters have preoccupied perceptive
minds since at least the beginning of the century. Chekhov had
some terrifying things to say about the destruction of the forests in
Russia, and a book published in 1911, F. Schrader's *Atlas de Géo-
graphie historique,* contains the following epilogue:

> As the various factors tending to promote disequilibrium work
> their effects... the planet is deteriorating... and growing im-
> poverished. Man... believes that he is exploiting its resources
> when he is actually destroying the vegetal wealth slowly accu-
> mulated over thousands of centuries' collaboration between
> atmosphere and soil. The vast forests of the northern hemi-
> sphere—once a cloak that protected the soil, balanced the
> climate, adjusted winds and rain—are daily being thinned out by
> insane exploitation, and value that is being squandered can never
> be replaced. What is taking the place of the forest is all too often
> either wasteland or large-scale agriculture which, by separating
> man from the land, invariably leads to barbarism. This time
> around, man thinks that he is proceeding scientifically because he
> uses machines.... The temperate zones are not the only ones in
> danger, however: the tropical regions... will be exploited in
> their turn.... Will this great climatic laboratory, this green
> belt... from which emanate the regular spiral currents that
> shape the world's weather... be exploited in a manner that
> respects man and nature and takes account of the intimate rela-

tionship between the earth and the atmosphere, or will man give in to the temptation to do violence to the earth and to attack the tropical forest in some quick and simple fashion? If the latter . . . it is mankind itself that will be placed in jeopardy . . . by atmospheric disequilibrium and destabilization of the world's weather.

The picture is a somber one. Let us hope that reality is not more somber still. . . . A now incontrovertible law of nature asserts that the duration of an organism is inversely related to its complexity. If that complexity is increased by artifice and competition, survival is impossible. As Montesquieu says, "Laws are necessary relations that derive from the nature of things." Examination of the world in its current state leads us ineluctably to the conclusion that these necessary relations are no longer being respected in our natural world, intoxicated as it is by its new powers and bent on destroying itself.

There can be no doubt, moreover, that the reality is indeed still more somber than even this scientist, writing in 1911, dared to imagine when he formulated conclusions that no doubt drew smiles from the technocrats and entrepreneurs of his day. He had no notion of such things as acid rain, pollution of the rivers and oceans by mercury and other chemical and atomic wastes, or thermal pollution from industrial coolant discharges. He did not predict that more than two thousand animal species would be extinct by the end of the century. He knew nothing of herbicides or of absurd nuclear-waste-disposal dumps, some hidden in outlying areas, some on the very outskirts of our cities—not to mention the clandestine disposal, at astronomical expense, of nuclear waste that is transported to the poorer continents and there allowed to continue its millennial cycle of destruction underground. Nor could Schrader have imagined our "black tides"; these are products of greed and negligence, for if our tankers had to be built more solidly and sensibly most existing ones would have to be taken out of service. And he had no way of foreseeing the destruction of the stratosphere, the depletion of oxygen and ozone in the atmosphere, or the thermal blanket that blots out the sunlight while artificially raising the temperature at the surface of the earth (the so-called greenhouse effect).

Yet he knew enough, obviously, to warn us against the path taken by our sorcerers' apprentices and temple merchants, who nowadays encumber not only the streets around the Temple but the entire earth. What he and a few others were saying (I am thinking of Albert Schweitzer, who was alerted to the danger somewhat later by precipitate changes he observed in the African climate), we today must shout from the rooftops.

G   I'm afraid shouting may prove futile, when a whole range of economic and national interests are impelling us in a direction that you deem destructive.

Y   Yet even here, in the region where I live, I have noted a few signs of change. Twenty years ago it was common to hear people say "You can't stop progress." They're saying that less now. Local governments are still making serious mistakes, but their decisions are immediately reported in the press and protests are raised against them. And it isn't only protest and demonstration that are producing results; quiet persuasion has proved no less effective in some cases. Some companies are of their own accord abandoning technologies that have turned out to have disastrous consequences for the environment, though invariably it has taken too long to recognize them. A young farmer, a man of twenty-five and a total stranger, came to see me yesterday to talk about ecology, *Coup de Grâce,* and Greece, which he visited last year. He came with his wife and two small children, who picnicked on the lawn, and with another famer of the same age, also an ecologist and a film buff with whom I had a long discussion about Pasolini and Bergman. The first young man was quite familiar with Central America, and especially Belize. These two young farmers pointed out to me that the big forest-product companies are in fact quite sensitive to what is here referred as their "image" and that they are therefore willing at times to try fresh approaches. It's the "old men," the fifty-year olds, who are most stubborn about sticking to methods that were new in their day but have since come under attack, for these were methods on which they once staked careers.

We found ourselves in such agreement about so many things that there were kisses all around when it came time to part. Not that I set too much store by their optimism. It does suggest, however, that, imperceptibly, things are changing.

My reason for mentioning this episode is that it relates two different strands in our previous conversations. It bears not only on ecology, which is the subject of the present chapter, but also on the myth that I live in "solitude"; it tells you something about the way in which new friends come into my supposedly isolated existence. It may also serve to qualify some of the negative remarks I made about American education. American schools do on occasion produce—perhaps in reaction against their deficiencies—young men who love Greece, follow literature and film, and dream of saving the earth.

G   To get back to the depredation of the earth, when do you think it began?

Y   A long time ago. Even Plato complains that Attica had in his day become a dry, semiarid land because of the cutting of trees during the Peloponnesian War, in order both to lay waste to enemy territory and to build ships. The Dalmatian coast was later stripped bare in the same way by the Republic of Venice, which needed raw material for its ships and pilings. This led to climatic changes, impoverishment of the soil, and so on. The ancients made mistakes just as we do. Nevertheless, they condemned what they referred to as "excess." The American Indians, like most other primitive peoples, also feared "excess." When the Indians killed the buffalo because they needed meat, they offered apologies, in the presence of the dead animal, for having been obliged to satisfy their hunger. They killed only when it was absoutely necessary.

G   When did the "excess" you're speaking of first make its appearance?

Y   It grew along with man. Wherever an opportunity for excess arose, man indulged himself, albeit sometimes with a bad conscience. In antiquity, however, it was far easier than it is now to suppose that the planet's resources were inexhaustible. Yet in Attica proof of the contrary was readily available, at least in a limited area. Man quickly managed to deplete the soil and make the land arid. Under the Roman Empire, moreover, the big trading monopolies wreaked havoc by forcing peasants off the land in order to clear the way for large-scale agriculture; the damage that was done then is comparable to what happened during the last century in similar circumstances.

G In other words, there was an exodus from rural areas in the Roman Empire comparable to the recent rural exodus in France?

Y Yes. People flocked to the cities and formed an urban proletariat. It might be possible to find traces of the same phenomenon in the ancient Middle East or Asia. A similar process affected Japan through most of its history. Rome, for its part, experienced crises of unemployment during which the state had to assume responsibility for idle or semi-idle workers and to impose moratoriums on debt repayments and monetary exchange, and it is not unreasonable to say that the empire died as much from exhaustion of the land and financial depletion as from the barbarian invasions and the spread of Christianity, factors whose importance has often been overemphasized. Rome died much as modern states die. A walk in the ruins of Ostia, Rome's ancient port and in a sense the precursor of today's wealthy seaside resorts, reveals the fact that wells and cisterns were dug in the courtyards of sumptuous villas because the municipality had grown too poor to repair the system of pipes and aqueducts intended to supply fresh water for baths, gardens, and fountains. In hard times people had to rebuild from the ground up.

G Do you think that a similar fate lies in store for us?

Y It wouldn't take much. Look how dependent we are on oil and electricity. All it would take would be a worsening of the oil crisis or the destruction of power plants in some nuclear or chemical catastrophe, of which monitory signs are readily visible in places like Love Canal, Three Mile Island, and Port Elizabeth, New Jersey; or perhaps a hurricane just a little stronger than those that strike our overpopulated, overbuilt seacoasts every autumn; or a series of exceptionally cold winters, which would block the roads; or the war which, as we all know too well, is one day sure to erupt. Here on Mount Desert Island, for example, we're all trying to minimize our dependence on commercial fuel by converting back to wood.

G Of course you're assuming that there will be enough wood.

Y Yet another problem, which, like the others, comes down to a question of overpopulation and overbuilding. We need to lower temperatures, reduce the height of ceilings and the size of rooms, and go back to the modest little houses of an earlier era.

G   Is waste the great sin of the current age?

Y   Remember that every day the world loses hundreds upon hundreds
    of acres of arable land. On every continent the amount of wasteland
    is growing year by year. These phenomena are related to the
    unchecked growth of cities, to overintensive methods of farming,
    to the use of fertilizers and other techniques that ruin and exhaust
    the soil, to the excessive numbers of livestock which destroy grass-
    lands, and to abuse of the water supply. Look at Sardinia, for
    example. Real estate promoters took it over, built villas and luxury
    apartments with bathrooms, swimming pools, and what have you,
    and now the island finds itself short of water. It can't sustain
    consumption at such a rate. Surely there were other ways to
    remedy Sardinia's poverty.

G   A central evil, then, is overpopulation.

Y   It's the worst of all the evils. Equilibrium can never be achieved
    until we eliminate the factors that threaten to produce environ-
    mental degradation and ecological imbalance of a kind never before
    seen, including artificially overdeveloped cities and coastal build-
    ups. Not only does humankind face the danger of extinction on a
    dead planet, but no human being can live a *truly human* life without
    the necessary air, without a liveable space, without an education,
    and without some sense of his or her utility. People need at least a
    shred of dignity and a few simple pleasures. If we create a waste-
    land inhabited by millions of abandoned children, we will dishonor
    the species.

G   That is the inevitable consequence of evolution.

Y   If that is the case, evolution must play the same role in modern
    thought as the "will of God" used to play for obtuse believers! But
    let us leave aside such abstractions (a favorite form of decit now-
    adays) and look unblinkingly at greed on the one hand and credulity
    and ignorance on the other: these are the forces that have created
    a world in which the air, the water, the earth, the things we eat, and
    even silence itself are polluted, a world in which gadgets substitute
    for realities, a world in which the tensions and frustrations unleased
    by uncontrolled population growth are laying the groundwork for
    the "unthinkable" wars of the future. When the beetles in the sack
    grow too many, they eat one another.

In *Archives du Nord* I tried to show the effects, still too minor to have been thought irreversible, of that kind of *evolution.* My grandfather, who was first a local councilor and then chairman of the prefectural council in his department for many years, should have known that packing proletarians into the "cellars" of Lille and later into jerry-built suburbs in order to assure a steady supply of factory hands was not the best way to secure a stable future.

G   What should he have done?

Y   He should have fought against housing that was inadequate or unhealthy, attempted to raise the standard of living in the city and suburbs of Lille, and, on his own property, done without certain luxuries, perhaps, in order to stay in closer contact with his tenants and workers.

G   Individual actions may seem rather silly when an entire society has gone off in the wrong direction.

Y   Everything begins with the individual. It's always a single individual who starts things moving: Dunant and Florence Nightingale for the foundation of the Red Cross, Rachel Carson for the fight against pesticides, Margaret Sanger for family planning. Speaking of God, I have Zeno say, "May it please the One who perchance is to expand the human heart ot life's full measure," and this, for me, is so important a statement that I've had it engraved on my tombstone in advance. Each of us must sympathetically share in the fate of all huminity, indeed, of all creatures.

For a writer, this means effacing one's own personality (have no fear—plenty will always remain!) in order to give oneself wholly to others. It's not so very different from true love, which consists in willing what is good for another creature or creatures. The Italians have a wonderful way of saying I love you: *Ti voglio bene.* We must try to approach everything we do with this same "good will" toward others.

G   But if we are acting alone, how are we to obtain the good will of others?

Y   Perhaps we need to love others in order to allay their mistrust, overcome their isolation. There is, in the United States, a group known as the Catholic Worker, headed by Dorothy Day, an exanarchist turned anarcho-Catholic. The group maintains homes in the most rundown neighborhoods of New York City and takes in people it picks up on the street (something like Mother Teresa but in New York rather than Calcutta). It also owns a farm, the running of which is entrusted to alcoholics and drug addicts. The residents work together making bread and tending the garden. When I send in my annual dues of twenty-five dollars (the minimum membership is twenty-five cents), I feel both humble and honored, because these people are doing what I could not do. I can't see myself serving soup all day long; I wouldn't have the strength.

G   Would you have had it in the past?

Y   Perhaps, but achieving detachment from ourselves and our own needs and projects takes a great deal of time, and by the time we've nearly succeeded it's often too late. Our paths through life seem different, though at bottom perhaps they are all the same. There are experiences one doesn't forget, however: living in the midst of extreme poverty, for example (and I came close to experiencing it myself once or twice); or watching animals suffer, as I did when I visited slaughterhouses; or seeing political prisoners in Greece, their hands bound, on a small boat sailing from island to island and filled with indifferent tourists.

G   Have you had any comparable experiences here in America?

Y   Well, I've done time in prison, though I must say it was a very short time. And once I carried a sign in a march, during the war in Vietnam, here in the island's main town, Bar Harbor. People passed us by; they weren't terribly interested in our little group of men and women wearing sandwich boards. There were quite a few of us, people of all sorts, including the sister of the Catholic priest and a number of blacks. One very angry gentleman drove past in a convertible and shouted, "Go back to Cuba!" The rather naïve woman standing next to me turned to me and asked, "Why did he say go back to Cuba? I've never been there." It was an experience worth having, rather like being locked in a pillory. But I no longer have the stamina necessary for that sort of thing. The truth of the matter is that it's the way people think that needs to be changed; they must be made to examine issues more closely than they do now.

G   What issues, specifically?

Y   The destruction of man by man, for instance. No permanent
    solution to this problem is possible until the problem of population
    growth has been solved. We have reached the point where society
    must agree to regress in order to cure its ills.

G   Is it then your view that the wealthier countries, whose population
    has remained stagnant or decreased, are headed in the right
    direction?

Y   Stagnant? What a bizarre way of putting it—I would not say that
    the population has remained stagnant but that it has achieved
    equilibrium. It is ignorance or sexual prejudice that induces so
    many people to go on procreating at random, producing children to
    serve as soldiers in future wars or as customers to would-be entre-
    preneurs. We are just beginning to prevent inopportune or unwanted
    pregnancies by means of contraceptives and legal abortion. Dazzled
    by new contraceptive technologies, we are too quick to forget,
    however, that precautions against pregnancy have been around as
    long as man has been on this earth. What is more, we are so im-
    moderate in our glorification of sexuality that the small groups of
    sterile but holy individuals that used to exist in almost every known
    civilization have been all but eliminated: I'm thinking of such insti-
    tutions as Christian and Buddhist monasteries, vestal virgins, celi-
    bate shamans, and even the priesthood in some respects, all of
    which once provided refuge for people who did not feel suited to
    family life or procreation or even sexuality. Our repudiation of this
    way of life is, I think, one more aspect of our unfortunate tendency
    toward conformity. It would be better if men could choose to
    become either fathers or monks.

G   What do you think of communes as an answer?

Y   Communes are an interesting answer because they require some
    measure of individual sacrifice for the common good, some measure
    of devotion to the life of the group. Conventual life demonstrated
    exactly how this was so. And the peasants of the Middle Ages,
    especially in eastern Europe, lived in circumstances not unlike our
    communes.

G   And they continue to live in similar circumstances, only now their
    communes are called kolkhozes.

Y When imposed from above, the communal way of life becomes yet
another form of coercion: Stalin's kolkhozes were abominable
places. What I am talking about is something rather different: a
voluntary renunciation of vain and limited forms of happiness. An
old poem by a Chinese monk concludes with the following lines:

> What a miracle!
> I sweep the courtyard and go to the well for water!

What a miracle indeed! If only each and every one of us could learn
this lesson, we would discover not only wisdom but pleasure in life,
and people would stop going places merely for the sake of going
and stop listening to the mechanical music that inundates the
airwaves, as they do now merely because they are bored.

G You haven't exactly chosen the ideal country for such a crusade.
Y I don't know about that, perhaps I have. What is nowadays most
frightening to contemplate is the effect of advertising and the
media on the poor countries.

G In an ideal society, would you go so far as to outlaw advertising?
Y Advertisers should in any case be required to be discreet. Advertisements should simply announce that a new type of footwear or a
new typewriter has arrived on the market and forgo making any
deceptive claims.

G But in that kind of society, would there be a place for writers?
They, too, are a luxury.
Y Genuine writers are necessary: they express what other people feel
without being able to give form to their feelings; that is why tyran-
nies always try to muzzle them. Besides, what is luxury? Not necessarily possession of material things. It is a luxury to go walking in a
meadow in springtime. It is a luxury to be happy when so many
people are suffering. It is a luxury to be healthy in the midst of so
many who are ill. I see nothing wrong if writing is a luxury for one
who writes, just as song and prayer are luxuries for those who sing
and pray.

G Provided one has the leisure to do it.
Y I will answer you by citing from *Hadrian*: "The liberty of a

238

vacation, of free time . . . Any ordered life has such moments, and anyone who does not know how to arrange them does not know how to live." I'm well aware, of course, that the man who utters these words is an emperor, but he's also a man busy to the point of exhaustion and active to a dizzying degree. Today's proletarian has his leisure time, his paid vacations, which are often put to ill use because people nowadays have so little idea about how to live. And when these vacations are "organized" to boot, we come right back to the servitude we want so much to escape. A banker or wealthy businessman may boast of having no leisure time and foolishly regard this as a point of pride. It is largely because individuals, and society as a whole, measure time and human effort in terms of useless or dangerous productive output that humankind lacks leisure. The farmer who, in winters past, sat by the fireside carving a spoon out of a piece of wood, every now and then spitting into the ashes, knew the meaning of leisure. He was a freer man than today's television watcher, whose actions are governed by advertising jingles.

G   So you condemn television as well?

Y   As it is currently offered to us, most assuredly. That's why I don't own one. I don't need salesmen coming into my home at various hours of the day to hawk their wares, and I don't need to trouble myself about the opinions of celebrities whom other people have told what to say. Have you read Orwell's *1984,* which describes a world in which television is compulsory? We've almost reached that state.

G   And what about newspapers? Do you read them every day?

Y   Not every day. I read piles of reports on economic, technological, and ecological questions. I read newsletters from Palestinian as well as Israeli sources. I read magazines put out by civil rights organizations. And many other things. The important things is always to check information stemming from any one source against information from other sources. But the Sunday *New York Times* and the weekly selection from *Le Monde* are quite enough for me—more than enough! In the first place, the press is all too often a distorting mirror, which deforms the people and events it represents, making them seem bigger or smaller than they really are. And anyway, we almost never read the inside story.

A Politics for Tomorrow

MATTHIEU GALEY:
You're also interested, I believe, in the campaign for purer food products.
MARGUERITE YOURCENAR:
Absolutely. The name of Ralph Nader is little known in France. Here, this lawyer who has for years been waging a campaign against the adulteration of foodstuffs is a celebrity. Of the many groups engaged in the struggle for purer food and dietary demystification, I decided to join one called simply the Homemakers' Association. This is a group of volunteers, all women, who put out a monthly or bimonthly newsletter, attend legislative hearings on dietary matters, and acquire the technical sophistication necessary to examine the methods used by meat packers, canners, frozen food suppliers, and so on.

Our work is closely allied with humanitarian concerns: for example, veal production methods currently in use make a miserable torture of the young calf's short life. "Assembly line" methods of egg production involve packing hundreds of hens together in cramped surroundings and forcing them to produce eggs day and night beneath the glare of electric floodlights. The birds are so close to one another that their beaks must be clipped to keep them from injuring their neighbors. Such methods inflict torture on the birds and yield eggs that are tasteless and probably harmful, since they come from sick hens. The association also issues warnings to the general public about hazardous technologies that reap handsome profits for a few industrialists.

I myself am 95-percent vegetarian. The major exception is that I eat fish perhaps twice a week for the sake of variety and in full knowledge that even the fish are now contaminated by what we have done to the oceans. And as I eat I am of course painfully aware of the agony of the dying fish squirming on the hook or thrashing about on the deck. Like Zeno, I don't like to "digest agonies." I eat as little poultry as I can, usually only on days when I have guests to dinner. I eat no veal, lamb, or pork, except on rare occasions a ham sandwich in a roadside restaurant. And of course I eat no beef or game.

G Why do you say "of course"?

Y Because I have a deep feeling of affection and respect for a species of which the female gives us milk and which symbolizes the earth's fecundity. Curiously enough, I first refused to eat meat when I was a small child, and those who raised me were wise enough not to force me to eat against my will. Later, when I was fifteen or so, a time in life when a person wants to be "just like everybody else," I changed my mind. But then, around the age of forty, I reverted to the views I had held at six.

I should also add that dietary and human rights issues are closely related. For years, no grapes were eaten in this house, in support of Cesar Chavez and his farm workers.

G Who is Cesar Chavez?

Y A Mexican emigrant[1] who became the leader of a movement to stand up for the rights of migrant farm workers in California, most of them illegal aliens who traveled from farm to farm picking grapes. Because their status was illegal, they were the victims of a great deal of abuse. The grape conflict has now been almost re-solved, not without violence, and the large vineyard operators have been forced to make some concessions.

Chavez subsequently took up the cause of migrant workers in the lettuce and tomato industries. Supporters of the movement, and I am one, buy almost no lettuce or tomatoes except from small, local farms and after checking the producer's name and the origin of the produce on the packing crates.

G Is this boycott the only action of the sort in which you are currently involved?

Y No. I'm also involved in the boycott of companies that have shipped certain powdered milk products to the Third World to be used in nursing infants. Some well-known corporations have sent women

1. Madame Yourcenar is mistaken. Chavez was born in Yuma, Arizona.— Trans.

242

sales representatives dressed in white jackets out to bush villages and nomad encampments, where humble women have mistaken them for nurses. Using such ruses they have sold products for what by Third World standards might as well be their weight in gold, and by so doing have discouraged mothers from breast feeding their babies. And since the milk substitutes are so expensive, the poor women feed their children too little or make them ill by mixing the powdered substances with polluted water.

My interest in this campaign was recently rekindled by the visit of an old friend with whom I once stayed in Lapland, a well-known Swedish physician who is now in charge of a United Nations study of nomadic peoples throughout the world. He is much more familiar than I am with the harmful effects of these artificial feeding techniques and particularly in favor of breast feeding by the mother because science has now proven what European women have believed for centuries, namely, that breast feeding acts as a sort of natural contraceptive.

But why emphasize these kinds of activities, which so many other people are pursuing with far greater energy than I? Many writers have shared these concerns: Rousseau fought artifice and inequality in his day and by so doing inspired Tolstoy, who for many years wore around his neck a medal depicting the Swiss reformer.[2] In England, writers like Ruskin and William Morris and Dickens took the lead in sponsoring social reforms.

G   Still, it wasn't Tolstoy who made the Revolution in Russia, was it?
Y   No, and doubtless he would have made a better job of it if he had. I am no idolator of revolutions. They ultimately provoke reactions more virulent than the disease that caused them; the societies they produce become bogged down in bureaucracy and hierarchy and end up establishing "gulags." It is reform rather than revolution that brings about improvement in the world. When one thinks of

2. It is odd that the social aspects of *La Nouvelle Héloïse,* utopian, perhaps, yet rich in useful observations, have been neglected in France, where the book is usually read as a novel of love (and an admirable one it is). Similarly, many people refuse to see *Lady Chatterley's Lover* as anything other than a tale of sexual fulfillment, which it is, and a very fine one indeed; but it is also more than that, since it has as its background a powerful depiction of the poverty and degradation of the miners.

the terrible massacres, the decimation of the peasantry in southern
Russia, it becomes apparent that Tsar Stalin was no better and no
worse than the Little Father, Ivan the Terrible, and Ivan was probably no less adulated.

G   You share Solzhenitsyn's mysticism.

Y   Such mysticism is a natural reaction on the part of a man victimized
    by a regime's deceit and errors, a man persecuted by his society and
    thrown into prison. Like André Gide, who can hardly be called a
    mystic, I believe that the social problem is more important than the
    political problem, and the moral problem more important than the
    social. One always comes back to the struggle between good and
    evil.

G   Were you ever actively involved in politics?

Y   In the narrow sense of the word, no, and I've just told you why.

G   Have you ever voted in France?

Y   No, because since I was a child I've never had a permanent resi-
    dence in France. Here, I do vote, though in doing so I am aware
    than I am taking positions on phony issues and voting for men
    whose worth I am not in a position to judge. In the United States,
    Democrats and Republicans hand down their opinions from father
    to son, so that the two parties sometimes look more like rival clans
    than political organizations; no independent, no matter how
    capable or intelligent, has ever been able to carve out a niche
    between these two blocs. The two parties have changed so much
    over the past century that it is now almost impossible to identify
    them with coherent positions or platforms. The Democrats are in
    theory at any rate a bit more liberal than the Republicans, whose
    policies tend to reflect the interests of big business. In practice,
    everything depends, as usual, on the individuals involved, but like it
    or not the individuals themselves resemble marionettes controlled
    by those who pull the strings. Despite all this mess some good and
    useful things do get done. Unfortunately, the large crowds that can
    be quickly mobilized for such issues as the war in Vietnam, Water-
    gate, or the Iranian hostage crisis, soon disperse as people settle
    back into their customary inertia or become preoccupied with petty
    private concerns. More extreme groups, which during periods of
    mass mobilization remain relatively obscure, are really just waiting

for an opportune moment to reemerge, fully armed and ready for battle (right now, for isntance, there seems to be a resurgence of the Ku Klux Klan). Special interest groups pass themselves off as champions of the public interest. The cost of campaigning for election and reelection is so high that democracy as it exists in the United States is actually plutocracy. Corruption is practically a sine qua non of politics. But then, am I really talking about the United States? Or is it some other democracy I've been describing, it hardly matters which—perhaps Rome in the time of Marius and Sulla?

G   You're also involved in a number of humanitarian causes, aren't you?

Y   People in France first learned of this part of my work from a letter that I published, in *Le Monde* I think, on the subject of the massacring of seals. Actually, I first became involved in this kind of activity many years ago, but the massacre of the baby seals was something that quite justifiably caught the imagination of the public. It has become a symbol of our indefensible, unthinking brutality toward nature. Who benefits from this atrocity? A few Canadian and Norwegian companies that operate in the area of Saint-Pierre and Miquelon, Newfoundland, and Labrador, now that the Bay of Fundy has fortunately been made off limits to the butchers, and a few American companies operating in the Pribilof Islands. And what is it all for? To enable these companies to sell women, and even a few men, fur jackets they would be better off without, or frightful knick-knacks, funny little toy animals and trolls made of tufts of fur from the slaughtered beasts. Apparently, too, denatured seal oil has been used as a secret ingredient in certain margarines. We are told that the natives of the seal-populated regions who do the actual bludgeoning (sometimes skinning and cutting up the baby seals while the frightened animals are still half-alive and just "playing dead" on the ice) need the wages they earn from this bloody business in order to live. If that is so, then let us find them another line of work in some nonpolluting industry: it is wrong to combine the ills of the atomic age with the savagery of the stone age. Our efforts have met with some success: Italy, Germany, and Holland have all agreed not to purchase any more seal fur, and I hope that France will soon follow suit, if it hasn't already. It is horrifying to have to think, late every winter when out on the ice floes mother seals are giving birth to their young, that nature is carrying out her important work only to have it immediately undone by the wholesale massacre of the newly born. By the same token, I can't feed the turtle doves in my woods without being reminded that this autumn alone sixty million birds will succumb to hunters' shells. "Animal overpopulation must be controlled," we are told by people who never give a thought to limiting the proliferation of their own species. And I can agree with them up to a point; but then I think of the millions of passenger pigeons, flocks of which used to blacken the skies above the United States: today the species is extinct, represented only by a wretched stuffed specimen in some New England museum, the rest having gone to make fricassees and decorate hats.

I've often thought that if only we had not, for generation after generation, allowed animals to be packed into cattle cars to die of asphyxiation or injure themselves on their way to slaughter, then none of us, not even the soldiers ordered to accompany the convoys, would have tolerated the prison trains of World War II. If only we were capable of hearing the cries of trapped animals (again taken for their fur) gnawing their own legs in desperation to escape, we would doubtless pay more attention to the frightful plight of our prison inmates—a plight we inflict on them for absurd reasons, because the punishment in fact accomplishes the opposite of its stated purpose, which is to improve and reeducate the prisoners, to make human beings of them. When autumn decks the woods in splendid colors and I see a man warmly dressed in waterproof clothing get out of his car beside some stretch of forest, as close as possible to his quarry in order to save himself the trouble of walking any distance, and equipped with a pint of whiskey in his pants pocket and a rifle with a telescopic sight to help him spy out the animals whose bloody remains he will fetch home at night lashed to the hood of his car, I say to myself that this fine fellow, who may well be a good husband, a fine father, or a wonderful son, is unwittingly laying the groundwork for the My Lais of the future. In any case he is no longer a homo sapiens.

G How do you participate in the movements you've described?
Y By giving money, as much as I possibly can; by sending letters and telegrams to the appropriate agencies; by speaking out when the occasion arises (in other words, whenever people are willing to

listen); and finally by what I am doing right now, speaking out in print. The most important thing, perhaps, is for interested groups to acquire, in the public interest, land that is still clean and virgin, land in Alaska, say, or along the "barrier reef" that protects the American coast. We must also combat the destruction of the forests, those marvelously complex constellations of living things, which as we discussed earlier are being supplanted by industrial tree farms. The paper companies grow acres of pine trees that will be cut down in five years for pulp to make paper (the paper, alas, on which this book will be printed), and still other vital plants are being destroyed by the use of herbicides even though they help stabilize the forests and impede the spread of tree diseases. I am a member of one of several groups that are working to purchase land for use as preserves, where the air and water can hopefully be kept unpolluted and plant as well as animal life protected. We now own several islands off the coast.

G Isn't what you're doing in the nature of a rearguard action?
Y I would say it's more in the nature of an avant-garde action, the purpose of which is to lay the groundwork for a cleaner, purer world to come.

G Isn't it too late?
Y It will never be too late to try to do the right thing, not as long as a single tree, animal, or human being remains on earth.

Sympathy through Intelligence

MATTHIEU GALEY:
When you think back over the past, when you reflect on the life you have lived, do you feel that you've kept the bargain you made with yourself?

MARGUERITE YOURCENAR:
I feel at any rate that I did my best playing the role that chance, fate, karma, or God chose to have me play. We are not free to choose our beginnings, though we are free to some extent—just how far I'm not sure—to choose our ends. Actually, to play on words a little, I would say that life as I see it has no definite pattern *(dessin)* or purpose *(dessein);* or, if it has, it's hidden so deeply that we can never know what it might be. This is a thought that Hadrian and Zeno have already expressed for me. I do not believe in an irrevocable, foreordained destiny: we change our destinies constantly as we make our way through life. Everything that we do affects our fate for better or for worse. The circumstances into which we are born also exert a tremendous influence; we come into the world with debits and credits for which we are not responsible already posted to our account; this teaches us humility. But everything is constantly changing inside us as well as outside. Even the words that I'm speaking at this very moment are working a change in me.

G   Nevertheless, there have been some constants in your life: for example, the two characters that you first conceived when you were twenty-years old, and who have accompanied you ever since.

Y   Yes, I can see that as something strange (where strange is a word we use to describe anything we don't understand). But no stranger than Wordsworth's reflections in his admirable "Intimations of Immortality," in which he shows the child as "father to the man." The adolescent I used to be, and even the child I remember having been, somehow did sense, obscurely and with the utmost confusion, something of what my life and work would turn out to be. But innumerable circumstances and countless events hide the broad outline of a life from view. Perhaps these "mysterious operations" will become clearer when (to borrow another image from *Hadrian*) the day's warm fog gives way to dusk's sharp outlines. Apparently I haven't quite reached that point. The question of a life's strangeness (and at the same time its ordinariness) will be the theme of *Quoi? l'Eternité.*

G Your life has indeed been rather well organized. But when you've finished the book you just mentioned, won't you feel that you've completed your work?

Y I never shut any door permanently. I have in mind other titles and other books that I probably won't have time to write. But our works should have something incomplete about them; Mexican potters, for instance, leave a broken line in their designs so that the spirit within won't be trapped. I shall mention just one of these projected works, to be entitled *Paysage avec des animaux* (Landscape with animals), which is to deal with animals in life and in history. Humans will appear in this work only as they relate to or use animals. Some use animals in order to commit crimes against other men: think of the Romans feeding Christians to the lions, or to cite another example that I find terrible to contemplate, the miniature by Fouquet that shows Philip Augustus seated on a horse caparisoned in blue velvet, watching heretics being burned; the smoke must have irritated the innocent beast. The reader will encounter some humans who loved animals and others who never learned to love them.

G Why this interest in animals?

Y I thought I explained that before. To put it more abstractly, if you'd rather, I think it is important to have some notion of what life is like when encased in a form different from our own. For us it's a major step forward to realize that the form we happen to be accustomed to living in is not the only one in which life dwells; life can come with wings instead of arms, with eyes more acute than ours, with gills instead of lungs. Then there are the mysteries of animal migration and communication; there is the intelligence of certain species (the dolphin, for example, is our equal in brainpower, though its image of the world is surely different from ours); and there is the phenomenon of adaptation to the changing environment, which has gone on for millions of centuries sometimes successfully, sometimes not. And it is still going on: those species that can adapt to the world as we have made it, live, and those that cannot, die.

What I find most moving, finally, about the world of animals is the fact that the animal possesses nothing but its life, when man doesn't rob it even of that. Animals are wonderfully free. Within their natural habitat they experience *being* in its purest form, with none of the specious trappings in which we wrap existence. That is why the suffering of animals affects me so profoundly. It is like the suffering of children: in both I see the very special horror that comes from inflicting our follies and our errors upon the innocent.[1] When *we* suffer hard blows, we can always console ourselves with the thought that intelligence will triumph over adversity, which up to a certain point is true. And it's also true, unfortunately, that we are in fact implicated, that we all of us have to some extent done wrong, or, what is worse, allowed it to be done. But to respond to the complete innocence of the animal or child with brutality, when that animal or child *cannot understand* what is happening to it, is an odious crime.

G   You're assuming that the animal has a quite anthropomorphic psychology.

Y   I think we'd do better to drop the word anthropomorphic, now obsolete thanks both to fascinating recent research on animal intelligence and communication and to work in anthropology which has shown that what man does is not so much to "anthropomorphize animals" as to "sacralize" himself by taking on animal characteristics. Primitive man does not "raise" the panther to the status of man; rather, he *makes himself* into a panther. The child who pretends to be a dog imagines that he really is a dog. The miracle—which is sensed by both the child and the primitive—is that it is precisely the same vital processes, the same viscera, the same digestive and reproductive functions (allowing, of course for some differences of

---

1. I am of course aware that from the standpoints of metaphysics and theology, not to mention mere psychology, the question of the child's, and even the animal's, complete innocence is open to question. But this is not the place to go into such profound matters.

physiological detail) that operate in all of life's multifarious forms, some of which possess powers not available to us. The same can be said for the emotions that arise out of the viscera. A warbler weeps for its young just as Andromache does. A cat plays with a mouse just as Célimène plays with her lovers. And there are even variations between species, and between individuals within species, not unlike the difference between an intelligent man and an imbecile; though we can be sure, at any rate, that the animal's beastliness is never due to the inculcation of slogans.

I am of course aware that France is said to be a Cartesian nation (and, I might add, rather prides itself on being so), and Descartes of course held the view that animals are machines. This metaphor would be beyond reproach if only Descartes had extended it to man as well, and I'm quite sure that, in the most secret recesses of his mind, he did so.

Now, I do not, mind you, deny that man has a grandeur all his own, which Pico della Mirandola has finely described in the passage I used as an epigraph to *The Abyss:* man the master, his own composer and sculptor, is free to choose between good and evil, wisdom and folly, and is thus gifted, and free, in a way the animal is not. But the point is that this relative freedom of choice (I say relative, for who would call it absolute?) makes us responsible. When we strike a child or let it go hungry, or when we raise a child in such a way as to warp its thinking or sap its enthusiasm for life, we are committing a crime against the universe, which manifests itself in that child. The same is true when we kill an animal for no purpose or cut down a tree without good reason. Each time we do these things we are betraying our mission as human beings, which should be to organize the universe a little better than it now is.

G For that, man would need to be good. How would you define goodness?

Y In its merely negative form, there is the well-known dictum: "Do not do unto others what you would not have them do unto you." But goodness involves more than that, or it would be limited to mere justice: goodness involves wishing well to others in the same measure as one wishes it for oneself. With sympathy (such a beautiful word, which means "to feel with") begins both love and goodness.

G   But it's not a question solely of sympathy; intelligence also comes
    into it.

Y   Of course. What would be the use of unintelligent sympathy? But
    sympathy and intelligence are, or ought to be, indissoluble. As the
    wise old alchemists used to say, "He who does not experiment or
    consent to be the subject of expeiment does not think." By the same
    token, he who does not *feel deeply* does not think. I am almost tempted
    to say that a kind of specialization has taken place in man: just as
    certain insects have transformed their bodies into useful tools, we
    have tended to transform a considerable part of our sensory and
    affective capacities into a kind of computer, which is what the
    brain is for us. If by so doing we have lost the almost visceral sym-
    pathy with which we were born, nothing has been gained.

G   Friendship might in some respects be classed along with sympathy.
    Has friendship been important to you?

Y   Infinitely important. I have many friends and am constantly acquir-
    ing new ones.

G   What age are your friends?

Y   All ages, because age is not something that concerns me. My dearest
    friends range in age from twenty-five to ninety-two.

G   But how do you make friends?

Y   Your question calls to mind a charming passage from a book by
    Montherlant. Surprised that a little girl has not given her cat a
    name, someone asks, "But how do you call him?" The little girl
    answers, "I don't call him. He comes when he wants." So, too, do
    friends often come to us through the most improbable of chances.

G   They come even to a place as out-of-the-way as this?

Y   Let's not rehash the myth of my solitude yet again. Sometimes one
    lives for years with one's friends, day in and day out. That is a rare
    stroke of luck. Other friends come and go, obliged by the require-
    ments of work or the accidents of residence to take their leave.
    Some may stay for weeks or months, some only for days. But every
    true friendship is a lasting possession. When true friends meet
    again, even after twenty-five years' separation, they embrace and
    nothing has changed.

I believe that friendship, like love, of which it is a particular kind, requires nearly as much art as a successful choreography. It requires much enthusiasm and just as much reserve, a lot of talk as well as a lot of silence, and above all plenty of respect.

G   What do you mean by respect?

Y   A feeling for the other person's freedom and dignity coupled with clear-sighted acceptance of that person as he or she really is, where by clear-sighted I mean without illusions but also without the slightest trace of hostility or disdain. Respect also requires a certain reciprocity (which may not be absolutely necessary in love, but what do I know about it?). Of course one can, if one wishes, make friends of animals, plants, or rocks, in which case reciprocity takes a different form: animals love us with an affectionate selfishness that isn't so different from the way many of our human friends love us—they love us (as is only natural) for what we give them. Plants also return our love: they thank us for the care we give them by the way in which they grow and blossom. And anyone who has crouched behind a boulder for protection from the wind or sat on a sun-heated ledge and tried to feel the hidden vibrations in the stone that elude our ordinary senses can hardly help feeling that in some obscure way the rocks are his friends.

G   No one can love all humankind.

Y   "Humankind" is a mere abstraction: we can sympathize with the people we meet, despite their faults (no doubt outweighed by our own); or at the very least we can think about the infinite possibilities that every person represents. In medieval Japan, monks given to just such a discipline of individual devotion used to kneel before each person they met and say, "I salute thee, O thou who may'st thousands of centuries hence become a bodhisattva." Even if we don't want to rest our faith on such a slow process of evolution, what is to prevent us from saying to everyone we meet, particularly those who are offensively ignorant, mean, or smug, something like this: "Greetings to thee who one day must die, may'st thou die a little wiser than thou seem'st right now." I myself am like Zeno, who hoped to "die a little less besotted than he was born." I don't mean to say that I will be fundamentally different—whatever I am I have probably been all my life—but I shall at least have gotten rid of a lot of excess baggage, or so I hope.

G   For you, then, life is primarily a matter of divestiture.

Y   Yes, certainly, but it is also a matter of enrichment. One sheds one's clothing in order to be bronzed by the sun's rays.

G   So when we say to people that they have acquired something, we're making a mistake.

Y   Not at all, not if they've acquired the things that are essential. Wisdom may well consist in the elimination of the accidental, or should I say, rather, that acquiring wisdom is like eating, in that we thrive by taking in what accidentally comes our way, carefully avoiding what is adulterated or spoiled, and then eliminating the useless residue. Wisdom also requires changing perspectives: every new friendship gives us a fresh view of the world, as do the things we experience and the trips we take. Some methods of mental discipline recommend listening to silence, or rather, to silences, since there are dozens of different kinds. Others advise staring at the night. One oriental technique recommends bending over and looking at the landscape between one's legs. That way you see it from a different angle.

G   It would look to be upside down.

Y   Only from your point of view. There are still other variations on the theme: lie down beneath a tree and look at the sky through its leaves—yet another way of shaping the universe.

G   Such contemplative disciplines are somewhat out of keeping with your taste for travel. You once wrote somewhere that it was necessary to "taste of the world's roundness."

Y   It's becoming increasingly difficult to follow you. One travels in order to contemplate. Every trip is contemplation in motion. But the phrase you quote, which is uttered by the young Henry Maximilian in *The Abyss,* echoes in a rather gayer key the young Zeno's question, "Who would be so besotted as to die without having made at least the round of this, his prison?" I've toured my prison as extensively as I could, but there are many countries I've never visited, for various reasons: I never went to Iran, for example, because the friend who invited me died before I had a chance to go. Many planned trips had to be cancelled at the last minute. I've always had a special liking for the frontier, for gateways to realms still more wild, like the Lapland region of Sweden and Norway, parts of the Middle East where the only roads are narrow mountain trails, and the now-threatened Alaskan wilderness.

When I have Hadrian speak of his love for the barbarian countries, his predilections echo my own at times.

Throughout my life I've found the prospect of travel very alluring. When, in recent years, various circumstances conspired to keep me here all but immobilized, I at first felt a distressing sense of *constraint*. I told myself that I was no doubt exaggerating the value of travel in a world that has become more and more homogeneous. I have also come to appreciate the benefits of standing still. To stay in one place and watch the seasons come and go is tantamount to constant travel: one is traveling with the earth.

In short, I learned to live with "immobility," much as Zeno did in the half of *The Abyss* (part 2) devoted to that theme. Oddly enough, immobility is described more than once in my works; indeed, I described it before I had experienced it myself, and it turned out almost exactly as I had described, except of course that the external circumstances were quite different. Yet the need to travel remained almost as powerful as carnal desire, so that lately I've "hit the road" again and will probably do so many more times in the future, until my strength is gone.

G You're by temperament rather adventurous.

Y I keep moving forward, that's all. But any trip, any adventure (in the true sense of the word, which is "that which arrives"), goes hand in hand with inner exploration. What we do and what we think bear the same relation to each other as the outer and inner curves of a vase: each models the other.

G Would you criticize your contemporaries for being too stay-at-home?

Y They crowd the highways, but what do they see along the way? In any case, I am suspicious of French people who say that France is enough for them and of Americans who say that you're only comfortable when you stay at home. That breed is dying out, fortunately, and is being replaced by another which does visit far-off places but only to give them a quick once-over. Like anything else, traveling requires contradictory qualities: enthusiasm, sustained attentiveness, and a certain lightheartedness, for as Baudelaire says,

> Real travelers are those who go for the sake of going,
> And who travel light, like balloons.

It also requires an ability to take pleasure in the outer spectacle of things combined with a definite willingness to go beyond that spectacle in order to discover the often hidden realities underneath. Every traveler is Ulysses and ought to be Proteus as well.

G Some great thinkers never left their studies: Descartes sat by his fire, and Montaigne had his library.

Y As it happens, the two men you mention both traveled fairly extensively. Descartes went off to war in Holland in 1618–19, visited Denmark and Germany, made an almost equally lengthy journey through central Europe in the following two years, and then stayed for nearly two years in Italy before finally settling for twenty years in Holland, only to die, ultimately, in Stockholm. If, as oversimplified legend has it, he lived and philosophized beside his hearth, he certainly warmed himself at many fires all over northern Europe. As for Montaigne, his seventeen months of travel in Switzerland, Tyrol, and Italy were undertaken ostensibly for reasons of health, but he speaks too highly of traveling for anyone not to sense his eagerness to leap into the saddle.[2]

Traveling is one kind of experience, just as staying in one place is another; and so are friendship, contemplation, love, illness, and for that matter gardening and cooking. Why discriminate among them?

G But these experiences, these insights, must be capable of being conveyed to othes if anyone else is to benefit from them. Writers are people who convey experiences and insights, but the question is, How? Why choose fiction?

2. In rereading some of Montaigne's remarks on travel, leafing idly, as is my wont, through his works, I stumbled upon certain comments he made in *L'apologie de Raymond Sebond* and the chapter that precedes it, on the treatment of animals and on their intelligence, comments that confirm my own thinking on these subjects. Montaigne, a man devoid of cruelty and prejudice, expressed my own thoughts much better than I could have done.

Y   Should I confess that I've never really felt that I was writing "fiction"? I've always waited until what I was writing was sufficiently a part of myself so as to blend in with my own memories. I believe in the reality of old Clement Roux walking through the streets of Rome as much as I believe in my own reality. Hadrian's illness seems as authentic to me as my own illnesses. I feel that I experienced Zeno's death, for otherwise I wouldn't have been able to write it. I should think that concocting "a fiction" would be quite a pointless thing to do.

G   No doubt that explains why your readers, when they read a "story" or "tale" by you, are inclined to look to you as someone who can teach them how to live.

Y   Perhaps they sense that my primary purpose has always been to discover how I might live a better life, how I might live the best life I am capable of. My books have been a series of explorations paralleling my personal explorations. People are likely to ask directions of someone they meet along a road somewhere, to find out about where he's coming from and where he thinks he's going.

With Open Eyes

MATTHIEU GALEY:
Have you been surprised by the way your books have been
received?
MARGUERITE YOURCENAR:
Yes, I have been, because I had absolutely no expectations. I was
surprised that when *Alexis* first appeared, Edmond Jaloux wrote a
review that brought me a few dozen readers and introduced me to
his friendship. I was surprised that once, by now a fairly long time
ago, a man of taste told me (as I mentioned earlier) that "For
certain men of my generation, Eric (in *Coup de Grâce*) was our
Werther," and surprised, too, that some veterans of the Baltic wars
let me know that the memories I had put down on paper were *theirs*.
I was dumbfounded when *Memoirs of Hadrian* was repeatedly reprinted until the number of extant copies must now be in the neighborhood of one million: I thought I had written it for three people. And
why was *The Abyss* translated into seventeen languages? One thing
is clear, however, and that is that after a certain point in a writer's
career many people read his work simply because it is fashionable.
It is also clear that many readers see in my works not what I put, or
tried to put, into them but what they want to find. At the same
time, friends come into our lives through the medium of the printed
page. Readers write, and all too often their letters go unanswered,
owing simply to lack of time (though a few forget to sign their
letters); these letters mention that this or that passage in one of our
books has meant something to them. Such news always brings joy to
the writer's heart.

G   Don't you feel that you're primarily an intermediary, a medium, in
    other words someone through whom something has passed?
Y   Absolutely. And that's why, basically, I have at most a limited
    interest in myself. I feel that I am an instrument through which
    currents, vibrations, have passed. That is true of all my books and I
    would even say of all my life. Perhaps of all life. The best of us,

perhaps, are mere crystal vessels. Thus, in thinking of my friends, those still living as well as those who are dead, I frequently find myself repeating the fine words that I was once told were uttered by the eighteenth century's "unknown philosopher," Saint-Martin, a man so unknown to me that I've never read a single line of his work or attempted to check the citation: "They are the beings through whom God loved me." Everything began before us and will continue after we are gone. Everything surpasses us, in other words, and we feel humble and amazed when we serve as instruments in this greater scheme.

G Don't such sentiments lead to a passive attitude toward life?

Y Not at all. One must toil and struggle to the bitter end, one must swim in the river that both lifts us up and carries us away, knowing in advance that the only way out is to drown in the vastness of the open sea. But the question is, *Who* drowns? We must accept all the evils, cares, and afflictions that beset us and others, as we must accept our own death and the deaths of others, as a *natural* part of life, as, say, Montaigne would have done—Montaigne, the man who of all Western thinkers comes closest to the Taoist philosophers and whom only superficial readers take to be an antimystic. Death, the supreme form of life—on this point my thinking is exactly contrary to that of Julius Caesar, whose wish (more or less fulfilled) was to die as quickly as possible. For my part, I would like to die fully conscious that I am dying, of an illness whose progress would be slow enough to allow death to insinuate itself into my body and fully unfold.

G Why?

Y So as not to miss the ultimate experience, the passage. Hadrian speaks of dying with his eyes open. It was in this spirit, moreover, that I had Zeno experience his death.

G You would like to emulate Proust, then, who changed his description of Bergotte's death by modeling it after his own.

Y I understand quite well why he attempted what he did. To use his own demise in this way is a novelist's form of heroism. For me, however, it would be more a matter of not missing out on an essential experience, and it is because I am determined to have this experience that I consider it detestable for any person to be robbed of his death. In the United States medical people are surprisingly honest, whereas in France doctors and especially families frequently do their utmost to keep things back from the patient. This is an attitude of which I disapprove. By the same token, I love and respect people who prepare for death.

G That means living in constant intimacy with one's demise.

Y Which is a very good thing indeed. We should think of death as a friend, even if we feel a certain instinctive repugnance to do so. It is true that animals don't think about death. Or do they? It is quite obvious that some animals do anticipate that they are going to die.

G Yet we are inevitably ill prepared for this passage.

Y So ill prepared that we end up snivelling wretches or cringing cowards, though these are no doubt mere physical reactions, like seasickness. The acceptance that matters will have occurred at an earlier stage.

And then, who knows? Perhaps we will be taken in hand by certain memories, as if by angels. Tibetan mystics tell us that the dying are supported by the presence of whatever it was they believed in: Siva or Buddha for some, Christ or Muhammad for others. Convinced skeptics and people without imagination will doubtless see nothing, like the fourth officer of Marlborough, who brought nothing. A friend of mine who was resuscitated after nearly drowning told me that the widespread belief that one sees one's whole life flash by in an instant is true. If so, it must be disagreeable at times. Greater selectivity is called for. But what would I like to see again?

Perhaps the hyacinths of Mont-Noir or the violets of Connecticut in springtime; the oranges my father cleverly hung from the branches in our garden in the Midi; a cemetery in Switzerland crushed by the weight of its roses; another buried in snow in the midst of white birches; and still other cemeteries whose names and locations escape me, but these, after all, are not the things that matter. The dunes of Flanders and of the Virginia sea islands, with the sound of the ocean that has persisted since the beginning of time. The modest little Swiss music box that plays pianissimo an arietta of Haydn, which I started playing at Grace's bedside one hour before her death, when she ceased to respond to word or touch. Or again, the huge icicles that form on the rocks here on Mount Desert Island, icicles which, come April, form channels for the melting snows that flow with a geyser's roar. Cape Sounion at sunset. Olympia at noon. Peasants on a road in Delphi, offering to give their mule's bells to a stranger. The mass of the Resurrection in a Euboean village, following a nocturnal mountain crossing on foot. A morning arrival in Segesta, on horseback, via trails that in those days were deserted and rocky and smelled of thyme. A walk at Versailles one sunless afternoon, or a day at Corbridge in Northumberland when, having fallen asleep in the middle of an archeological dig overgrown with grass, I passively allowed the rain to penetrate my bones, as it penetrated the bones of the dead Romans. Some cats I picked up with the help of André Embiricos in an Anatolian village. The "angels game" in the snow. A mad toboggan ride down a Tyrolian hillside under stars full of omens. Or again, from more recent times and still hardly distilled enough to qualify as memories, the green sea of the tropics, stained here and there by oil. A triangular flight of wild swans en route to the Arctic. Easter's rising sun (which didn't know that it was the sun of Easter), viewed this year from a rocky spur of Mount Desert, high above a half-frozen lake hatched with fissures by the approach of spring.

I toss out these images at random with no intention of making them into symbols. And I should probably add the faces of a few loved ones, living and dead, along with other faces, drawn from history or my imagination.

Or perhaps none of these things, but only the great blue-white void which, in Mishima's last novel completed only hours before his death, is contemplated by the octogenarian Honda—a perspicacious judge who is also a voyeur (in the worst sense of the word)—at the end of his life. What he sees is a flamboyant emptiness like that of the summer sky, which devours all things and reduces the rest to a train of shadows.

G   Perhaps it isn't accidental that you should take this example from a Japanese novel. Buddhism it seems to me has had great influence on you.

Y   I have several religions, just as I have several homelands, so that in a sense, perhaps, I belong to none of them. Naturally I don't entertain the slightest thought of renouncing the Man who said that those who are hungry and thirsty for justice would be satisfied (in another world to be sure, for they are surely not satisfied in this one) and that those who were pure of heart would see the face of God, and who was crucified for his trouble ("Oh sometimes I tremble at that spirit," as one of the finest of the Negro spirituals puts it); still less do I renounce the wisdom of Tao, which is like a limpid pool, sometimes clear, sometimes dark, beneath whose surface the innermost depths of things are revealed. I am grateful, too, to Tantrism, with its almost physiological methods of awakening the powers of mind and body, and to Zen, that sparkling sword, for the invaluable lessons each taught me about myself in reward for the effort I devoted to their study and practice. Above all, I remain deeply attached to Buddhist thought; I have studied its various schools, and, like the different denominations of Christianity, these seem to me not so much to contradict as to complement one another. Not only does Buddhism's compassion for all living things extend our often quite restricted notions of charity; and not only does Buddhism attempt, as did the pre-Socratic philosophers, to situate man, that transitory creature, in his proper place in an ephemeral universe; but even more, Buddhist philosophy, like Socrates, warns us against (even as it indulges) ambitious metaphysical speculation and urges us instead to know ourselves. And, to a degree that rivals the boldest of modern philosophers, Buddhism insists on our need to rely only on ourselves: "Be a lamp unto yourselves."

G   Is that one of the "Buddhist vows" to which you have alluded several times?

Y   The four Buddhist vows, which I have indeed recited to myself quite often in the course of my life, I hesitate to repeat right now in front of you, because a vow is a prayer, indeed even more secret than a prayer. (People who tell you to "make a vow" while eating the first strawberries of the year or gazing upon the new moon wisely tell you to keep that vow to yourself.) But, simply put, the four vows are as follows: to fight against one's wicked tendencies; to devote oneself fully to study; to perfect oneself insofar as one is able; and finally, "as numerous as are the creatures that range over the three worlds," that is, over the universe, "to work to save them." From moral conscience to intellectual pursuits, from self-improvement to love for and compassion toward others, the vows seem to contain everything that matters, in a text some twenty-six-centuries old.

G   And have you put those vows into practice?
Y   One time out of a thousand. But it's something just to think about them.

Bibliography

NOVELS AND STORIES

Alexis ou le traité du vain combat. Sans Pareil, 1929; rev. ed., Plon, 1952; Gallimard, 1971. (Translated into English as *Alexis or the Treatise of Vain Struggle* by Walter Kaiser in collaboration with the author, forthcoming).

La nouvelle Eurydice. Grasset, 1931.

La mort conduit l'attelage. Grasset, 1934.

Denier du rêve. Grasset, 1934; 2d ed., 1963. (Translated into English as *A Coin in Nine Hands* by Dori Katz in collaboration with the author. Farrar, Straus, & Giroux, 1982).

Nouvelles orientales. Gallimard, 1938; rev. ed., 1953.

Le coup de grâce. Gallimard, 1938; rev. ed., 1963. (Translated into English as *Coup de Grâce* by Dori Katz in collaboration with the author. Farrar, Straus, & Giroux, 1957).

Mémoires d'Hadrian. Plon, 1951; Gallimard, 1971, 1974; Folio collection, 1977. (Translated into English as *Memoirs of Hadrian* by Grace Frick in collaboration with the author. Farrar, Straus, & Giroux, 1954, 1957, 1963).

L'œuvre au noir. Gallimard, 1968. (Translated into English as *The Abyss* by Grace Frick in collaboration with the author. Farrar, Straus, & Giroux, 1976).

ESSAYS AND AUTOBIOGRAPHY

Pindare. Grasset, 1932.

Les songes et les sorts. Grasset, 1938.

Sous bénéfice d'inventaire. Gallimard, 1962, 1978.

Le labyrinthe du monde. Vol. 1, *Souvenirs pieux.* Editions de Monaco, 1973; Gallimard, 1974; Folio collection, 1980. Vol. 2, *Archives du Nord.* Gallimard, 1977.

Discours de réception de Marguerite Yourcenar à l'Académie royale belge de Langue et de Littérature françaises, précédé du discours de bienvenue de Carlo Bronne. Gallimard, 1971.

PLAYS

Electre ou la chute des masques. Plon, 1954.

Le mystère d'Alceste and *qui n'a pas son Minotaure?* Plon, 1963.
Théâtre. 2 vols. Gallimard, 1971.

POEMS AND PROSE POEMS
Le jardin des chimères. Perrin, 1922.
Les dieux ne sont pas morts. Sansot, 1924.
Feux. Grasset, 1936; rev. ed., Plon, 1957; Gallimard, 1974. (Translated into
English as *Fires* by Dori Katz in collaboration with the author. Farrar,
Straus, & Giroux, 1981).
Les charités d'Alcippe. La Flûte enchantée, 1956.

TRANSLATIONS
Woolf, Virginia. *Les vagues.* Stock, 1947, 1974; Plon, 1957.
James, Henry. *Ce que Maisie savait.* Laffont, 1947, 1980.
Cavafy, Constantin. *Poemes.* Gallimard, 1958, 1978. Critical introduction to
the poetry followed by a translation of his poems by M. Yourcenar and
C. Dimaras. Gallimard, 1964, 1974.
Fleuve profond, sombre rivière. Gallimard, 1964, 1974. Translations, with
commentary, of American Negro spirituals.
Flexner, Hortense. *Poèmes.* Gallimard, 1969. Critical introduction to the
poetry, followed by translations of selected poems.
La couronne et la lyre. Gallimard, 1979. Critical introduction with
translations of selected Greek poets.

Index